THE UNSIGNED ESSAYS OF SUPREME COURT JUSTICE Joseph Story

Early American Views of Law

ENCYCLOPÆDIA AMERICANA

A

POPULAR DICTIONARY

OF

ARTS, SCIENCES, LITERATURE, HISTORY, POLITICS AND BIOGRAPHY,

A NEW EDITION;

INCLUDING

A COPIOUS COLLECTION OF ORIGINAL ARTICLES

IN

AMERICAN BIOGRAPHY;

ON

THE BASIS OF THE SEVENTH EDITION OF THE GERMAN

CONVERSATIONS-LEXICON.

EDITED BY

FRANCIS LIEBER,

ASSISTED BY

E. WIGGLESWORTH.

VOL. I.

PHILADELPHIA:

LEA & BLANCHARD

1843.

THE UNSIGNED ESSAYS OF SUPREME COURT JUSTICE Joseph Story

Early American Views of Law

Edited by

VALERIE L. HOROWITZ

Introduction by

MORRIS L. COHEN

Yale Law School

TALBOT PUBLISHING
Clark, New Jersey

ISBN 978-1-61619-454-3 (Hardcover)
ISBN 978-1-61619-456-7 (Paperback)

TALBOT PUBLISHING

AN IMPRINT OF

THE LAWBOOK EXCHANGE, LTD.

33 Terminal Avenue
Clark, New Jersey 07066-1321

Please see our website for a selection of our other publications and fine facsimile reprints of classic works of legal history:
www.lawbookexchange.com

Library of Congress Cataloging-in-Publication Data

Story, Joseph, 1779-1845, author.
[Joseph Story and the Encyclopedia Americana]
The unsigned essays of Supreme Court Justice Joseph Story : early American views of law / Valerie L. Horowitz, editor ; introduction by Morris L. Cohen, Yale Law School.
pages cm
Contains a little-known series of legal essays written by Joseph Story for the first edition of the Encyclopedia Americana, edited by Francis Lieber, published in 1844.
Includes bibliographical references and index.
ISBN 978-1-61619-454-3 (hardcover : alk. paper) -- ISBN 978-1-61619-456-7 (pbk. : alk. paper)
1. Law--United States. I. Horowitz, Valerie L., editor. II. Cohen, Morris L., 1927-2010, writer of introduction. III. Encyclopædia americana. IV. Title.
KF213.S7S76 2015
349.73--dc23 2014049750

Printed in the United States of America on acid-free paper

CONTENTS

ESSAYS BY JOSEPH STORY

From *Encyclopedia Americana,* Philadelphia, 1843–1844

FROM VOLUME III

FROM VOLUME IV

FROM VOLUME V

PREFACE

WHEN WE PUBLISHED *Joseph Story and the Encyclopedia Americana* in 2006, we were delighted to offer, gathered in one volume for the first time, the anonymous essays written by Joseph Story for the *Encyclopedia Americana* during the prime of his judicial career. Although we published the facsimiles of the two-column encyclopedia pages in an oversized (8-1/2" x 11") format, the small columns and encyclopedia font size were not comfortable to read. For this volume we have typeset the essays in a 12 point typeface, which should ensure readability and access to these important writings.

The *Encyclopedia Americana* was the first significant American encyclopedia. Kent Newmyer notes Story's anonymous authorship and confirms the publishing success of the first edition:

> Story's response came in his "Law, Legislation and Codes," one of his several anonymous essays published in Francis Lieber's *Encyclopedia Americana* (1829–33), which, it should be noted, sold one hundred thousand copies.[1]

Although it is now available online by subscription, when it was first published the *Encyclopedia Americana* was not generally available in law libraries. A well-advertised, "popular" work as defined by its sub-title, it was purchased primarily by public libraries and student organizations for reference use. Fewer than half of the colleges and universities that existed during the early and mid-19th-

[1] R. Kent Newmyer, *Supreme Court Justice Joseph Story: Statesman of the Old Republic* (Chapel Hill: University of North Carolina Press, 1985) 275.

century held copies of the set.[2] Over time those colleges and universities that held a set in their main library collections came to regard the set as a rare book item. Consequently, these essays have not been widely known and studied.

Joseph Story insisted that the essays be published anonymously; however the piece on *Jury* gives us a clue to its authorship in the note that ends "written by an American jurist."[3]

I recall fondly the eureka moment when I read the list of anonymous essays in William Wetmore Story's *Life and Letters of Joseph Story.*[4] I knew that they were not available in one volume in print as such. I discussed them with our publisher, Greg Talbot, and we decided to publish them in facsimile.

When I met with Morris L. Cohen at the American Association of Law Schools conference in New Orleans in 2002, I proposed the idea of publishing the anonymous essays in one volume. Morris not only gave the project his blessing but offered to write the introduction.

He delved into the heretofore anonymous essays expecting that Story would have written the essays about the Constitution for the *Encyclopedia*, and was surprised that he did not. In his Introduction he speculates as to the reasons for that decision. Morris' enthusiasm and guidance are sorely missed, and we dedicate this revised edition to him. He would have been pleased to see the essays typeset as they are now.

I have since learned that Drake de Kay published an article on the first edition of the *Encyclopedia Americana* in which he quotes William Wetmore Story's list of his

---

[2] Drake de Kay, "Encyclopedia Americana, First Edition," 3 *Journal of Library History* 214–220 (1968).

[3] Francis Lieber, editor, *Encyclopedia Americana* vol. VII (Philadelphia: Lea & Blanchard, 1844) 278, reproduced herein at page 151.

[4] William W. Story, editor, Life and Letters of Joseph Story Vol. II (Boston: Charles C. Little and James Brown, 1851), 26–27.

father's essays in the work.[5] He quotes Nicholas Murray Butler (1862–1947), President of Columbia University for forty-four years, in his description of a conversation Butler had with Robert Lincoln, son of Abraham Lincoln, who told him that Lincoln owned a copy of the set and had read the essays on political topics. De Kay goes on to speculate that:

> Since Judge Story's authorship of a score of the *Americana's* juridical and legal articles was well known, at least to the American bench and bar, in all probability Mr. Lincoln read those entries with keen professional interest.[6]

John C. Hogan also published several law review articles on the anonymous essays.[7] Hogan describes Story's enthusiasm to help the editor of the *Encyclopedia*, his friend Francis Leiber, by compiling a list of the essays he planned to write, and quotes from Story's letters to Lieber that showed his conscientious attention to the writing of the essays. He points out that the essays:

> ...attracted little attention in legal circles when they were first published, and in time they seem to have been forgotten. This may have been due in part to the fact that they were published anonymously; but equally important is the fact that the first edition of the *Encyclopedia*

---

[5] De Kay, 206.

[6] Ibid., 213.

[7] "Comments: Legal History—Joseph Story's Anonymous Law Articles," 52 *Michigan Law Review* 869 1953–1954, "Three Essays on the Law by Joseph Story," 28 *Southern California Law Review* 19 1954–1955, "Joseph Story's Encyclopedia Americana 'Law Articles,'" 48 *Law Library Journal* 117 1955, "Joseph Story on Capital Punishment," 43 California Law Review 76 (1955), Joseph Story's Essay on 'Domicil,'" 35 *Boston University Law Review* 215 1955, "Justice Story on the Common Law of Evidence" 9 *Vanderbilt Law Review* 51 (1955–1956), "Joseph Story on Juries," 37 *Oregon Law Review* 234 1957–1958, and "Joseph Story on the Law of Contract," 12 *Rutgers Law Review* 366 (1957–1958).

> *Americana* was introduced as a popular priced general work with no special emphasis on legal subjects. One would not expect to find scholarly articles on the law by a Supreme Court Justice in such a work.[8]

Hogan later reminds us that the author of the anonymous essays should not have been such a mystery:

> From the tone of the articles it is clear that they were written by someone schooled in the common law; their richness in Latin phraseology suggested a scholar; their depth of reasoning and learning, a judge; their fluent literary diction, an educator, perhaps a law teacher; and their subject matter, a man with a wide and varied judicial experience, a fluent lawyer-writer, a judge or college teacher, or, perhaps, both. Few men in 1833, or since that time, have been endowed with all these characteristics.[9]

It is to all of our benefit that Joseph Story's authorship of these remarkable essays is known. We hope that you will find that the accessibility of this volume offers the opportunity to study previously anonymous writings, on key subjects, from the mind of a remarkable jurist.

Valerie L. Horowitz
Clark, New Jersey
2015

---

[8] "Three Essays on the Law by Joseph Story," 28 Southern *California Law Review* 19 1954–1955.

[9] "Comments: Legal History—Joseph Story's Anonymous Law Articles," 52 *Michigan Law Review* 870 1953–1954.

INTRODUCTION

THIS VOLUME CONTAINS a little-known series of legal essays written for the first edition of the *Encyclopedia Americana*[1] by Joseph Story (1779–1845), one of America's greatest scholars and jurists. In the following introduction I aim to sketch the genesis of these articles and some of their main ideas. I will also discuss the crucial role played by the founding editor of the *Encyclopedia*, Francis Lieber (1798–1872), then a recent immigrant and political refugee from Germany and later to be America's first great political scientist.

Joseph Story[2] was born and raised in Marblehead, Massachusetts. He graduated with honors from Harvard College in 1798. After reading law with Samuel Sewall, a distinguished Federalist lawyer and member of Congress, he was admitted to the bar in 1801. While practicing in Salem, Massachusetts, Story became active in the Jeffersonian Democratic-Republican Party. With that party's backing, he served in the Massachusetts legislature (1805–1811) and in Congress (1808–1809), where his Federalist leanings led Jefferson and the party leadership to consider him unreliable. Nevertheless, when a vacancy occurred on the Supreme Court in 1811 and President James Madison's first two choices declined to serve and the third was rejected by the Senate, Madison reluctantly nominated Story to the Court over Jefferson's objections. The seat required a New Englander since the occupant would also serve on the lower

---

[1] Philadelphia: Carey, Lea & Carey, 1829–1835.

[2] The three leading biographies of Story are R. Kent Newmyer, *Supreme Court Justice Joseph Story: Statesman of the Old Republic* (Chapel Hill: University of North Carolina Press, 1985), James McClellan, *Joseph Story and the American Constitution* (Norman: University of Oklahoma Press, 1971) and Gerald T. Dunne, *Justice Joseph Story and the Rise of the Supreme Court* (New York: Simon and Schuster, 1971).

federal courts of the first circuit, and there was no other obviously viable candidate. Madison was also less fearful of the Court than Jefferson, and Story, who had been a Democratic-Republican, seemed a likely solution to the problem. Story served on the Court for thirty-four years, until his death in 1845. During that service, he confirmed Jefferson's suspicions by becoming Chief Justice John Marshall's closest collaborator in his efforts to move the government toward Federalist-oriented policies.

In 1829, when Nathan Dane endowed a professorship at the Harvard Law School, Story was appointed to that chair, and continued there until his death. The law school had been in disarray or doldrums in the years before Story's appointment; there had been only one student registered in the previous year. When Story began teaching there were 27 students; by 1842 the number was up to 120. During his tenure Story taught commercial law, constitutional law, equity, and maritime law. In addition to his several works on the Constitution, Story wrote ten legal treatises on a number of other subjects. The first of these, on bailments, appeared in 1832,[3] and the last, on promissory notes, was published in 1845.[4] Each went through numerous revisions prepared by him or later editors; many were standard texts until the twentieth century. James Kent expressed a general opinion when he wrote "I think all the treatises of my friend Story are, upon the whole, the most finished and perfect of their kind, to be met with in any language, foreign or domestic; and for learning, industry, and talent, he is the most extraordinary jurist of the age."[5] The treatises, like his

---

[3] *Commentaries on the Law of Bailments, with Illustrations from the Civil and Foreign Law* (Cambridge: Hilliard and Brown, 1832).

[4] *Commentaries on the Law of Promissory Notes and Guaranties of Notes and Checks on Banks and Bankers* (Boston: C.C. Little & J. Brown, 1845).

[5] Extract from a letter of James Kent to the editor of the *Louisiana Law Journal*, July 31, 1841, quoted in William W. Story, ed., *Life and*

contributions to the *Encyclopedia Americana,* were marked by Story's comparative law approach whereby American law was viewed in a larger context and related to English law, the law of various civil law countries, Roman law and other ancient legal systems.

Since the Supreme Court met in Washington for only a short time each year, Story was able to maintain his two careers throughout his mature life. It is important to note, however, that Story's interests were not limited to the classroom and the bench. Convinced that the new American republic's success and survival depended on a popular understanding of the nation's laws and constitution, he recast his ideas for a variety of non-specialist readers. When he published his monumental three volume treatise on the Constitution in 1833, he also published a one-volume abridgement for general readers and two smaller versions for younger and older students.[6]

Story had literary interests and ambitions since his youth, and he read widely in both the ancient classics and contemporary works throughout his life. When he was twenty-one he published a book-length poem[7] and when a

---

Letters of Joseph Story (Boston: Little and Brown, 1851, reprinted Union: The Lawbook Exchange, Ltd., 2000) Vol. II, 648.

[6] *Commentaries on the Constitution of the United States: With a Preliminary Review of the Constitutional History of the Colonies and States Before the Adoption of the Constitution* (Boston: Hilliard, Gray, and Company, 1833), *Commentaries on the Constitution of the United States...Abridged by the Author, for the Use of Colleges and High Schools* (Boston: Hilliard, Gray, and Company, 1833), *The Constitutional Class Book: Being a Brief Exposition of the Constitution of the United States. Designed for the Use of the Higher Classes in Common Schools* (Boston: Hilliard, Gray, and Company, 1834) and *A Familiar Exposition of the Constitution of the United States; Containing a Brief Commentary on Every Clause, Explaining the true Nature, Reasons, and Objects Thereof; Designed for the Use of School Libraries and General Readers...* (Boston: Marsh, Capen, Lyon and Webb, 1840).

[7] *The Power of Solitude: a Poem, in Two Parts* (Boston: Printed by John Russell, 1800).

"new and improved edition" of that work was published in 1804, Story added seventy-one pages of other poems. Another collection of poetry and prose was published in 1835.[8] Several examples of his prose and an often anthologized poem, "Advice to a Young Lawyer," were included in *A Library of American Literature from the Earliest Settlement to the Present Time.*[9] Many other poems and prose excerpts appear in the two volume compilation, *Life and Letters of Joseph Story* (1851).[10]

Story's son, William Wetmore Story, who left a promising career in the law to become a successful sculptor, wrote of his father's wide-ranging intellect and prodigious memory:

> His knowledge of the law had scarcely any boundaries… he had read nearly everything of any value in the range of jurisprudence. And he remembered with wonderful accuracy what he had read. It did not, however, lie in his mind like a dull, cumbrous load of facts, cases, rules, and precedents, but like a living organization held together and vivified by principles. But not only this; he remembered all the leading cases in every branch of the law, by name and volume, and many of them by page…. His mind was not a lumber-room, with all sorts of things tumbled into it without classification or order, but everything there was completely arranged and in its place.[11]

* * * * * *

[8] *Miscellaneous Writings: Literary, Critical, Juridical, and Political of Joseph Story, Now First Collected* (1835).

[9] Edited by Edmund Clarence Stedman. 11 vols. (1892) at vol. IV, 421–426.

[10] Edited by William Wetmore Story (1851).

[11] W.W. Story, *Conversations in a Studio* (Boston and New York: Houghton, Mifflin and Company, 1890) 448–450.

The other central figure in this volume, Francis Lieber,[12] was born in Berlin in 1798 into a large middle class family with strong liberal and nationalistic beliefs, which he inherited. He was a boy when he saw Napoleon's army capture Berlin, and this event led him to develop a hatred of the invader. Lieber joined the Prussian army when he was old enough to enlist and was wounded at Waterloo.[13] He maintained his liberal political beliefs after the restoration of the Prussian monarchy in 1815. During this repressive period his liberalism and membership in secret patriotic societies were viewed with suspicion by government authorities. He was imprisoned twice. Despite these setbacks he received a Ph.D. in mathematics in 1820, but subsequently became more interested in politics, law and history. His youthful political idealism still intact, he turned his attention to the Greek revolution in 1821. Like Lord Byron before him, he joined a multi-national group of young radicals then forming in Marseilles to support the Greek cause. Unfortunately, their expedition to Greece was a disaster; their meager resources were depleted by Greek thieves, official ineptitude and the chaos of the failed uprising. Penniless, ill and thoroughly disheartened, Lieber stopped in Rome on his way home to Germany. While in Rome, he met and befriended the great German historian, Barthold George Niebuhr, who was then Prussia's minister to Rome. Niebuhr became Lieber's teacher and protector, and under his influence Lieber's revolutionary outlook was gradually replaced by the conservative political doctrines of Edmund Burke.

---

[12] The major biography of Lieber is Frank Freidel, *Francis Lieber, Nineteenth-Century Liberal* (Baton Rouge: Louisiana State University Press, 1947, reprinted Clark: The Lawbook Exchange, Ltd., 2003).

[13] Lieber gives an account of his army experiences including the battle of Waterloo in "Personal Reminiscences of the Battle of Waterloo." See *The Miscellaneous Writings of Francis Lieber* (Philadelphia: J.B. Lippincott, 1881, reprinted Clark: The Lawbook Exchange, Ltd., 2003) Vol. I, 149–175.

With Niebuhr's support and some promise of an academic career, Lieber returned to Germany. The police, however, continued to hound him. In fear of the authorities, he fled to England in 1826 with letters of introduction from Niebuhr to influential Germans living in London. While there, Lieber received encouragement from many sympathetic intellectuals, including John Stuart Mill and Jeremy Bentham. Lieber hoped to receive an academic appointment in England, but he was unsuccessful. Instead, his next job offer came from another field in which Lieber was active: gymnastics. Like many German progressives, he was a disciple of Friedrich Ludwig Jahn, the German physical culturist and political liberal. Known as "*Turnvater Jahn*" [the father of gymnastics Jahn], he was the author of an influential treatise on the physical, intellectual, moral and political benefits of gymnastics that was translated into several languages. A deeply influential book, it inspired the establishment of several gymnasia and related facilities in Germany and elsewhere. In 1825 George Bancroft and some other prominent Bostonians who had encountered Jahn's work while studying in Germany wished to establish a similar institution in Boston that would include a gymnasium and a swimming pool. Upon Jahn's recommendation, they invited Lieber to establish and direct it. He arrived in the United States in 1827. In part through contacts he made at work, Lieber came to know such distinguished members of America's intellectual, literary and political elite as George Bancroft, John Quincy Adams, Caleb Cushing, Edward Everett, George Ticknor and, most important, Joseph Story.

Lieber's biographer Frank Freidel quotes a letter from Lieber to his parents describing a visit to the swimming school by John Quincy Adams, who was a remarkably good swimmer:

> [I asked Adams] if he would do me the honour to swim with me, and if he preferred, we would go outside

> the enclosure, in order to avoid the frolicking boys.... The old man looked at the boys, and said: "No, I prefer to stay here, if they will not laugh at me...." We prepared ourselves...and this man of sixty-one sprang headlong into the water from a spring-board six feet high.... He praised the school, and expressed the wish that there were many establishments of the kind in the country, which would greatly tend to promote the public health.[14]

Unfortunately, the Boston gymnasium soon proved to be only a passing fad and the pool also failed to maintain its initial popularity. Casting about for a new venture, Lieber decided to return to scholarship, hoping to find a project with good financial prospects. While in England, Lieber had begun a relationship with an attractive young woman named Mathilda Oppenheimer and he needed money to bring her over from England, marry her, and establish a proper home in America. So in January 1828, Lieber approached the leading publishing firm of Philadelphia, Carey, Lea, and Carey, with several publication ideas. The proprietors of the company were Henry Carey and Isaac Lea, son and son-in-law, respectively, of Mathew Carey, the great Irish radical printer and pamphleteer. The idea that appealed to them most was Lieber's plan for a new American encyclopedia. It would be based on the most influential encyclopedia in Europe, the *Conversations-Lexikon*,[15] a popular German work first published in 1812. It had already been translated and published successfully in Danish, Dutch, French and Swedish with great commercial success, but Lieber did not intend to restrict himself to yet another translation—he would add many new articles of American content and interest by leading American scholars and,

---

[14] Freidel, *op. cit.,* quoting letter from Lieber to his parents, September 6, 1827.

[15] *Allgemeine deutsche Real-Encyklopädie für die gebildeten stand* [*Conversations-Lexikon*] (Leipzig: F.A. Brockhaus, 1827–1829), that is the 7th edition of a work originally published in Leipzig in 1812.

where appropriate, supplement or revise existing articles with new American content. Rather than receiving royalties, Lieber agreed to accept a flat fee of $20,000 for producing the encyclopedia. From that sum, however, he had to pay his own writers, translators and editors. Mathilda joined Lieber in New York in September, 1829. They were married and lived happily ever after.

Lieber hired as his assistant editor Edward Wigglesworth, a twenty-four year old member of a distinguished Boston family who had been trained in the law. They set up offices in Boston, and hired a dozen translators to convert the German text into English at fifty cents a page. Writers of new articles were paid a dollar a page, the same rate as was paid by *North American Review,* the leading literary and current affairs magazine of the day. That rate, however, was only half of what the Carey firm paid contributors to their own periodical, *American Quarterly.*[16] After seventeen months of preparation, the first volume appeared in September 1829. Although it was originally conceived as a twelve-volume set, the editors needed a thirteenth volume to accommodate the balance of the final text, which appeared in 1833. A fourteenth, or supplementary volume prepared by a new editor, was issued years later in 1847.

The first edition cost purchasers $32.50 for the set and it was a smashing success. The *North American Review*[17] gave it lavish praise, saying:

> This work...deserves to be recommended to the great body of our people, as a library of itself; —cheap, com-

---

[16] D. Kaser, *Messrs. Carey & Lea of Philadelphia, A Study in the History of the Booktrade* (Philadelphia: University of Pennsylvania, 1857) 134.

[17] Unsigned but probably by John Neal, *North American Review,* vol. XXXIV (1832) 265; *American Quarterly Review*, by Robert Walsh, Vol. VI (1829) 347–349.

> prehensive, exceedingly well executed, and of the highest authority.

The review, which is included in this volume at pp. 329–335, went on to compare the size and price of the American encyclopedia with a hypothetically similar English publication. Because of the double columns, the size and quality of paper and the small type size, the reviewer suggested that each of Lieber's volumes contained the equivalent of three or four English octavo volumes, which would have cost twelve shillings sterling per volume. Thus, by English practice, the same set would have filled 36 to 48 octavo volumes and would have cost $150 in America, compared to the $32.50 price of Lieber's set.

The publishers promoted their new publication aggressively by issuing an eight page prospectus that they placed in the *North American Review* and other periodicals.[18] It included testimonials from such distinguished figures (who were also contributors) as Ticknor, Bancroft, Everett and Story.[19] (The prospectus is set forth in this volume at p. 361.) Lieber said later that over a hundred thousand sets of the *Americana* were sold, but he, pursuant to his agreement, received no royalties.[20] In a letter, Lieber angrily noted that upon the completion of the thirteen volume encyclopedia he had only a few hundred dollars left. That anger grew, as Carey and Lea sold or licensed the work to other publishers and sales continued without any return to Lieber.[21] Although ultimately disappointing from a financial standpoint, the encyclopedia helped him to launch a scholarly career

[18] *North American Review*, vol. XXVII (1828) and in *American Quarterly Review*, vol. X (June 1829).

[19] It seems that Carey and Lea were not bothered by this conflict of interest. Since the articles were unsigned, and only a partial list of contributors was revealed in Volume 13, most readers would not have been fully aware of the conflict, if they noticed it at all.

[20] Freidel, *op. cit.,* 80.

[21] Freidel, *op. cit.,* 66.

that brought the great success and prominence he sought. In 1835 he accepted an appointment as professor of history and political economy in the University of South Carolina. After publishing *Legal and Political Hermeneutics* (1839) and other important treatises in law and political science, he moved to Columbia College in New York in 1856, and then to its Law School in 1860. In addition to *On Civil Liberty and Self-Government* (1859) and the path-breaking *Code for the Government of the Armies of the United States* (1863), he continued to publish scholarly works, translations of European writers, and books for the general public until his death in 1872. While his mentor, Jahn, was known as the "father of gymnastics," Lieber became known as the father of American political science.

* * * * * *

Lieber met the fifty-year old Joseph Story when Story had been an associate justice of the Supreme Court for some seventeen years, and was at the beginning of his career as professor of law and legal scholar. The warmth of their friendship and intellectual compatibility is indicated in many of the letters which passed between them.[22] Given those factors, it is not surprising that Lieber asked Story to write for his encyclopedia. Story agreed to write all of the major articles on American law and ultimately completed eighteen articles, totaling over 120 pages in double columns and small print. The first of these (including "Common Law," "Congress of the United States" and "Contracts") appeared in Volume Three. Story insisted that the articles appear anonymously, as were most but not all of the articles in the *Encyclopedia*. In at least two of the articles, "Jury"

[22] For example, Story writes in a letter to Lieber dated August 16, 1834: "I can scarcely tell you, how much I wish that you lived in Cambridge. I should not even then (so constant are my occupations) see you often; but then I could catch a lazy hour and sit down and talk straight forward to you, on all you thought and wished. I want a mind that can stir my own."

and "Law, Legislation, Codes,"[23] which included a section from the *Conversations-Lexicon* and a section newly written for the *Americana,* the author of the new material is identified as "an eminent American jurist." In the thirteenth volume of the *Encyclopedia*, the editors included a partial list of the contributors that included "Joseph Story of Washington." They further noted:

> In preparing this *Encyclopedia*, the conductors have endeavored to obtain the best materials and the best assistance within their power. Their labors have been lightened by the kind contributions which they received from various quarters. To the Hon. Judge Story, and to John Pickering, Esq., of Boston, they are under peculiar obligations. The longest and most elaborate articles in the law department are from the pen of the former gentleman; and it is needless to say how much these add to the value of the work. From Mr. Pickering they have received, in a variety of ways, the most important aid."[24]

As Story's son William Wetmore Story suggests, his father was not paid for this work. Instead, "[t]hey were labors dedicated purely to friendship, and illustrate a generosity which is as beautiful as it is rare."[25] Years later, Lieber fondly remembered:

> I shall never forget the offer he made to contribute some articles when I complained of my embarrassment as to getting proper articles on the main subjects of law for my work intended for the general reader. Many of them

[23] *Encyclopedia Americana*, Vol. VII, 278, 576.

[24] *Encyclopedia Americana*, Vol. XIII, 3–4. John Pickering (1777–1846), distinguished Boston lawyer, political figure and philologist, wrote several articles on law for the *Encyclopedia*, including one on Agrarian laws (mostly Roman law which was a major interest of his) and another on public lands. He also wrote several entries on linguistics.

[25] W.W. Story, ed., *Life and Letters of Joseph Story*, *op. cit.*, Vol. II, 27.

> were sent from Washington while he was fully occupied with the important business of the Supreme Court. He himself made out the list of articles to be contributed by him, and I do not remember ever having been obliged to wait for one. The only condition this kind-hearted man made was that I should not publish the fact that he had contributed the articles in the work until some period subsequent to their appearance...[26]

The following is a list of Story's articles:

VOLUME III

Common Law
Congress of the United States
Conquest
Contract
Corpus Delicti
Courts

VOLUME IV

Criminal Law
Death, Punishment of
Domicile
Equity

VOLUME V

Evidence

VOLUME VII

Jury
Lien
Law, Legislation and Codes

VOLUME IX

Law of Nations
Natural Law

[26] *The Life and Letters of Francis Lieber*, *op. cit.*, 79–80.

VOLUME X
Prize

VOLUME XII
Usury

Several of Story's articles contain his Federalist political philosophy, supporting the primacy of the federal government over the states, and implying the danger of dissolution of the union if the states were given too much autonomy. It is therefore surprising that Story didn't write the article on the Constitution of the United States. At first, I wondered whether Story's son might have inadvertently, by oversight or mistake, omitted that article from his list. In reading the article entitled, "Constitution," which was an original contribution to the *Americana*, it is clear that it is not by Story. The article begins with six columns on the political concept of a constitution followed by sixteen columns on European constitutions and, finally, three columns and twelve tables on the American Constitutions —meaning the state constitutions and the federal constitution. Those comparative tables treat the federal text as just another constitution among many. The table, entitled "Abstracts of the Constitutions of the United States" compares the provisions of 24 state constitutions and the federal constitution on their legislatures, executive, and judiciary branches. The text of the article offers no discussion of the topics about which Story felt so strongly, particularly those dealing with federal-state relations. Ironically, that constitution article appeared in the encyclopedia volume published in 1833, the same year as Story's *Commentaries on the Constitution of the United States.*

A reference in a letter written by Story to Lieber, accompanying his submission of the article "Congress," confuses the issue further. The letter, dated December 16, 1829, states:

> I now enclose the article *Congress of the United States of America.* You will please take notice that it includes a full account of all the powers of the Legislature. Still to give a full view of the Constitution of the United States it will be necessary to give under other articles, say, Constitution of the United States, President of the United States, Courts of the United States, etc., etc., a like description of all the other Departments.[27]

Note that Story here refers to Constitution in the singular. The article that he's suggesting, i.e., on the Federal Constitution, seems to have never been written, or perhaps if written, it was not included in the encyclopedia.

It's not clear whether this omission was Story's choice, or the preference of either Lieber or Carey and Lea. The motivation for such a choice (on Story's part) or preference (on the part of either the editor or the publishers) is also puzzling. I can't think of any reason why Story would not have wanted to write the Constitution article. Someone suggested that perhaps either Lieber or the publishers were concerned that Story's Federalist views might have hampered the marketing of the *Encyclopedia* in the South where such views were an anathema. That's possible, I guess, but why then did they take a chance that his Federalism would pervade this article, as it in fact does in the articles they accepted? Perhaps they realized that his ideological stance was potentially the most dangerous on the federal-state question and they didn't want to lose the prestige of Story's participation entirely. Or, maybe Story was just sick and tired of writing about the Constitution because he just finished his three-volume *Commentaries* and its one-volume abridgment.

---

[27] Francis Lieber Manuscript Collection, Henry E. Huntington Library, San Marino, California; quoted in John C. Hogan, "Comments: Legal History - Joseph Story's Anonymous Law Articles," 52 *Michigan Law Review* (1954) 874.

In his articles Story frequently makes reference to other law writers and the historical sources of English and American law. For example, in the article on the Common Law, he refers several times to Blackstone's *Commentarie*s and notes that the United States did not adopt all of English common law. Story states:

> When we say that the common law constitutes the basis of American jurisprudence, we do not mean that the whole common law, as it exists in England, is adopted here...many portions were never enforced at all in America. For instance, the ecclesiastical establishment, and much of the law growing out of it, was never introduced or recognized here.[28]

In his article "Contracts" and in his other articles on private law, Story includes extensive references to Roman law, and to English and French law. As in his many treatises, Story contrasts common law principles with those of the civil law system. The wide scope of Story's interests and the breadth of his scholarly view can also be seen in his article on the punishment of death. In justifying the death penalty, Story refers to Biblical, Greek, and Roman law, and then to contemporary French, German and Turkish law, and, of course, the common law of England. He makes frequent references to foreign and comparative law, and to the writings of continental legal scholars in many of his articles.

Although Story did not write the article on the Constitution, the views which he expressed in his *Commentaries on the Constitution* are reflected in his other articles. For example, in "Congress," "Courts," "Punishment by Death" and "Jury" he refers to particular provisions of the Federal Constitution. Story's article on the Courts of the United States assumes that the doctrine of judicial review was

---

[28] *Encyclopedia, op.cit.*, Vol. III, 394.

settled law. Judicial review, of course, had been established in various decisions by Chief Justice John Marshall and by Story himself. This power of judicial review extended not only to "final decisions of the State courts," but also to acts of the federal Congress and the executive. He states:

> The constitution is deemed the supreme law of the land, which rulers, and magistrates, and legislatures are bound to obey; and if, unintentionally or otherwise, they overleap the proper boundary, and the supreme court so decide, the act of the legislatures or rulers becomes a mere nullity, and receives no sanction or support whatsoever.[29]

Perhaps Story felt, and Lieber agreed, that the extensive coverage of Constitutional issues, particularly in the articles on Congress and the courts was sufficient and that a separate essay wasn't necessary.

Story's articles were not, however, the only ones on law in the *Encyclopedia*. Lieber commissioned others from several scholars. In fact, I was able to count almost two hundred such articles, but most of those were not on American law. The highlights of Lieber's coverage of American law were those eighteen articles by Joseph Story.

Story's article on *Natural Law* reveals his deep commitment to the natural law tradition which he had previously called "the foundation of all other laws."[30] The article reveals him in agreement with Blackstone that the natural law is God-given. He notes: "The obligatory force of the law of nature upon man is derived from its presumed coincidence with the will of his Creator."[31] Story's biographer, James McClellan, notes: "This conservative

---

[29] *Encyclopedia, op. cit.*, Vol. III, 596.

[30] "Discourse pronounced upon the inauguration of the author, as Dane Professor of Law in Harvard University, August 25th, 1829," in Joseph Story, *The Miscellaneous Writings, Literary, Critical, Juridical, and Political of Joseph Story, LL.D. , Now First Collected*, 465.

[31] *Encyclopedia, op. cit.*, Vol. III, 150.

religious orthodoxy, lying at the heart of his natural law philosophy, forms the thesis of his essay, "Natural Law," which he wrote for Francis Lieber's *Encyclopedia Americana* in 1832."[32]

As McClellan and other biographers have noted at length, Story's conception of natural law was very much influenced by his reading of Edmund Burke, the conservative political philosopher. McClellan, who notes that Burke was the thinker Story admired most, observes: "Story's frequent references to Burke are also instructive; inasmuch as Burke greatly influenced Story, and Story in turn permanently influenced the growth and development of American constitutional law, there is good cause to suspect that Burke's influence on American law has been far more extensive than usually is believed."[33] He then says: "Indeed, the mainstay of the *Commentaries* is Burke, whose conservative philosophy Story weaves into the constitutional fabric as though Burke himself had written the document.[34] Although, earlier in his life, Burke supported the American Revolution, he was appalled by the excesses of the French Revolution and actively opposed its British supporters. Burke's influence on Story was in turn extended to Lieber, not only through their discussions about the encyclopedia, but even more directly in Story's advice to Lieber in connection with the latter's first book, *A Manual of Political Ethics* (1838). Story's conservatism was most apparent in his economic decisions, but he also upheld the Fugitive Slave Acts and permitted the forcible return of runaway slaves to their owners. Although Story's son and other defenders noted that he was only doing his judicial duty in enforcing a valid law, critics felt that he went further in invalidating as unconstitutional personal liberty laws enacted by some northern states to protect the fugitives.

---

[32] McClellan, 66.
[33] McClellan, 83, n. 75.
[34] McClellan, 310.

One of Story's most interesting articles is "Law, Legislation, and Codes," which appeared in the Appendix to Volume Seven. In it, after a long and learned exposition on the history of legislation and on principles of statutory interpretation, he focuses on codification by asking: "how far it is practicable to give a complete system of positive law, or a complete code of direct legislation."[35] Spurred on by Jeremy Bentham's writings, American law reformers were exploring the possibilities of codification to correct the uncertainties of the common law. Although Story was usually an ardent supporter of the common law and disliked Bentham and most of his ideas, here he seems to favor a qualified notion of codification and the adoption of a uniform code of laws for all jurisdictions. Story concludes this discussion, as follows: "…in every civilized country, much may be done to simplify the principles and practice of the law by judicious codification, and to give it uniformity and certainty."[36] Maybe in this instance Story's Federalist leanings trumped his advocacy of the common law.

Story's conservative economic philosophy can be seen in "Usury," where he supports freedom of contract unrestrained by governmental interference. That was the last one he contributed to the *Encyclopedia.*[37] He asserts: "There is, however, not the slightest foundation, either in natural or revealed religion, for any prohibition against the taking of interest upon money, any more than against the taking of a profit for the use of any other thing loaned." He thus opposes absolute legislative restrictions on particular rates of interest. With compassion in his conservatism, he goes on to say, however, that "the object of laws is to prevent oppression and imposition, and undue advantage of the strong over the weak and credulous…." He therefore favors "providing, by general principles of law, that

[35] *Encyclopedia, op. cit.*, vol. VII, 585.
[36] *Ibid*, 590.
[37] *Ibid*, vol. XII, 485–488.

unconscionable and oppressive contracts, where undue advantage is taken of the weakness, or credulity, or necessity, of the other party, shall be either wholly set aside, or reduced to moderation, upon a full trial of each particular cause, and an examination of all the facts...." That may, of course, be an expensive and uncertain means of relief for the weak and oppressed.

Another example of Story's writing for a wider audience is an article he wrote for a German legal periodical. That article, called by Story "Sketch of American Law,"[38] was written in response to a request made to him by Francis Lieber. A German friend of Lieber's, Carl Joseph Anton Mittermaier, professor of criminal law at Heidelberg University, had asked Lieber for information on American law and for names of American jurists who might write for his new comparative law journal, *Kritische Zeitschrift fur Rechtswissenschaft und Gesetzgebung des Auslandes.*[39] Lieber solicited Story and the latter wrote the *Sketch,* reproduced below at pp. 343–360, which was sent to Mittermaier. It appeared a year later, after being translated into German, as the lead article in Volume Nine.[40] Story had great interest in developing closer contacts between American lawyers and their German counterparts. He thought that foreign influences would be very helpful in the development of American law and that Lieber could play an important role in facilitating them. He wrote to Lieber:

---

[38] Letter by Joseph Story to Francis Lieber, dated Aug. 16, 1834, referring to its completion.

[39] These events are described in Kurt H. Nadelmann, "Joseph Story's Sketch of American Law," 3 *American Journal of Comparative Law* 3–8 (1954) reproduced below at pp. 337–342.

[40] Its publication was noted in 17 *American Jurist and Law Magazine* 496 (1837), with the following editorial comment: "It will do much to diffuse correct information, throughout Germany, in relation to our government and laws, and to the different functions of the federal and State courts, in the administration of Justice."

> I look chiefly to the study of foreign law, and especially foreign commercial law, for the most important improvements which are likely to be made in our commercial jurisprudence.[41]

Lieber's biographer, Frank Freidel, nicely summarized Story's contribution to the *Encyclopedia*: "Erudite but understandable, these articles on both American and Roman law made the *Encyclopedia* a worth-while acquisition for any young lawyer and gave the publication a prestige it otherwise could not have enjoyed."[42] For modern readers, these articles offer insights into the development of Joseph Story's thinking on a variety of legal topics and illustrate his wide-ranging intellectual interests in law. They also demonstrate his determination to educate all Americans in the law of their nation. The sketch on American law which Story wrote for Carl Mittermaier's German journal reflects his desire to maintain close connections with the Continental legal community and to keep European academic and jurists apprised of America's intellectual development.

Morris L. Cohen
Yale Law School
October 2005

---

[41] Letter from Story to Lieber, July 24, 1833, Francis Lieber Manuscript Collection, Huntington Library, quoted in an excellent article on these overseas exchanges: M.H.Hoeflich, "Transatlantic Friendships & the German Influence on American Law in the First Half of the Nineteenth Century," 35 *American Journal of Comparative Law* 599–611 (1987) at 604.

[42] Freidel, *op. cit.*, 69.

Essays by Joseph Story

from

Encyclopedia Americana

Philadelphia, 1843–1844

ENCYCLOPÆDIA AMERICANA.

A

POPULAR DICTIONARY

OF

ARTS, SCIENCES, LITERATURE, HISTORY, POLITICS AND BIOGRAPHY,

A NEW EDITION;

INCLUDING

A COPIOUS COLLECTION OF ORIGINAL ARTICLES

IN

AMERICAN BIOGRAPHY;

ON

THE BASIS OF THE SEVENTH EDITION OF THE GERMAN

CONVERSATIONS-LEXICON.

EDITED BY

FRANCIS LIEBER,

ASSISTED BY

E. WIGGLESWORTH.

VOL. III.

PHILADELPHIA:
LEA & BLANCHARD.
1844.

Common Law

The phrase "the common law" is a very familiar expression in English jurisprudence, and, has various significations, or, rather, is used sometimes in a limited and sometimes in a more enlarged sense. In a large sense, it comprehends the whole body of English law, as well the statutes passed by parliament as the general customary law of the realm. In this manner, it is used in contradistinction to the Roman, or, as we call it, the civil law. In a more limited sense, "the common law" expresses that portion of English jurisprudence which is unwritten (*lex non scripta*), in contradistinction to the parliamentary statutes, which are the positive written code (*lex scripta*). For instance, we say that a particular remedy for a wrong is given by the common law, and that another remedy, by way of penalty, is provided by statute; meaning that the latter depends upon some known act of the legislature; but the former rests altogether upon immemorial usage or general principles, which cannot be traced back to any such act. There is yet a still more limited sense, in which the expression is used to designate that portion of the English common law, which is strictly the custom of the realm, and local and municipal in its origin, in contradistinction to the law of nations, and the maritime and commercial law, which are drawn from the general usages and principles recognised among civilized nations. Correctly speaking, the common law now comprehends the law of nations and the law merchant. But these are of much later introduction into English jurisprudence, than the other general customs of the realm, of which we have been speaking. They have been borrowed, for the most part, from the general usages of merchants, in the commercial nations, which, upon the revival of commerce and letters, inhabited the shores of the Mediterranean. For instance, the law of foreign bills of exchange, of insurance, and of general average, is of comparatively recent adoption in England, and cannot be traced back far in her annals. The law of insurance has almost entirely grown up since the time when Lord Mansfield became the chief-justice of England (1756). The name of the *common law*, which is thus given to this collection of maxims and customs in England, Blackstone (1 *Bl. Comm.* 67) says, was either given to it in contradistinction to other laws, as the statute law, the civil law, the law merchant, and the like; or, more probably, as a law common to the realm (*jus commune*, or *folk-right*), mentioned by King Edward the Elder, after the abolition of the several provincial customs and particular laws by king Alfred and his successors. But though it is called the *lex non scripta* (or *unwritten law*),we are not to imagine that it is, at present, merely oral, and transmitted, from age to age, by word of mouth. In the dark ages, indeed, amidst the general ignorance of the times, few laws were reduced to writing; and still fewer of these maxims and customs were to be found in books or manuscripts. But (as Blackstone has observed, 1 *Bl. Comm.* 63) with us, at present, the monuments and evidences of our legal customs are contained in the records of the several courts of justice, in books of reports and judicial decisions, and in the treatises of learned sages of the profession, preserved and handed down to us from times of the highest antiquity. They are, however, still styled the *unwritten law*, because they are not set down in a code, as acts of parliament are, in writing, but they derive their authority from long and immemorial usage, and the universal recognition of them throughout the realm. The origin of this common law is now lost in remote antiquity. It probably began in the early customs of the aboriginal Britons, and was successively augmented, in different ages, by the admixture of some of the laws and usages of the Romans, the Picts, the Saxons, the Danes and the Normans, who spread themselves over the country. It was feeble and narrow at first; but, expanding with, the exigencies of society and with the progress of knowledge and refinement, it has now become a very complex and intricate system, and presents a singular combination of the strict principles of the old feudal law, with the elegant reasoning of public and commercial jurisprudence, which are so much admired for their general equity. Of such a gradual formation and expansion is, doubtless, the law of most civilized countries. The Roman or civil law is made up, not merely of the positive legislation of the senate and the people, and the edicts of the emperors, but also of the decrees of courts of justice, of the opinions of learned jurists, and of the silent but irresistible usages of the people in the arrangements of their business and domestic policy. These usages, at first voluntary and arbitrary, generally acquired the force of custom; and tradition made them operate as laws to regulate like concerns in other ages; and, as they were generally founded in public convenience, they were adhered to, first from habit, and at last from an anxious desire, natural in all governments, to profit by the experience of the past, and to fix rights by some certain rules coinciding with the existing state of the people. The common law is usually divided into 3 kinds:—1. general customs, which are the universal rule of the whole kingdom, and form the common law in its more usual signification; 2. particular customs, which, for the most part, affect only the inhabitants of particular districts; 3. certain particular laws, which, by custom, are adopted and used by some particular courts of pretty general and extensive jurisdiction. (1 *Bl. Comm.* 67.) The first embraces the general maxims and principles of English jurisprudence, such as the regulation of the descent of estates, the exposition of contracts and wills, the remedies for civil injuries, and the definition and punishment of crimes, &c. The second embraces the jurisprudence of a peculiar nature existing in certain local districts, such as the custom of gavelkind, in Kent county, where all the sons inherit the estate of their parent, and not (as is the general law of England) the eldest son; so the custom of Borough English, where the youngest son inherits the estate: such, also, are the peculiar customs of the city of London. The third embraces those portions of the civil law and the canon law which are of force in the ecclesiastical and admiralty and other courts, and have long constituted the system which regulates the rights and remedies administered in those courts. This subject will be found discussed at large in1 *Bl. Comm.* from p. 63 top. 92, and in Lord Hale's *History of the Common Law*. A further discussion here would occupy too much space.

The common law of England constitutes the general basis of the jurisprudence of all the U. States of America, except only Louisiana, where the civil law prevails. This common law consists only of the first and third kinds of customary law above mentioned, there being no local or provincial law existing in any particular county or district of any state, as contradistinguished from that which prevails in the state at large. When we say that the common law constitutes the basis of American jurisprudence, we do not mean that the whole common law, as it exists in England, is adopted here. The general doctrine is, that such portions of the common law only as were adapted to the situation of the colonies at their first settlement, and were thence afterwards used and recognised, are now of force in the states. But many portions were never in force at all in America. For instance, the ecclesiastical establishment, and much of the law growing out of it, was never introduced or recognised here. We, too, consider that all the statutes made in England before the emigration of our ancestors, which were in amendment of the law, and in melioration of it, constitute a part of our common law, and, as such, were brought thither by our ancestors, at their emigration. But statutes since enacted have no force at all here, unless they have been sanctioned by the legislature, or have been adopted into our local practice, by general usage, as amendments of the law. And, indeed, many of the fundamental principles of the common law have been altered, repealed or modified by positive legislation of the various states, as well while they were colonies as since their independence; so that, though the general basis is the same, there are almost infinite shades of difference in the actual jurisprudence of the different states. There is another sense in which we speak of the common law, in contradistinction to what is called *equity jurisprudence*. The administration of a distinct system of jurisprudence by distinct tribunals of this nature seems peculiar to England and the colonies which derive their origin from her. Blackstone (3 *Bl. Comm.* 50) has well observed, that the distinction between law and equity, as administered in different courts, is not at present known, nor seems ever to have been known in any other country at any other time; and yet the difference of one from the other, when administered by the same tribunal, was perfectly familiar to the Romans; the *jus prætorium*, or discretion of the *prætor*, being distinct from the *leges*, or standing laws. It would occupy too much space to enter into a full development of this distinction in the actual administration of justice in England. In general, courts of equity administer remedies *ex æquo et bono* only in cases where the courts of common law cannot administer an adequate remedy. Hence a very familiar expression is, that a right is an *equitable right*, or an *equity*; by which we mean, that it is a right recognised only in courts of equity, and for which the common law, in its ordinary tribunals, affords no remedy, and of which it takes no notice. (See *Courts and Equity*.)

Congress of the United States of America

The national legislature of the U. States of America is designated, in the constitution of the general government, by this title. It consists of a Senate and a House of Representatives, each constituting a distinct and independent branch. The House of Representatives is composed of members chosen every second year, by the people of the several states; and the voters or electors are required to have the same qualifications as are requisite for choosing the members of the most numerous branch of the state legislature of the state in which they vote. The representatives are apportioned among the several states according to their respective population; and, in estimating the population, three fifths of the slaves are added to the whole number of free persons. A census of the population is taken once in every ten years, and an apportionment is then made of the representatives for each state. The representatives are then elected in each state, either in districts, or by a general ticket, as the state legislature directs. There cannot be more than 1 representative for every 30,000 persons. The present apportionment is 1 representative for every 40,000 persons. Each state, however small may be its population, is entitled to at least 1 representative. No person can be a representative who shall not have attained the age of 25 years, and have been 7 years a citizen of the U. States, and who shall not, when elected, be an inhabitant of that state in which he shall be chosen. No other qualifications are required. When vacancies happen in the representation of any state, by death, resignation, or otherwise, new writs of election are issued by the executive thereof to fill the vacancy. The House of Representatives chooses its own speaker and other officers, and possesses the sole power of impeachment. Each representative has a single vote.

The Senate of the United States is composed of 2 senators from each state; and, there being 24 states, the Senate now consists of 48 members. The senators of each state are chosen by the legislature of the state for six years, and each senator has one vote. They are divided into three classes, so that one third thereof is, or may be, changed by a new election every second year. When vacancies happen, they are supplied by the state legislature, if in session; if not, the state executive makes a temporary appointment until the legislature meets. No person can be a senator who is not 30 years of age, and has not been 9 years a citizen of the U. States, and is not, when elected, an inhabitant of the state for which he is chosen. The vice president is, *ex officio*, president of the Senate; but he has no vote unless they be equally divided. The Senate chooses all its other officers, and a president, *pro tempore*, in the absence of the vice president, or when he exercises the office of president of the U. States. The Senate has the sole power of trying all impeachments; and, when sitting for this purpose, the Senators take an oath or affirmation. If the president of the U. States should be impeached, the chief justice is to preside. A conviction on impeachment cannot be without the concurrence of two thirds of the members present. The judgment extends only to a removal from office and future disqualification for office. But the party is, nevertheless, liable to punishment on indictment, by the common trial and course of law.

The times, places and manner of holding elections for Senators and Representatives, are appointed by the state legislatures; but the Congress may, by law, fix and alter the time and manner of holding such elections. Each of the two houses, viz., the Senate and Representatives, is the judge of the elections, returns and qualifications of its own members. Each house determines the rules of its own proceedings, and has power to punish its members for disorderly conduct, and, with the concurrence of two thirds, to expel a member. A majority of each house constitutes a quorum to do business; but a smaller number may adjourn from day to day, and has power to compel the attendance of absent members, in such manner as it may provide. Each house is required to keep a journal of its proceedings, and, from time to time, to publish the same, excepting such parts as, in its judgment, may require secrecy. In point of fact, they are published every day or two, during the session, and collected in volumes at the end thereof. The yeas and nays of the members of each house, on any question, are required, at the desire of one fifth of those present, to be entered on the journal. The congress is required to assemble at least once ever year; and such meeting is on the first Monday of December annually, unless a different day is provided by law. The president of the U. States has authority to convene extra sessions. Neither house, during the session of congress, can, without the consent of the other, adjourn more than 3 days, nor to any other place than that in which the two houses shall be sitting. In case of disagreement between the two houses, as to the time of adjournment, the president of the U. States may adjourn them to such time as he shall think proper. The Senators and representatives are entitled to receive a compensation, provided by law, for their services, from the treasury of the U. States. They are also privileged from arrests, except in cases of treason, felony, or breaches of the peace, during their attendance at the session of their respective houses, and in going to and returning from the same. This does not mean merely their daily attendance; but, also, in going from or returning to their respective homes, in the several states. They have liberty of speech, and are not liable to be questioned, in any other place, for any speech or debate in either house. No Senator or representative can be appointed to any civil office under the authority of the U. States, which is created, or its emoluments increased, during the time for which he is elected; and no person, holding an office under the U. States, can be a member of either house during his continuance in office. It has been already stated, that each house determines the rules of its own proceedings; and, in point of fact, each house now has a large collection of rules, which are printed for the use of the members, and for the public at large. In a general sense, the rules and practice of the British House of Commons form the basis of their proceedings, modified from time to time, as each house deems fit. The rules are too numerous to admit of any useful summary in this place. There are, however, certain constitutional provisions, as to the proceedings of the two houses, which deserve to be mentioned. All bills for raising revenue must originate in the House of Representatives; but the Senate may propose or concur with amendments, as on other bills. Every bill which has passed the Senate and House of Representatives, before it can become a law, must be presented to the president of the U. States. If he approves, he signs it; if not, he returns it to the house in which it originated, with his objections, and these objections are entered at large on their journals, and they then proceed to reconsider. If, upon reconsideration, two thirds of such house agree to pass the bill, it is sent, with the objections, to the other house, by which it is also to be reconsidered; and, if approved by two thirds of that house also, it becomes a law. But in all such cases, the votes of both houses are determined by yeas and nays, and the names entered on the journals. No instance has, as yet, occurred, in which any bill, returned by the president with objections, has ever become a law by a vote of two thirds of each house. If any bill is not returned by the president within 10 days (Sundays excepted) after it is presented to him, it becomes a law, in the same way as if he had signed it, unless congress, by their adjournment, prevent its return. Every order, resolution or vote, to which the concurrence of both houses is necessary, must, in like manner, be presented to the president, and similar proceedings are to be had thereon. The legislative powers belonging to congress will now be stated, in the words of the constitution itself, since different modes of interpretation of the same language have, at different times, been insisted on by different parties in the U. States. Congress, then, by the constitution, has power to lay and collect taxes, duties, imposts and excises, to pay the debts, and provide for the common defence and general welfare of the U. States; but all duties, imposts, and excises shall be uniform throughout the U. States:—to borrow money on the credit of the U. States:—to regulate commerce with foreign nations and among the several states, and with the Indian tribes:—to establish a uniform rule of naturalization, and uniform laws on the subject of bankruptcy throughout the U. States:—to coin money, regulate the value thereof, and of foreign coins, and to fix the standard of weights and measures :—to provide for the punishment of counterfeiting the securities and current coin of the U. States:—to establish post offices and post roads:—to promote the progress of science and useful arts, by securing, for limited times, to authors and inventors, the exclusive right to their respective writings and discoveries:—to constitute tribunals inferior to the Supreme Court to define and punish piracies and felonies committed on the high seas, and offences against the law of nations:—to declare war, grant letters of marque and reprisal, and make rules concerning captures on land or water:—to raise and support armies; but no appropriation of money to that use shall be for a longer term than two years:—to provide and maintain a navy:—to make rules for the government and regulation of the land and naval forces:—to provide for calling forth the militia to execute the laws of the union, suppress insurrections and repel invasions:—to provide for organizing, arming, and disciplining the militia, and for governing such part of them as may be employed in the service of the U. States, reserving to the states, respectively, the appointment of the officers, and the authority of training the militia according to the discipline prescribed by congress:—to exercise exclusive legislation in all cases whatsoever over such district, not exceeding 10 miles square, as may by cession of particular states, and the acceptance of congress, become the seat of the government of the U. States; and to exercise like authority over all places purchased by the consent of the legislature of the state in which the same shall be, for the erection of forts, magazines, arsenals, dockyards, amid other needful buildings and:—to "make all laws which shall be necessary and proper for carrying into effect the foregoing powers, and all other powers vested by this constitution in the government of the U. States, or in any department or office thereof."

Congress has also power to organize the Supreme Court, and to ordain and establish, from time to time, inferior courts. In some cases, the original jurisdiction of the Supreme Court is expressly given in the constitution; but its appellate jurisdiction is under the regulation of congress. Congress has, in other cases, an unlimited authority, as to the jurisdiction which shall be vested in other inferior courts, to which the judicial power given by the constitution extends. Congress has also power to declare the punishment of treason; but no attainder works any corruption of blood, or forfeiture, except for the life of the person attainted. The crime of treason is expressly defined, by the constitution, to consist in levying war against the U. States, or in adhering to their enemies, giving them aid and comfort. Congress has also power to prescribe, by general laws, the manner in which the public acts, records and judicial proceedings of the states shall be proved, and the effect thereof, the constitution declaring that full faith and credit shall be given in each state to them. Congress has also power to dispose of, and make all needful rules and regulations respecting the territory or other property belonging to the U. States; and also to admit new states into the union;

and also to propose, by a majority of two thirds of both houses, amendments to the constitution; or, on the application of the legislatures of two thirds of the several states, to call a convention for proposing amendments. But such amendments, to be binding, must be ratified by the legislatures of three fourths of the states, or by conventions in three fourths thereof, as the one or the other mode may be proposed by congress. But no state, without its consent, can be deprived of its equal suffrage in the Senate. There are also certain restrictions upon the powers of congress; the most material of which are, that the privilege of the writ of *habeas corpus* shall not be suspended, unless, in cases of rebellion or invasion, the public safety require it. No bill of attainder, or *ex post facto* law, shall be passed. No capitation or other direct tax shall be laid, unless in proportion to the census or enumeration before taken. No tax or duty shall be laid on articles exported from any state. No preference shall be given, by any regulation of commerce or revenue, to the ports of one state over those of another; nor shall vessels bound to or from one state be obliged to enter, clear, or pay duties in another. No money shall be drawn from the treasury but inconsequence of appropriations made bylaw; and a regular statement and account of all receipts and expenditures of all public money shall be published from time to time. No title of nobility shall be granted by the U. States; and no person holding any office of profit or trust under them shall, without the consent of congress, accept of any present, emolument, office or title of any kind whatever from any king, prince, or foreign state. These restrictions are found in the original constitution. Certain other restrictions and rights are secured by amendments made soon after the constitution was adopted. Among the most material are these:—Congress shall make no law respecting an establishment of religion, or prohibiting the free exercise thereof, or abridging the freedom of speech or of the press, or the right of the people peaceably to assemble and petition the government for a redress of grievances. The right also is secured to the people to bear arms, to be free from having soldiers quartered upon them in time of peace, or in war in any other manner than prescribed by law:—to be secure in their persons, houses, papers and effects against unreasonable searches and seizures, and to be liable to search and seizure only upon warrants upon probable cause supported by oath or affirmation; to answer for capital or otherwise infamous crimes only upon a presentment or indictment of a grand jury:—to be exempted from being twice put in jeopardy of life or limb for the same offence; not to be compelled, in any criminal case, to be witness against themselves; nor to be deprived of life, liberty or property, without due process of law; nor to have private property taken for public use, without just compensation. In criminal prosecutions, too, the accused enjoys the right to a speedy and public trial by an impartial jury of the state or district wherein the crime shall have been committed, which district shall have been previously ascertained by law; and to be informed of the nature and cause of the accusation; to be confronted with the witnesses against him; to have compulsory process for obtaining witnesses in his favor; and to have the assistance of counsel for his defence. In suits at common law, where the value in controversy exceeds $20, the right of a trial by jury is preserved. And no fact tried by a jury is to be otherwise reexamined in any court of the U. States, than according to the rules of the common law. Excessive bail is not to be required, nor excessive fines imposed, nor cruel or unusual punishments inflicted. This enumeration in the constitution of certain rights is not to be construed to deny or disparage others retained by the people. And the powers not delegated to the U. States by the constitution, nor prohibited by it to the states, are reserved to the states respectively, or to the people. (For other provisions of the constitution, see the titles *Constitution of the United States, Courts of the United States, President of the United States*, &c. &c.*)

* It will not be uninteresting to our readers if we add here a statement of the expenses of congress for the session of 1829–1830. The expense of this session is set down, in the estimate of the treasury department, at $665,050. The session is estimated to last 175 days, or nearly 6 months; so that the pay of each member will amount to $1400, or $375,800 for the whole number of members and delegates, besides the round sum of $120,000 for travelling expenses. The stationary, fuel, printing, &c., for the Senate, are estimated at $35,000, and for the House of Representatives, $100,000. It is worthwhile to compare these expenses with those of the chambers of France and the two houses in England.

Conquest

By *conquest* is now generally understood the right over property acquired in war, or by superior force. In the feudal law, it had a somewhat different sense, meaning any means of acquiring an estate out of the common course of inheritance. (2 *Bl. Comm.* 243.) The right of conquest has been deduced as an inference of natural law, from the right to weaken our enemy, to compel him to make compensation for injuries, to force him to an equitable peace, and to deter or prevent him from future injuries. It presupposes a just war, and a right of appropriation growing out of it. It is now generally admitted as a part of the law of nations. If a war be unjust, it is plain that it can receive no sanction from the law of nature or the law of nations; and, therefore, no just acquisitions can arise from it. But who is to decide whether the war be just or unjust? If neutral nations attempt to decide the question without consent, they draw themselves into the quarrel, and may be involved in the war. The parties who wage war never avow that they are acting unjustly, and will not admit any superior, who has a right to decide such questions for them. Nations claim a perfect equality and independence, and therefore will not submit to the decision of any other sovereign. The only answer, in a practical view, that can be given to the question is, that every free and sovereign state must decide for itself, whether it is carrying on a just war, and what are the duties required of it in such a war. With a view to public safety and repose, neutral nations are understood to be bound to act upon certain rules, which may be called the *voluntary law of nations*. Among these rules the following are universally admitted:

1. that every regular war, as to its effects, is to be deemed, by neutral nations, just on both sides; 2. that whatever is permitted to the one to do, in virtue of the state

of war, is also permitted to the other; 3. that the acquisitions made by each belligerent in the war are to be held lawful, and to be respected; 4. that neutral nations are bound to impartiality in their conduct to each of the belligerents. Many questions are discussed by jurists, in respect to the rights of conquest, some of which are of great nicety and subtlety. To enumerate them, without adverting to the various shades of opinion, would itself occupy a large discourse. We shall content ourselves, therefore, by enumerating a few only of the principles, which, by the benignity of religion and the enlarged influence of knowledge and public opinion, are now generally received among civilized nations. Conquest may respect either persons or things. It may respect movable or immovable property. It may apply to a whole nation, or only to a single town or province. It may be temporary or permanent.

Conquest over Persons

Persons captured in war are called *prisoners of war*, especially if they are taken in arms. If they are included in a mere surrender of territory, without being in arms, they are commonly deemed *subjects*, for the time being, upon their submission. But the conqueror may, if he chooses, consider all his enemies who surrender as prisoners of war, though it would be deemed a harsh and vindictive course.

The conqueror has no right to inflict upon prisoners of war any unnecessary injury or violence. He has no right to take away their lives, or subject them to cruel punishments. Formerly, they were sometimes removed into other countries, or reduced to a state of slavery for life. But these would now be thought such extreme exercises of power, as no Christian sovereign ought to authorize. Christian sovereigns now usually keep prisoners of war under guard, in suitable depots, until they are ransomed, or exchanged by cartel, or restored upon there turn of peace. Upon their return to their own country, all such prisoners are, by the law of *postliminy*, as it is called, considered as re-integrated to all their original rights and privileges. Officers in the public service are often released upon their parole of honor, by which they promise not to serve again in the war, until they are regularly exchanged; and, if they remain in the country of the conqueror, they are required to keep within certain limits, and report themselves at stated seasons to some proper officers. If they break their parole, they are universally esteemed infamous, and, if again taken in war, may be treated with great severity for their conduct.

Where persons are not found in arms, but are included as inhabitants of a town or province which has surrendered, they are treated generally as subjects. The original allegiance to their own government is suspended, and they come under the implied obligation to the conqueror, to violate none of his rights, to submit to his orders, and to demean themselves, for the time, as faithful subjects. Under such circumstances, the conqueror generally leaves them in possession of their property, and exercises his power with moderation, usually quartering his troops upon them, levying taxes, and punishing them only for rebellious or traitorous conduct.

Where the conquest is of a whole state (as, indeed, is true also of a town or small territory), the conqueror has authority either to rule the inhabitants by their former laws, or to create a new form of government; or perhaps, in an extreme case, to dissolve their society. Where the conquest is temporary, while war rages, it is rare for the conqueror to change the laws. But, where the conquest is permanent, or is recognised by a treaty of peace, the conqueror usually exercises his sovereign power to annul or vary the laws, or form of government, according to his own pleasure. It is not usual, in modern times, to change the fundamental laws of a country, in cases of conquest, unless under very pressing circumstances. But the sovereign power of the conqueror so to do is conceded by the law of nations.

Conquest of Property

This may be of movable or immovable property. In the former case, it is commonly called *plunder*, or *booty*, or *prize of war*, according to the circumstances under which it is taken. In the latter case, it merely follows from the right of occupation and superior force; and, therefore, the right of property continues no longer than such occupation by superior force. The original proprietor is reinstated in his rights the moment the conquest is abandoned.

As the law of nations allows the conqueror, in its utmost strictness, to appropriate to himself all the property of his enemies, as soon as it is within his reach by conquest, the extent to which he shall exercise this harsh power must depend upon his own moderation and sense of justice. Neutral nations always respect the title conferred by conquest when it is already established; and enemies respect it only so far as it suits their own convenience and policy, when in the hands of enemies. But, when acquired by a neutral, they also respect the title; for that which, by the law of nations, is lawfully acquired by an enemy, may be lawfully transferred to a neutral, and thus the latter may acquire a valid title. There is a distinction, in this respect, between movable and immovable property. No conquest of the latter is esteemed absolute, so as to divest the original proprietor, unless confirmed by a treaty of peace, or an entire submission and extinction of the state to which it belongs, or by an acquiescence so long, that it amounts to an abandonment of all prior right and title. But movable property, which is capable of being conveyed from one country to another, becomes the absolute right of the conquerors from the moment of conquest and complete possession. Movable property, captured in the heat of battle, or as an immediate result of victory, by an army on land, is often called *booty* or *plunder*. It belongs to the conquering sovereign, and portions of it are usually distributed among the officers and soldiers. It seldom happens now, that any place which is captured is given up to indiscriminate plunder. Private property is, for the most part, respected; but public property is appropriated by the sovereign to such purposes as he pleases. All property captured in war may be justly denominated prize. But, in a more limited sense, that is called *prize property*, which is acquired by capture and surrender upon land or upon the ocean, and is disposed of by some formal proceedings, under the sovereign authority. Thus, in England and America, all property captured on the ocean, by public or private armed ships, is required to be brought into port, and condemned as prize by the lawful prize tribunals, before the captors acquire any rights under the capture; and, in cases of joint captures, by land and naval forces, a similar proceeding is usually had.

A question is often discussed, at what time, movable property captured is so completely in the power of the captors, as to give them a perfect title to it. Writers on the law of nations differ on the point; and the practice of nations also differs. Some writers hold that it should be carried to a place of safety; as, for instance, if captured at sea, that it should be carried into port (*infra præsidia*) before the title of the original proprietor is divested. Others contend that it is sufficient that the property has remained in possession of the captors 24 hours. But, at present, in England and America at least, a sentence of condemnation is considered indispensable to divest the right of the original proprietor in movable property. Nevertheless, if a treaty of peace takes place between the belligerents, and no contrary provision is made, the actual state of things, in relation to captures, is deemed rightful; and neither can reclaim any thing of the other on account of such captures, whether there has been a condemnation or not.

This question, with regard to the title to movable property, chiefly arises in cases of recapture, or other cases where the *jus postliminii*, or right upon repossession or return of the property to the country of the original proprietor, occurs.

Conquest of Immovable Property

It has been already observed that, of such property, the title by conquest is not deemed perfect or complete, unless recognised by a treaty of peace, or cession, by an extinction of the state, or by a long acquiescence, amounting to an admission of right. The conqueror usually appropriates the public domains to himself, and generally leaves private property in possession of the original proprietors.

Whenever there is a reconquest or reoccupation by the original proprietors, their original right returns by the *jus postlininii*; and no intervening title, unless confirmed by treaty, or by some other mode, as above stated, is recognised, although it may have passed into the hands of a neutral. Where a conquest is temporary, it gives validity to titles to immovable property only while it lasts. It merely suspends the rights of the former proprietors at the conqueror's choice; but these rights revive as soon as the conquest is abandoned. The same thing is true as to the laws of the conquered territory, whether it be a town, province or state. The conqueror may, if he chooses, suspend all the common laws which regulate persons or property, during his occupation, and impose new ones; but the old laws revive as soon as the conquest is surrendered or abandoned. Acts, however, done during the possession by the conqueror, according to his laws, are considered as rightful for many purposes. Thus, if goods are imported into a conquered territory, with the consent of the conqueror, they are not liable to forfeiture afterwards, although prohibited by the laws of the country antecedent to the conquest. But the prohibitory laws revive, as soon as the territory is regained, by their own force, *proprio vigore*.

In general, the laws of a conquered territory remain in full force until they are altered by the conqueror. As soon as the conqueror receives the parties under his protection by capitulation or otherwise, they become his subjects; and they are entitled to have their persons and property secure from violation.

The question is often asked, To whom do things taken in war belong to the captors, or to their sovereign? The true answer is, To the sovereign. Whatever is acquired in war is acquired by the state; and the manner in which the property so acquired shall be disposed of or distributed depends upon the orders of the state. In cases of prizes upon the ocean, it is usual for the state to distribute the property captured, after condemnation, as a bounty among the captors.

CONTRACT

An agreement or covenant between two or more persons, in which each party binds himself to do or forbear some act, and each acquires a right to what the other promises. Natural law requires that if one person accepts from another a service, he should render to him something in return, whether this be expressly agreed upon, or only implied from the nature of the undertaking. Mutual promises of future good offices also are binding, at least by the natural law, if one of the contracting parties has thereby been induced to act; for, if he does not receive the thing stipulated for, he suffers wrong. We may go further, and say, that confidence in promises is so essential to the existence of social intercourse among men, that even the bare promise of one of the parties, when given and received in earnest, that is, with the idea of its being binding, is not entirely destitute of the force of obligation. In every state, it will be necessary to retain these principles, since the idea of justice implanted in the human mind should not be violated. It is the part of legislation to provide for special cases, to establish certain forms, and to fix, according to rules founded upon experience, the effects of each promise; also to withdraw from certain contracts their natural obligation, or to determine this in others, in which it is uncertain according to natural law. Such has been the course of the Roman law, which, by its consistency and justice in regard to contracts, has obtained, on the continent of Europe, a host universal authority. In that law, at an early period, a contract (*contractus*), in the proper sense of the word, was an agreement binding on both parties. It was required to be in a determinate form; and there was an equally determinate mode of impeaching it. A contract was distinguished from a simple pact or promise (*pactum*); and it was a fundamental doctrine, that a simple pact (*pactum*) would not entitle one to maintain a legal action, but merely to raise an objection in defence. The essential character of contracts in the stricter sense, is founded on the circumstance that such a legal relation is necessary for the most simple social intercourse, and imposes, according to its nature, certain duties. The most simple of these relations arise from a positive act, as the transfer of a thing to be returned (*contractus realis*), in which the object and extent of the obligation are determined by the real benefit conferred. Such a contract arises from delivering a thing, with or without pay; as, for instance, a deposit, a *mutuum*, or a pawn. A determinate form of agreement, however, is not always necessary. Civil intercourse allows another kind of contract, in which the simple consent of the parties gives obligation to agreements, so that they may constitute the ground of an action (*contractus consensuales*). Such, according to the Roman law, is sale, hire (as well the lending of a thing as services done for money), partnership, an accepted commission, and the contract for a fee farm rent (*emphyteusis*). But the same obligatory power, and this in the strictest sense, was allowed, also, to a verbal promise given in a certain solemn form, called a *stipulation* (*contractus verbalis*), as well as to a written obligation (*contractus literalis, chirographarius*). The form of a stipulation became continually more lax, approaching nearer to a simple promise, and, at last, amounted to nothing more than this, that he who wanted to bind another (*stipulator*) asked him, in a form of his own choosing, "Do you promise to give me such a thing?" and the other, who was to be bound, answered, "I promise it." It is obvious that, in this way, every simple promise (*pactum*) could be made actionable, and that the alteration, in modern times, in the law of some parts of Europe, which admits of an action upon every compact, amounts, in fact, only to this, that the form of a stipulation has become even more lax, so that there is no longer any necessity for the claimant (*promissarius*) to commence with his question, but the compact can as well begin with the declaration of the party under obligation (*promissor*). These forms of contracts are, in their essential parts, settled; and the legal relation, together with the action arising from it, has a fixed name (*contractus noninati*). But other relations, also, as exchanges of things and services, service for service, gift for gift, gift for service, service for gift (*do ut des*, *facio ut facias*, *do ut facias*, *facio ut des*), gave rise to rights and obligations, but in such diversified ways, that an appropriate form of action could be framed only from the statement of each particular case (*actio in factum præscriptis verbis*); and there were, accordingly, no technical terms adapted to such variously combined relations. Hence arose the *contractus innominati*, which were considered as real contracts so far only that the actual performance of one party entitled him to an action; and, even in this case, there was not an absolute obligation on the other party to the performance of his part of the contract; but, in most cases, simply the duty of restoring what had been received. But the modern law creates here (though not without dispute) a perfect duty to perform the very thing promised. Finally, the Roman law attributed the effect of actionable obligations even to some partial promises and agreements (*pacta*); not only to those which were added as appendices to other real contracts (*pacta adjecta*), but also to some of a different kind. These were either declared obligatory by a formal law, or were admitted as grounds of action by the pretor (*pacta legitima* and *prætoria*). Most of the technical designations of these are indeed new, yet the ancients had several, as, for instance, *re*, *consensu*, *verbis*, *literis*, *contrahitur obligatio*, &c. In this way donations, promises of dowry, promises of interest, acknowledgments of debt, &c., were made actionable. It is always implied in the idea of a contract, that the real cause of its obligation is founded on some particular rational object of the party who promises (*causa civilis*), and that mere promises and agreements are not binding.

Even stipulations, which have no ground, or an unlawful one (*nullam aut injustam causam*), are valid, indeed, with regard to their form, but are open to the objection of intrinsic groundlessness, except when they are donations. With these views were also connected certain divisions of these legal relations, and of the actions arising from them, according to which, in some cases, the object of the obligation was strictly enforced (*actiones stricti juris*); but, in others, the liability could be settled only by the decree depending upon all the circumstances of the special action before the court (*actiones bonæ fidei*). Other divisions refer to the relation of the parties, as, in some of them, the obligation is only on one side, as to return the thing received in lending (*contractus unilaterales*); and, in others, there are reciprocal obligations, as in a sale, a partnership (*contractus bilaterales*); or they concern the subject of the contracts, whether relating to property or to some other object. To the conditions necessary for the formation of a contract belongs the consent of the contracting parties. Accordingly, when this is wanting, either because the parties were not capable of taking upon themselves the obligation (as minors, madmen, prodigals), or because the contract was founded on an error (an innocent error on the side of the party making the mistake, or one occasioned by the deceit of the other party), or when the engagement was extorted by force and fear, there can be no valid contract. To contracts may also be added conditions, which either delay or dissolve them, and also precise determinations of time, place and object (*modus*), which coincide, at times, with the condition. A contract must be possible and legal, else it is without force. No one can be obliged to undertake what is impossible, or decidedly immoral (*causa turpis*). According to the Roman law, it is a matter of dispute, whether an obligation to do something or to leave something undone gives a right to compel a specific performance, or whether it gives merely a claim to indemnification.

The English and French laws have adopted the latter doctrine (*toute obligation de faire ou de ne pas faire se résoud en dommages et intérets*). Obligations resembling express contracts arise if one person does something for another, without the knowledge and desire of the latter; so that the latter is bound to give a recompense for what has been thus beneficially done for him (*obligatio quasi ex contractu*). In this case, there is no consent existing, neither is it supposed, but the consent could not have been refused, or it was not necessary. Such relations, resembling express contracts, arise in cases of guardianship, between guardian and ward, by the receipt of money for a nonexisting debt by mistake, the amount of which ought to be restored; so by a beneficial performance of some business for another, without any actual commission from him, where the circumstances raise a presumption of obligation.—Thus far the present article refers to the general theory of contracts, founded either upon natural justice or the principles of the civil and Roman law. A short account will now be added of the nature and obligation of contracts by the common law; that is, by the law which regulates this subject in the jurisprudence of England and America. The original basis of the common law, as to contracts, was, without doubt, the civil or Roman law; but it has undergone some modifications in its incorporation into our jurisprudence. A contract may be defined, in the common law, to be an agreement made in one form, between parties capable of contracting, for a legal object or purpose, and upon a sufficient consideration. It must be an agreement or mutual bargain, voluntary, and without force or fraud; and therefore it includes an assent given *bona fide*. The notion of an assent includes a physical and moral power of assenting, and the deliberate and free use of this power. And this leads us to the consideration of the next point, which is, that it must be between parties capable of contracting. Upon principles of universal law, an infant, having no discretion or moral power of perception, cannot make a contract; nor can a person who is insane or mad; nor an idiot, or person laboring under such mental debility or such natural defects as prevent a just exercise of reason. The common law recognizes these principles, and therefore it treats as nullities all contracts entered into by such persons; it treats in like manner contracts made by aged and imbecile men, whose understanding has become so weak and inefficient that they are liable to imposition, and cannot act with a reasonable discretion. In respect to persons who enter into contracts in a state of intoxication, the old law, with a view to determine from such practices, did not hold the contracts void, so that the party might set them aside at his own suit, upon the ground that no man should be allowed to stultify himself, or allege his own vice to excuse his nonperformance of a contract. But this principle, if it is now acted upon at all, is received with great modifications; and, if there be any undue advantage taken of the party's situation, he will be relieved. The common law, indeed, seems originally to have disabled a party who was insane from avoiding, after the recovery of his reason, any contract made during his insanity; partly upon the maxim that no man should be permitted to stultify himself, and partly upon the supposed danger, in admitting such defences, of overturning deliberate and solemn contracts. But his legal representatives, after his death, were always allowed to avoid them; and when he has a guardian appointed, the guardian may avoid his contracts in a proper suit; so that the doctrine, if it now exists (and it has been much questioned), is more a matter of form than of substance. The general inclination, in American courts, has been to allow the party himself to show that the contract was void by reason of insanity, &c. In respect to who shall be deemed infants or minors, the laws of every civilized country have provided a certain age, at which persons shall be deemed capable of all sorts of contracts, and for all purposes *sui juris*. The time differs in different countries, and different times are assigned for different acts. By the common law, all persons are infants until twenty one years of age, and then are considered as of full age for all purposes whatsoever. By the same law, the ages of males and females are different for different purposes. A male at *fourteen* is at years of discretion, and may consent or disagree to marriage, may choose his guardian, and, if his discretion is actually proved, he may make a testament of his personal estate, though not of his lands; at *seventeen*, he may be an executor. A female may, at *seven* years, be betrothed in marriage; at *nine*, is entitled to dower; at *twelve*, may consent or agree to marriage; at *fourteen*, may choose a guardian; at *seventeen*, may be an executrix; and at *twenty-one*, is of full age for all purposes. Both males and females are capable of making contracts for necessaries during their minority; but, in general, other contracts do not bind them, unless manifestly for their benefit; and, though contracts made with them cannot be avoided by the other side, the infants themselves, when they arrive at age, may ratify them; for, as to them, they are generally voidable, and not void. A contract, too, must be for some legal object or purpose; that is, for something which the law allows to be done or omitted for it is a general principle, that all contracts which are prohibited by law, whether they involve moral turpitude, or are merely prohibited by positive law, are void and incapable of binding the parties. A contract, too, must have a sufficient consideration to support it. Considerations are either *valuable* in themselves, or *good*. A good consideration is such as flows from blood or natural affection between near relations, such as parent and child. In respect to such considerations, it may be said, that they are, as between the parties, generally sufficient to support an executed contract; that is, a contract which has completed its operation by a transfer of the thing, such as a gift or grant, or assignment and delivery of a thing. But where the rights of third persons, such as creditors, intervene, such gifts, or grants, or assignments, are not always valid, as against them. For a man must be just before he is generous. But in respect to good considerations, if the contract is not executed, but is a mere *chose in action*, such as a promise to pay money, or to deliver goods, or to give a thing, such a contract has no legal obligation, and cannot been forced in a suit, in a court of law. It is generally deemed a voluntary promise or naked pact. A *valuable* consideration is one arising from, or on account of, money or goods received, or services done, or other contracts of reciprocal benefit, or marriage, or a loss or injury, or forbearance of right. In all such cases, if a promise is made on any of these or the like accounts, it is binding in law. If A promises to pay ten dollars to B for goods sold to A, or money borrowed, &c., it is a binding contract. So if A promises to pay B a debt due from C, if B will forbear, for a certain time, to sue C, it is a binding contract. So, if A has done an injury to B's lands or goods, and promises to indemnify him, it is a good contract. In all these cases, there is a mutuality of interest or consideration—a *quid pro quo*. But a mere moral obligation creates no contract; as if A promises to give a pauper his clothes, or to supply him with necessaries. But though, in general, a contract is not binding, unless made upon a valuable consideration, there are certain forms in the common law, as there are in the civil law, by which a party may bind himself without such consideration. If, therefore, A enter into a written contract, under his seal, with B, to pay him a sum of money, or do any other act, there the common law considers the deed of such high solemnity, that it will hold it binding. It deems it as importing a valuable consideration, or rather will not suffer the contrary to be proved, and acts upon the solemnity of the instrument as, of itself, of paramount obligation. There are certain contracts which the common law requires to be done in a particular mode to give them validity, and therefore another requisite is, that the contract must be in due form. There are certain things, which can be conveyed or transferred only by some written instrument or deed, such as incorporeal hereditaments, as rights of ways, easements, &c.; and, generally speaking, lands can now be granted only by deed. There are, also, many cases specially provided for by statutes, in which contracts are not binding, unless reduced to writing, and signed by the party or his agent. Among these are contracts for the debts of another, contracts respecting lands, and contracts respecting goods beyond a certain value. Indeed, many of the regulations, here referred to as part of the common law, are, in the different states of the American union, variously modified by the local jurisprudence, and, principally, by statutes.

CORPUS DELICTI

(literally, the *body of the crime or offence*). It is a figurative expression, used to denote those external marks, facts or circumstances which accompany a crime, and without the proof of which the crime is not supposed to be established. We have no correspondent expression in English, and the preceding exposition is peculiar to the civil law of continental Europe. We should say, that certain proofs are indispensable to establish a crime, and that, unless they exist, there is no legal ground to convict the party; so that *corpus delicti* is equivalent to the proofs essential to establish a crime. The following observations have reference to the Jurisprudence of Germany. The marks of guilt, which constitute the *corpus delicti*, are, in many cases, perceptible in the traces remaining (*facta permanentia*); for instance, the wounds inflicted upon a man; a lampoon posted up; written or printed words; counterfeit writings; in other cases, such traces exist only in the memory (*facta transeuntia*); as words merely spoken, &c. A criminal trial must always rest upon a *corpus delicti* clearly substantiated. Unless the death of a man is fully proved, and shown to have been occasioned by the cooperation of another, no sentence of homicide can be passed. An inspection of the body, in case of murder, or the statement of the injured party, in less heinous offences, confirmed, with an oath, &c., is, accordingly, the first condition of a criminal process. Entire deficiency of the *corpus delicti* can be supplied by no confession; and the latter remains without any effect; as, for instance, if a person should accuse himself of having stolen something from another, or of having killed some one, and no person could be found from whom such thing had been stolen, or who had been killed. In the cases where the *corpus delicti* cannot be discovered by means of immediate examination, because the doer has destroyed all traces of it (for instance, by a total burning of the corpse of a murdered person), other circumstances must be sought for, which can afford certain proof of the crime; and without them punishment cannot be legally pronounced by the court. It must further be ascertained, in a case of murder, that death has ensued in consequence of the wound; or, rather, that the wound inflicted was, in itself, a sufficient cause for the death. In this respect, the courts in Germany often go too far, by seeking for the most remote possibility, by which the *corpus delicti* may be rendered uncertain. In the famous trial of Fonk, in Cologne, it was one of the greatest faults, that the *corpus delicti* (the wounds in the head of the dead man, Cönen) had not been examined with sufficient medical accuracy, and that there was a search for a murderer before the murder was ascertained. It has happened more than once that a person has been executed as a murderer of a missing person, who, after some time, has reappeared. No reliance ought, in most cases, to be placed upon the circumstance, that several persons pretend to have seen the corpse of the individual believed to have been murdered, until the corpse has actually been discovered, or until infallible, evidence of the murder has been adduced. In crimes which leave no traces, the whole possible proof rests on witnesses and confessions. Even a confession of guilt by an accused party must be supported by other circumstances; e.g. actions which have been observed by other persons, and which have a bearing on the crime, and render it probable. In the investigation of the *corpus delicti*, in a great many cases, the science of medicine must assist the law. Nevertheless, great uncertainty often remains, after all the aid which can be thus attained; for instance, in poisonings, and in cases where the point in question is, whether an infant was born alive or not. Frequently, questions are proposed to the physicians, which they cannot answer at all. In such cases, nothing is required of them but the declaration that nothing can be said with certainty. It is a very important question, whether preference ought to be given to the testimony of the physician who has attended the deceased till his death, or to the opinion of the physician of the court at the official examination.* In a famous case, in Germany, the inquest found traces of poisoning by arsenic, though not the arsenic itself; whilst the physician attending during the last illness of the deceased asserted that no symptom of poisoning had shown itself, and that the disease had taken its natural course. In another case, the physician declared that the deceased had died of the lock-jaw, occasioned by a wound, whilst the legal examiners maintained that the wound had been without influence upon his death.

* In many parts of Germany, a physician, in the employ of the government, is attached to each district, who sees that proper health regulations are observed, makes reports respecting births, deaths, &c., inquires into the causes of deaths which are attended with suspicions circumstances, and is *ex officio*, the medical adviser of the judicial courts.

Courts

[In the following article, we shall give, at some length, a view of the courts of England, followed by an account of the courts of the U. States.]

Courts of England

Inferior Courts

In describing the courts of England, it will be sufficient to take a cursory view of those of inferior and limited jurisdiction; among the most inconsiderable of which is the *pipowders* court, which is commonly said to derive its appellation from words signifying the *dusty foot*, either in allusion to the suitors who frequented it, or, as some say, because justice was as speedily done in this court as the dust could be shaken from the feet. Barrington, however, derives the name from the old French *pied-pouldreaux*, a pedlar, because the chapmen frequented these courts. The *pipowders* court is incident to fairs and markets, having two branches, one held by the lord of the franchise or his steward, the other by the clerk of the market. In this court are settled all disputes respecting contracts made, and all suits for injuries and offences committed during the fair. An appeal lies from this court to those of Westminster hall. The *pipowders* court has fallen very much into disuse.

Courts of *manors and hundreds*. The lord of every manor is entitled to hold a court, not of record, called a *court baron*, by himself or his steward, having a civil jurisdiction. A *hundred* court is similar, only embracing a wider district.

The *coroner's* court is held by a coroner, who assembles a jury to inquire concerning the death of any person, wherever any violence is suspected. (Coroners hold similar courts in the U. States).

The *sheriff's* court. The sheriff of each county formerly held a court, called the *sheriff's tourn* or *torn*, twice a year, in each hundred of his county, at which every person over 12 years of age, and not specially privileged, was obliged to attend, for the reformation of common grievances and nuisances, the trial of offences, and the preservation of peace and good government. It has also a considerable jurisdiction in civil suits. Though the jurisdiction of this court remains, its business has, it seems, long since ceased, except in regard to actions of replevin, which, professor Wooddeson says, are frequently commenced in the *sheriff's torn*, and almost as frequently removed into a superior judicature.

The court *leet* has the same jurisdiction, in particular districts, that the sheriff's court has in the county, and, like the sheriff's court, is now almost obsolete.

Justices Court

The jurisdiction of justices of the peace has superseded that of most of the small courts. These officers are now the conservators of the peace, scattered in every town and parish of the kingdom. We have a minute account of the qualifications and powers of these officers in Burn's *Justice*. A justice of the peace is required to have a yearly income, clear of all encumbrances of £100, or property estimated to be equivalent. The justices are commissioned by the king, their appointment being made through the lord chancellor. A justice is a judge of record, and causes are removed from his court to the superior courts by *certiorari*. The justices of each county hold quarterly sessions; but any justice is empowered to hold a court at any time for the examination and committing of offenders, and also for the trial of such actions as come within his commission.

The *quarter sessions*, as well as the individual justices, are instituted for the suppression and punishment of offences, and their power extends to the committing to prison for trial for crimes, with but few exceptions. Two justices may determine the settlement of a pauper, but an appeal lies from their decisions to the quarter sessions.

Assizes

Courts of assize and *nisi prius* are treated at length under the article *Assizes*. (q. v.) These courts are branches of those of Westminster hall, the great centre of the judicial administration in England, according to the forms of the common law. Besides the above courts, there are others of a limited and special jurisdiction; namely, three in London.— 1. the *hustings* court, which has a jurisdiction in civil actions, and at which some of the city elections are held (among others, that of members of parliament from that city), and from which an appeal lies to certain justices of the city; 2. the *sheriffs'* courts; 3. a court of *conscience*, of summary jurisdiction in actions under 40 shillings, held by the lord mayor:—the court of *commissioners of sewers*, to provide for the repair of seawalls, ditches, sewers, &c.—the court of *stannaries*, for the tin mines in Cornwall and Devonshire, for the trial of suits in which the tinners are parties:—courts of the *forest*, having jurisdiction over the royal forests:—the court of the *royal franchise of Ely*, belonging to the bishopric of that name, but held by justices, not by the bishop himself and having jurisdiction of causes arising within the bishopric:—courts *palatinate*, of the counties palatine of Durham, Chester and Lancaster, which are courts of record, of superior jurisdiction, commensurate with that of the courts of Westminster, from which Writs do not run into these counties palatine:—the court, of the *Marshalsea* and of the *palace*, still held weekly at Southwark, whose jurisdiction embraces a circuit of 12 miles about the king's palace, for the determination of causes arising among the servants of the king's household; and the court of the *earl marshal*, authorized by the statute of 13 Richard II, chap.2, to take cognizance "of deeds of arms and war out of the realm, which cannot be discussed by the courts of the common law:"—besides the *ecclesiastical* courts and those of *admiralty* and *chancery*, of which a more particular account will be given.

The Superior Courts of Westminster hall are the courts of *exchequer*, *common pleas*, and *king's bench*. These three courts, and also that of *chancery* and the *house of lords*, are the remains and successors of the great court established in the Norman period, under the title of *aula regis*, which was divided, very naturally, into several departments, for the trial of different kinds of pleas; and, at length, these several branches of one jurisdiction became so many distinct courts. The *king's bench* is considered as the most direct successor to the *aula regis*, in Westminster hall. In this court, the sovereign is, by a fiction, supposed to preside in person, and the writs are, accordingly, made returnable "before the king, wherever he may be in England," because the court formerly followed the king to different parts of the kingdom, and was once held, in the 21st year of Edward I, at Roxburgh, in Scotland; but, for many centuries, its sittings have been held in Westminster hall, and the king never presides at its sittings. Sir Edward Coke says, if he were present, still justice could be administered only by the justices, in the same manner as if he were absent; and sir William Blackstone says, when James II sat there, he was told by the judges that he must not give his opinion. The three courts of Westminster hall, at the time when they were constituted out of the *aula regis*, had jurisdiction of distinct kinds of actions; the king's bench having cognizance of criminal suits, the common pleas of suits between party and party respecting land titles and on contracts, and the exchequer in matters of revenue. These courts have also a jurisdiction in respect to the person, and not resting wholly on the kind of action. Every one, for instance, has jurisdiction of suits in which its own attorneys, or some other of its officers, are parties; and through this right of jurisdiction, in relation to the person, the king's bench has drawn to itself cognizance of actions of almost all descriptions, in which the proceedings are at common law, except real actions; nor does this exception much abridge its jurisdiction, for title to lands, in England, as in the state of N. York, is tried in personal suits, between the parties to a real or supposed lease of the lands in dispute. This general jurisdiction was acquired upon the principle that no other court could bring before it a person imprisoned by the king's bench; and, in respect to every such person, therefore, suits must be brought against him in that court, or there would be a failure of justice, as long as lie should thus continue to be imprisoned. A defendant being, accordingly, once arrested and imprisoned, in an action brought before this court, might, while so in custody, be sued in any civil action, in the same court. By taking one step farther, the jurisdiction was made general in such actions, namely, by adopting the fiction that the defendant was imprisoned by the court. The great mass of the present business of this court, which fills the reports of its proceedings, is brought under its cognizance by this fiction. It has also supervision of all the inferior courts of common law throughout the kingdom, from all which a writ of error lies to this court. It may also punish magistrates and officers of justice for wilful and corrupt abuses of their authority. This species of supervision has, in some cases, been extended to other than civil and judicial officers, as in the case mentioned by Noy, where the court issued a *mandamus* to the bishop of Exon to allow the sacred unction and baptismal oil to the people of a certain parish, to whom they had been denied by him. This power of supervision is frequently exercised by ordering officers of corporations to discharge the duties incumbent upon them. This court does not take cognizance of any civil action in which the amount in dispute is less than 40 shillings. Actions are brought from the common pleas to this court, and are also carried from the king's bench to the exchequer chamber or the house of lords by writ of error. The *common pleas*, originally having jurisdiction of civil causes, between party and party, was, like the king's bench, ambulatory, moving with the king wherever he went in the kingdom. But, by the 11th chapter of *Magna Charta*, it was ordained that it "should not follow the court, but be held in some certain place." This court is still distinguished by some of the characteristics of its original constitution, for it has the jurisdiction of real actions, and has no jurisdiction in felony and treason. Like the king's bench, it may issue writs of *habeas corpus*, which may be issued by the whole court or any one of its judges, to bring up a person imprisoned, and inquire into the cause of his imprisonment, and set him at liberty if he is confined without lawful cause. A writ of error lies from it to the king's bench. It consists of a chief justice and three justices.

The court of *exchequer*, having jurisdiction of that part of the general business of the *aula regis* which relates to the revenue, derives its name from a chequered cloth (*exchequier*, a chessboard, or chequerwork) on the table. There are reckoned 7 courts in the exchequer; viz., 1. of *pleas*; 2. of *accounts*; 3. of *receipts*; 4. of *exchequer chamber* (where all the 12 judges of England assemble to consult on difficult matters of law); 5. of *exchequer chamber* for errors in the exchequer; 6. for errors in the king's bench; 7. of *equity*. The court of equity is held by the lord treasurer, the chancellor of the exchequer and four barons of the exchequer. The four barons, in fact, are the regular and constant judges of this court, in which is transacted the business originally belonging to the exchequer, namely, the calling the king's debtors to account, on bills being filed against them by the attorney general, and the recovering lands, chattels or profits belonging to the king. A court of common law is also held by these four barons. And, in both these courts, civil actions, in general, may be brought, under pretence or on the fiction that the plaintiff is the king's debtor, and the less able to discharge the dues to the king, because his own debtor, the defendant, neglects to make the payment or do the act demanded; the fact whether the plaintiff is, as he alleges in his writ, the king's debtor, being never inquired into. One of these courts of exchequer chamber is merely an assembly of all the judges of the three superior courts, for consultation in matters of law. The court of exchequer chamber, for the correction of errors in the common law courts of exchequer, constituted by the statute of the 31 Edw. III, chap. 12, consists of the lord chancellor, the lord treasurer, and the judges of the king's bench and common pleas. The other court of exchequer chamber, for the correction of errors in the king's bench, in certain cases, is constituted by the statute of 27 Elizabeth, chap. 8, and consists of the judges of the common pleas and the barons of the exchequer. We have seen that the three courts of king's bench, common pleas and, exchequer have, all of them, by means of the fictions above mentioned, concurrent jurisdiction of civil actions in general; and, if there were no higher tribunal for the supervision and correction of their decisions, they might diverge into different principles of adjudication, so that what was law in one would not be so in another, and thus uncertainty might be introduced into rights and obligations of every kind. Accordingly, every community requires to have one ultimate tribunal of appeal on all questions of the same description; and the judicial system of Great Britain is constituted upon this principle. The king's bench may, on writ of error, revise the decisions and correct the errors of the common pleas; the exchequer chamber, consisting of the judges of the common pleas and court of exchequer, may revise those of the king's bench;

and the court of exchequer chamber, consisting of the lord chancellor and lord treasurer, with the judges of the king's bench and common pleas, may revise those of the common law courts of exchequer; and from all these, as also from the court of chancery, the equity side of the court of exchequer, and from the superior courts of Scotland and Ireland, actions may be carried, by writ of error or appeal, to, the house of lords, the highest judicial tribunal in the kingdom.

The judges of each of the courts of king's bench, common pleas and exchequer are usually four; and this number is so well established by usage, that the expression the "twelve judges of England" is used to signify the court of exchequer chamber already mentioned, including all the judges of these courts. But the number of these judges has, as we learn from Mr. Wooddeson, sometimes been five, and again, at others, less than four, there having been but two in the beginning of Trinity term, 1655, in Cromwell's time, in the king's bench, then called the *upper bench*. The judges anciently held their office during the pleasure of the king; but now, by the statutes of 12 and 13 of William III, chap. 2, and 1 George III, chap.23, during good behavior; and their commissions do not expire on the demise of the crown. When the judges of either of the courts are equally divided, a meeting of the twelve judges is held in the exchequer chamber, to consult on the matter. The *house of lords*, in its character of a judicial court, is the highest tribunal in the kingdom, to which civil actions are carried, by writ of error, from the two courts of error already mentioned, as held in the exchequer chamber, and from the court consisting of the twelve judges; also from the king's bench, from which latter court some actions may be carried, as we have already seen, to the court of exchequer chamber; but the party aggrieved by the judgment of the king's bench has his election, in actions of that description, to go immediately to the house of lords, if he so chooses. So civil actions may be brought before this court by appeal from the, chancery and the equity side of the exchequer, and by writ of error or by appeal from the highest courts of Scotland and Ireland. Actions were formerly brought, in the first instance, before the *aula regis*, to which, of all its surviving successors, the house of lords bears the greatest resemblance; and petitions continued to be presented to the house of lords, from the reign of Edward I to that of Henry VI, to take cognizance of suits in the first instance; but the lords uniformly referred the petitioners to the other courts; and they entertain no civil action except on appeal or writ of error. The practice of bringing cases, by writ of error, from the courts of common law, has prevailed ever since the establishment of those courts; but appeals from the court of chancery are of later date, having commenced in the latter part of the reign of Charles I, after the court of chancery had succeeded in establishing its present extensive jurisdiction against the opposition of the common law courts. The reason commonly given in favor of this right of appeal is, that it ought not to be left to the chancellor to bind the whole property of the kingdom, by his decrees, without any power of revision. The house of lords, also, exercises a very important original criminal jurisdiction, in respect to the person; for all peers, including all the Scotch nobility, whether of the 16 who are members of the house or not, and the queen, duchesses, countesses and baronesses, are exempt from a trial by jury, for treason or felony, being liable to be tried for those crimes only by the house of lords; and they are not only entitled to this mode of trial for these crimes, but are bound to it, and cannot waive it, and put themselves upon trial by jury. In case a peer marries a woman not of noble blood, she is to be tried only by the lords for the above offences; but if she afterwards lose her rank by marrying a commoner, she ceases to be entitled to this mode of trial. The question does not seem to be fully settled, whether bishops, who have a seat in the house of lords, must be tried by that body, or are subject to be tried for treason or felony by jury. It has always been customary, in all capital trials, in the house of lords, for the bishops to withdraw before the taking of the vote of guilty or not guilty; and it is made a question whether they have a right to vote upon that question; and Mr. Wooddeson seems to be of the opinion that they have not this right. The reason for this distinction between them and the temporal peers is, that the character of their profession ought to exclude, as well as excuse, them from taking a part in the final decision of a question of life and death. The proceeding of which we have been speaking is by indictment before this tribunal as a court of judicature, during the session of parliament; and, during the recess of parliament, such trials take place before a court of peers, summoned by the lord high steward, consisting of not less than 35 peers, who formerly might be summoned at the discretion of that officer; but, to avoid the abuses to which such a power might be liable, the statute of 7 and 8 William III, chap. 3, provides that all the peers shall be summoned to attend. A majority of 12 is necessary in order to a conviction in this court. The last trial before this court, up to the present time (1830), was that of lord Delamere, in the reign of James II. There is still another form of proceeding before this tribunal, as a court of judicature, namely, that by impeachment by the house of commons, which suggested the trial before the Senate of the U. States, on impeachment by the House of Representatives, and similar trials by the senates in the separate states. Impeachments may be made, in Great Britain, against any person and for any misdemeanor, though it is a mode of accusation ordinarily adopted only against public officers in relation to some abuse of their trusts; as the trial of Warren Hastings, for alleged maladministration as governor of India, which lasted for seven years. As all these judicial proceedings, both civil and criminal, are analogous to those of other courts, they are not dissolved by the prorogation or dissolution of the parliament; and though, in the ordinary business of legislation, any peer may vote by proxy, he cannot so vote in his judicial capacity. At the first view, it would seem to admit of a question whether a body constituted like that of the house of lords would be the best calculated to act as the judicial tribunal of ultimate jurisdiction; but it is to be considered, that the chancellor, who is necessarily one of the ablest law officers of the kingdom, presides in all the civil trials, and in those and all other cases, the judges of the superior courts and the attorney general are present, and their opinions are taken on all difficult questions. The court, therefore, combines the collected wisdom, talent, learning and dignity of the kingdom. Bills of attainder, and of pains and penalties, an anomalous kind of jurisdiction, is also exercised by parliament, as constituted for the ordinary purposes of legislation, consisting of the king, lords and commons, who, by their concurrent voices, have occasionally acted as judges, in particular cases, at the same time making the law, if they choose, and punishing the offence (already committed) for which the law is made. This is one kind of *ex post facto* law prohibited to congress by the constitution of the U. States; the abuses to which this power has been subject, having impressed upon the framers of that instrument the strong necessity of guarding against its exercise. When a bill of this description was introduced into the house of lords, in 1820, against the queen, Mr. Brougham commenced the defence by urging objections to this mode of proceeding in any case. Though such a bill is passed like any other in parliament, yet witnesses may be examined, and the party heard by counsel, as in any trial before a judicial tribunal.

Admiralty Courts

The *admiralty* court, in England, is coëval at least, perhaps anterior, to the others in its origin, as we meet with it in the most remote periods of the judicial history of the country. This court formerly maintained a long and arduous, and, in some respects, an unsuccessful struggle for jurisdiction against the common law courts, in which strife it was encumbered with the disadvantage of being allied, in its forms of proceeding, to the ecclesiastical courts; since both these descriptions of judicial tribunals, as well as the chancery, borrow their forms of process from the civil law; and they, therefore, had formerly to encounter the prejudices of the nation, which set very strongly against the civil law, as associated with the papal usurpations. By a comparison with the French courts, we shall see how much the jurisdiction of the British admiralty has been curtailed. The French code assigns the jurisdiction of prize questions to a distinct court. The tribunals of commerce have jurisdiction of all disputes relative to engagements and transactions between merchants, traders and bankers, and all commercial contracts or affairs, viz., purchases of goods for the purpose of selling them, either in the same state or after labor done upon them, and agreements for hiring the use of chattels; all undertakings in manufacturers for commissions, or for transportation by land or water; all agreements for supplying provisions, and for agencies; all those relating to sale by auction; all operations of banking, exchange and brokerage; all those of the public banking companies; all obligations between merchants, traders and bankers; all bills of exchange, or remittances of money between whatever persons; all agreements for the purchase, building, sale or resale of vessels, used either in foreign or domestic trade; all maritime undertakings; every purchase or sale of rigging, apparel or provisions for vessels; agreements for freight or charter-party; loans on bottomry, or *respondentia*; contracts of insurance, or other contracts respecting marine commerce; every contract with seamen in regard to their services on board the merchant vessels. The boundaries of the jurisdiction of the corresponding courts in England and the U. States are much narrower, and the reasons and principles on which its extent has been settled, are, as stated in the reports, involved in the greatest confusion, obscurity and contradiction, as is fully shown in the learned and profound investigation of the subject by judge Story, in the case of De Lovio against Boit, in the 1st volume of Gallison's *Reports*. The judge of the high court of admiralty in England holds his office by two commissions. (See the article *Admiralty Courts*.) It does not appear that the English admiralty ever had a jurisdiction commensurate with that of the present French tribunals of commerce; but it does appear that a part of that which it formerly enjoyed has been extorted from it by the common law courts. In a great part of what now remains to it, the common law courts have a concurrent jurisdiction. As a prize court, the admiralty has retained its jurisdiction unimpaired; and it is in the administration of this branch of the jurisdiction, for the most part, that sir William Scott (since Lord Stowell), has shed so much splendor upon his court, and given so many profound and luminous expositions of the law of nations and of commerce. In regard to the other branches of its jurisdiction, all piracies, robberies and felonies committed on the high seas, are exclusively within its cognizance, and they are tried, not according to the forms of the civil law, but, by the statute of the 28th year of Henry VIII, in the same manner as similar offences committed on land are tried by the courts of common law. In respect to minor offences, it has a concurrent jurisdiction with the common law courts. In matters of commerce, these latter courts have, in the most important subjects, a jurisdiction exclusive of the admiralty; as, for example, over bills of exchange, promissory notes, charter parties, bills of lading, and policies of insurance. In others, the jurisdiction is again concurrent, as in respect to victualling and repairing ships, mariners' wages, hypothecation of the ship or goods by instruments of bottomry, or *respondentia*. In matters of salvage, or the recovery, at sea, of lost goods, the jurisdiction is in the admiralty; and so are also questions of seamen's wages; and it is resorted to for the purpose of enforcing liens against the ship, as in bottomry or suits for mariners' wages. It has also jurisdiction of all stipulations made by the parties to a suit in reference to the subject of dispute in a case pending in the court; as, for example, where the goods, which are the subject of controversy, are delivered to one party on his agreement, in the nature of a recognizance to answer for their value in case the opposite party prevails; in which case execution is forthwith issued on the stipulation. The admiralty jurisdiction of the courts of the U. States is adopted into the American from the English laws.

Court of Chancery (*See Equity*)

Ecclesiastical Courts

There are still subsisting in England divers ecclesiastical courts, of which the most important jurisdiction remaining is that relating to the goods of persons deceased, which belongs to the prerogative courts of the archbishops of Canterbury and York, if the deceased leaves goods to the amount of £5 (*bona notabilia*) in two different dioceses; otherwise it belongs to the court of the bishop of the diocese. But much of the business of administering upon and determining the distribution of the estates of persons deceased passes into the court of chancery, under its jurisdiction of trusts; a large amount of property in Great Britain being put in trust under grants and wills.

Courts of the U. States

By the constitution of the U. States, which went into operation in the year 1789, a limited extent of judicial power was confided to the government of the union, the nature of which will be best explained by quoting the very words in which it is given. The third article of the constitution declares, 1. that "The judicial power of the U. States shall be vested in one supreme court, and in such inferior courts as the congress may, from time to time, ordain and establish. The judges, both of the supreme and inferior courts, shall hold their offices during good behavior, and shall, at stated times, receive for their services a compensation, which shall not be diminished during their continuance in office." 2. "The judicial power shall extend to all cases in law and equity arising under this constitution, the laws of the U. States, and treaties made, or which shall be made, under their authority; to all cases of admiralty and maritime jurisdiction; to controversies to which the U. States shall be a party; to controversies between two or more states; between a state and citizens of another state; between citizens of different states; between citizens of the same state claiming lands under grants of different states; and between a state, or the citizens thereof; and foreign states, citizens or subjects." 3. "In all cases affecting ambassadors, other public ministers and consuls, and those in which a state shall be a party, the supreme court shall have original jurisdiction. In all the other cases before mentioned, the supreme court shall have appellate jurisdiction, both as to law and fact, with such exceptions, and under such regulations, as the congress shall make." It is observable, that this enumeration of the various classes of cases to which the judicial power may extend, does not make it imperative upon congress to vest the whole jurisdiction in courts created by the general government; but leaves much to the discretion of congress, as to the establishment of courts, and the jurisdiction with which they shall be clothed. In point of fact, congress has never legislated to the extent of the judicial power authorized by the constitution. Some branches of it remain undisposed of; and the courts of the several states are left to act upon them as matters not exclusively confided to the courts of the U. States. At the first session of congress, under the constitution, the organization of the judicial establishment was made, which has substantially remained in force ever since. By a statute passed Sept. 24, 1789, a supreme court was created, consisting of a chief justice and five associate justices, since increased to six; and two classes of inferior courts, viz., circuit courts and district courts, were also created. All the judges of the courts of the U. States are appointed by the president, by and with the consent of the senate of the U. States, and cannot otherwise be appointed. We will now proceed to give a summary view of each of these courts, beginning with those which are the lowest in point of rank, and of the first instance.

1. *The District Courts*

Each state in the confederacy constitutes at least one judicial district, and the states of New York, Pennsylvania and Virginia are divided into two districts by certain local limits. In each district, a court is appointed to hold sessions, consisting of a single judge. The district courts possess criminal jurisdiction, exclusively of the state courts, of all crimes and offences against the U. States, where the punishment of whipping, not exceeding 30 stripes (which is now generally abolished), or a fine not exceeding $100, or a term of imprisonment not exceeding 6 months, is to be inflicted. It also possesses civil jurisdiction of all civil causes of admiralty and maritime jurisdiction; that is, of suits upon maritime contracts and maritime *torts*; of seizures *in rem*, and of suits *in personam* for penalties and forfeitures incurred under the laws of the U. States; of all causes where an alien sues for a tort only, in violation of the law of nations, or a treaty of the U. States; of all suits at common law, where the government of the U. States sue, or any officer thereof sues, under the authority of any act of congress. Whatever may be the matter in dispute, and of all suits against consuls and viceconsuls. The district courts also possess the jurisdiction of circuit courts in those districts where no circuit courts are held, and also certain limited authorities under special laws.

2. *The Circuit Courts*

The U. States are now divided into seven circuits, in each of which a court is held, called a circuit court. It consists of two judges, one of whom is a justice of the supreme court of the U. States, and the other is the district judge of the particular district in which the court sits. The court may be held by either judge in the absence of the other; but the district judge cannot try causes brought by appeal from his own decisions. Each circuit consists of at least two states, and some of three states, and one of four states. There are six states in which no circuit court sits; and there the like duties are performed by the district judges. The circuit courts possess original jurisdiction in all civil suits at common law, or in equity, where the matter in dispute is of the sum or value of $500, or upwards, and the U. States are plaintiffs; or where an alien is a party; or where the suit is between a citizen of the state where the suit is brought, and a citizen of another state. They also possess jurisdiction in cases of patents for useful inventions, and of copyrights for books, &c. They have also exclusive jurisdiction of all crimes and offences against the U. States, not cognizable in the district courts; and concurrent jurisdiction with those courts of all crimes and offences cognizable therein. They have appellate jurisdiction of all final judgments and decrees of the district courts, in all cases where the matter in dispute exceeds $50. Civil suits can be brought in the Circuit and district courts, by original process, against an inhabitant of the U. States, only in the district whereof he is an inhabitant, or in which, at the time of serving the process, he may be found; and, in cases of negotiable securities for money, except foreign bills, these courts cannot, by any transfer or assignment of such securities, maintain jurisdiction, unless their jurisdiction could have attached independent of such transfer or assignment. If a suit is commenced in a state court against an alien or citizen of another state, and the matter in dispute exceed $500, it may be removed into the circuit court, which sits in the same state, and tried there according to certain regulations prescribed by law; and a like removal may take place where, in a suit in the state court, the parties claim title to lands under a grant thereof from different states, that is, where one party claims title under the state in which the suit is brought, and the other under another state.

3. The *Supreme Court*

Consists of seven judges, as above stated. It sits annually at the seat of government, on the 2d Monday of January. It possesses exclusive original jurisdiction of all controversies of a civil nature, where a state is a party, except between a state and its citizens, and except, also, between a state and citizens of other states and aliens, in which latter case it has original but not exclusive jurisdiction. It possesses also, exclusively, all such jurisdiction of suits and proceedings against ambassadors, and other public ministers, or their domestics, or domestic servants, as a court of law can have or exercise consistently with the law of nations; and original, but not exclusive jurisdiction of all suits brought by ambassadors, or other public ministers, or in which a consul or viceconsul is a party. It possesses, also, appellate jurisdiction from the final judgments and decrees of the circuit courts, and of the district courts exercising circuit court powers, in all civil cases where the matter in dispute exceeds $2000 in value or amount, and the causes were originally brought in or removed into such circuit or district courts. It has also jurisdiction in cases brought by way of appeal into the circuit court from the district courts (which word *appeal* has here a technical and somewhat peculiar sense), but not in cases brought by writs of error from the district courts into the circuit courts. This difference is more accidental than intentional, and proceeds from the different modes of process by which suits are brought into the appellate courts according to the course of the common law. The terms of the statute conferring the jurisdiction are supposed to limit the appellate jurisdiction to cases which did not get into the circuit courts by the process of a writ of error, in its technical sense. It is difficult to make the distinction clear to lawyers bred in the civil law; it is obvious to those bred in the common law. The supreme court also possesses appellate jurisdiction from the final decisions of the state courts, in cases in which there is drawn in question the validity of a treaty or statute of, or an authority exercised under, the U. States, and the state court decides against its validity; or where is drawn in question the validity of a statute of, or an authority exercised under, any state, on the ground of its being repugnant to the constitution, treaties or laws of the U. States, and the decision is in favor of its validity; or where is drawn in question the construction of any clause of the constitution, or of a treaty or statute of, or commission held under, the U. States, and the decision is against the title, right, privilege or exemption specially set up or claimed by either party, under such clause of the constitution, treaty, statute or commission. The appellate jurisdiction, however, so exercised in these cases, coming from the state courts, is confined to the points above-mentioned, and does not extend to the other merits of the case, not connected there-with, nor flowing there from. From this sketch, it will be perceived that the supreme court exercises, or may exercise, jurisdiction in the following classes of cases: 1. In cases where the construction of the constitution, treaties and statutes of the U. States is involved; 2. in cases where the state laws are supposed to be inconsistent with the constitution, treaties or laws of the U. States; 3. in cases of rights derived under the constitution, treaties or laws of the U. States; 4. in cases where a state is a party to the suit, or a foreign ambassador, or minister, or consul, or viceconsul; 5. in cases of controversies of a civil nature between aliens and citizens, or between citizens of one state and citizens of another state; 6. in cases of admiralty and maritime jurisdiction. As a general description, this is sufficiently precise for the common reader. The supreme court has authority, also, in various other modes, to exercise a supervision over the acts of inferior tribunals; as, by granting writs of *mandamus*, to direct them to do their duty in certain cases; by granting writs of *prohibition*, where they exceed their authority; by granting writs of *habeas corpus*, to relieve parties from unjust imprisonment, &c. &c. In cases also where no appeal lies to the supreme court, the judges of the circuit courts are allowed to obtain the opinion of the supreme court, by certifying cases to that court, in which they are divided in opinion. This course is often pursued in important and difficult questions, both of civil and criminal law, and in the latter especially, because, in criminal cases, the supreme court has no direct appellate jurisdiction. The general mass of business, which employs the supreme court, consists of private controversies respecting property, or personal rights and contracts. In times of war, it also exercises a final appellate jurisdiction in prize causes, and other causes in which belligerent and neutral rights and duties are involved. For the most part, questions of national and public law are there finally discussed and settled. Its most important function, however, in a practical view, is the decision of the great constitutional questions, which, from time to time, arise in the different parts of the Union. These questions are not brought forward, in a formal manner, by the government itself, to be adjudged upon a mere reference of them to the court. The court cannot take cognizance of them in such a shape, but only in a suit regularly brought before it, in which the point arises, and is essential to the rights of one of the parties. Hence it happens that a private person may litigate any question respecting the constitutionality of a law of the national or state government, whenever it is connected with his own rights, which are in controversy in a suit. Such a person may not only litigate the constitutionality of such laws, independently of the government, but even against the will of the government; and it not unfrequently happens that such questions are discussed and decided without the government having any opportunity of interposing itself in the discussion. The constitution is deemed the supreme law of the land, which rulers, and magistrates, and legislatures are bound to obey; and if, unintentionally or otherwise, they overleap the proper boundary, and the supreme court so decide, the act of the legislatures or rulers becomes a mere nullity, and receives no sanction or support whatsoever. It may naturally be supposed, that, in many instances, such questions must involve interests of a public nature to a vast extent, as well as contests respecting the just exercise of political power, and thus give rise to very heated discussions, and sometimes to violent political struggles, which might threaten the very existence of the national government. But hitherto, however warm have been the preliminary controversies, and however important the rights to state sovereignty or state pride, the decisions of the supreme court have been universally respected. Indeed, the people are so well satisfied, that the great security of their civil and political liberties essentially depends upon the independent exercise of this great function, and the supreme Court is accustomed to expound its opinion with so much fulness and moderation, that no instance has occurred, in which a great majority of the nation has not hitherto rested satisfied with the decision. Such is the supremacy of law in the U. States. If it be asked, in what respects the supreme court of the U. States differs, in its functions and organization, from the highest courts of England, the following will be found the most important particulars:

1. In England, the prize and admiralty jurisdiction, the equity jurisdiction, and the common law jurisdiction, are severally intrusted to distinct courts. The supreme court of the U. States exercises all these jurisdictions, as, indeed, do the circuit courts.

2. The highest courts in England have a general jurisdiction as to all persons and all suits. The supreme court of the U. States has a limited and restricted jurisdiction over particular persons only, and particular classes of suits. 3. The courts in England have no jurisdiction over constitutional questions: an act of parliament is an act of uncontrollable sovereignty, which all courts must obey and enforce. 4. The courts in England do not exercise jurisdiction in cases between state sovereignties; or, if they do, it is a very limited and incidental jurisdiction in many particulars, the highest courts in England and the supreme court of the U. States exercise the same powers substantially in the same way. In the first place, the general system of jurisprudence to be administered by them is, in most respects, the same. The common law governs in England. It constitutes the general basis of the jurisprudence of all the states in the Union, with the exception of Louisiana, where the civil law prevails, as it did while that territory belonged to France and Spain. The common law is, indeed, modified by the legislation of the several states, according to their pleasure, as it is by the parliament in England; and, in some of the

states, there are some customs and peculiarities which grew up in early times. But they are few, and, in a general sense, unimportant. The statutes passed by the states, and the judicial constructions or interpretations of them, constitute the principal peculiarities of what is denominated *local law*; and these are far more uniform than at first thought would be supposed. The original circumstances of the colonies were not, as to most political and municipal arrangements, materially different. Inheriting from England the common law, they generally adopted such amendments of it as were, from time to time, made in the mother country; and, in their colonial legislation, they borrowed from each other such portions of the statutes, which were enacted and in use, as were suited to their own wants. Hence, at an early day, in almost all the colonies, they enacted nearly uniform laws as to the making of wills, as to registering of conveyances of lands, as to the descent of estates among all the children, giving, in some cases, a double share to the eldest son, but excluding the English law of primogeniture. The system of land law, that is, the system adopted in relation to the sale and distribution of the public lands belonging to the states, constitutes, at this very time, a more important feature of difference in the legislation, and judicial interpretation of rights to landed property, than any other in the whole code of positive law. It may naturally be presumed, too, that, though the common law was the general basis of the jurisprudence of all the states, yet, in the course of time, the judicial interpretations thereof, especially when there were no printed reports, might essentially vary in the different states, in many cases; and that these diversities, as well from the different talents and acquirements of the judges, as from the uncertainty of many of the principles of decision, might create other heads of local law. It would surprise a foreigner, however, to learn how few, comparatively speaking, these now are. The regular publication of reports; the desire to give uniformity to the system; the influence of the decision in the mother country and in the national courts, have a powerful operation upon the whole profession in this respect, and the more powerful and beneficial, because it is silent and insensible. In this way, it conduces to a general harmony and coincidence in the administration of the law, by the gentle means of juridical reasoning and argument. From this general prevalence of the common law, the decisions made from time to time in England are cited in the discussions in the American courts, not as absolute authorities, but as very able expositions of the law; and, on that account, they are generally adopted. In the next place, the modes of administering justice are the same in the courts of the U. States as they are in England in like cases. In the prize and admiralty proceedings, the principles and practice of the English courts of admiralty are adopted; in equity causes, the principles and practice of the court of chancery in England; in suits at common law, the principles and practice of the courts of *commendam* in England. There are no courts in America which possess a general jurisdiction in ecclesiastical affairs, like the ecclesiastical courts in England; for, in America, there is no church establishment. But the business of the probate of wills, and granting administration on the estate of deceased persons, and appointing guardians to minors and others, is generally confided to orphan courts, or probate courts, exercising a jurisdiction over these subjects very similar to the summary jurisdiction exercised by the ecclesiastical courts in England over the same subjects. The jurisprudence in America, then, not being entirely homogeneous, the supreme court, in the exercise of its jurisdiction, has an invariable regard to the local law, where it applies, and, consequently, is called upon to administer justice in many cases of a conflict of laws. In this part of its functions, it acts upon the same general principles which regulate, or ought to regulate, the tribunals of other independent states. It acts upon the same principles which the English courts would act upon; but it is called more frequently to decide on such questions, and therefore it refers more, as guides in its decisions, to the civil law writers, who have discussed this complicated subject with ability and learning. Indeed, it may be stated as a general fact, that the American courts, in questions of public and commercial law, are in the habit of paying great attention to the works of the continental jurists. The supreme court of the U. States exercises no political functions whatsoever, except the administration of public and prize law, and the decision of constitutional questions, may be so considered. It is wholly independent of the executive government, the judges holding their offices during good behavior, and receiving a salary which cannot be diminished during their continuance in office. The present salary of the chief justice is $5000, and that of each of the other judges, $4500. They are liable to impeachment for high crimes and misdemeanors; before the senate of the U. States, and, upon conviction by two thirds of the members present, are liable to be removed from office. Cases of impeachment of public officers are exclusively triable before the senate; and, when the president of the U. States is on trial, the chief justice of the U. States is required by the constitution to preside. As to the modes of trial: in cases of impeachment, as has been already stated, the trial is before the senate, without any jury. The trial of all crimes, in other cases, is required by the constitution to be by jury. So is the trial of all civil suits at common law, where the value in controversy exceeds $20. And, in all cases where the facts are tried by a jury, their verdict, as to the facts, has the conclusiveness given it by the common law of England. In admiralty and prize causes, and in equity causes, the questions of fact, as well as of law, are decided by the court, as they are decided in the English courts. The general practice, in the trials by jury, is the same as in England. The mode of appointing and selecting the jurors is not uniform. In some of the states, the marshal or sheriff selects them; in others, they are drawn out of ballot boxes, which contain the names of all the persons whom the municipal authorities deem qualified to sit as jurors. The selections thus made usually embrace a very large proportion of the voters; and as many are selected and returned for a particular session of the court as the court deems the occasion to require. In some states, the same jurors sit in all causes tried at the same term; in others, a distinct jury is, or may be, returned for each cause. The courts of the U. States, sitting in any particular district, follow the local practice as to the selection of juries. In all criminal trials, the constitution guaranties to the party accused a public trial, upon a written indictment or accusation, a right to be confronted with the witnesses brought against him, and to have compulsive process for the attendance of his own witnesses, and a right to have the assistance of counselor lawyers in his defence. The statutes of the U. States generally secure to him, in civil cases, the same privileges, except that depositions of witnesses may be used therein, in certain cases, where the witnesses cannot attend by reason of infirmity, or distance of place, &c. The power of pardon is exclusively confided to the president of the U. States. The judges have no express authority to recommend any person, after conviction, for a pardon; but, where the case requires it, it is not unfrequently done by them, as private persons, upon their own responsibility and sense of justice. It may be asked, Who determine finally what causes do or do not belong to the jurisdiction of the courts of the U. States? The general answer should be, that the court, before which the suit is brought, must, in the first instance, decide that question for itself; and it is finally to be decided by the highest court to which an appeal lies from that court if it depend on matter of fact, the fact is ascertained in the usual way in which other facts are ascertained in cases of a like nature; if it depend on matter of law, then the court primarily decides on its own view of the law. In general, the judgments and decrees of courts of competent jurisdiction are held conclusive in the U. States, as they are in England. Few conflicts, as to jurisdiction, arise in the American courts, as, for the most part the jurisdiction of the state courts is concurrent with that of the U. States courts in civil cases; and where it is not, the line of exclusive jurisdiction is broadly marked out. For instance, the admiralty and prize jurisdiction is exclusive in the courts of the U. States; but in controversies between citizens of different states, the jurisdiction is concurrent. One state cannot sue another in its own courts. The suit must be in the supreme court of the U. States. The courts of the U. States, like the courts in England, have general authority to make rules for the orderly course of their business, to issue writs and executions, to take bail, to grant injunctions, to permit amendments, to punish for contempts, &c., in the same way as the courts in England. Writs and executions do not run, that is to say, cannot be executed, beyond the limits of the particular district in which the court sits, with a few exceptions, among which are *subpoenas* for witnesses and executions on judgments in suits in favor of the U. States. There are various sorts of process to compel the performance of judgments, as in England. Such are writs of *fieri facias*, on which the goods and chattels of the debtor or defendant may be taken or sold; writs of *levari facias*, on which his lands may be taken for a term; writs of *capias*, on which his person may be arrested and imprisoned; and other writs, on which his lands may be taken and set off to the creditor, at an appraised value, or sold at public auction. In criminal cases, the courts of the U. States direct the punishment against the party according to the rules prescribed by the law. If the punishment is death, the court, before which the trial is had, declares the time and place when and where the execution of it shall take place. If the punishment is discretionary, as by fine, or by imprisonment, or by fine not exceeding a certain sum, or by imprisonment not exceeding ascertain period of time, the court fixes the fine, or imprisonment, or both, in its sentence, according to the circumstances of each particular case. As all trials, both civil and criminal, are public; and reports are printed, from time to time, of those which are most interesting either as to law, or facts; as the opinion of the court is always publicly given, and, generally, the reasons of that opinion, it is not easy for any court to trespass upon the known principles of law or the rights of the parties. In the U. States, as in England, the citizens at large watch with jealousy the proceedings of courts of justice. The very great number of lawyers engaged in the profession also furnishes an additional security. The rules of admission to the bar are not very strict; and usually, after three years' preparatory study, any citizen of good education and character is admissible to the inferior courts, and, after two or three years' practice there, is admissible to the highest courts. Generally speaking, lawyers are entitled to the same privileges, upon the same terms, in the U. States courts, as in the state courts. Few but eminent lawyers, in fact, practise in the supreme court of the U. States, although the admission to it is quite easy. Throughout the U. States, the bar of the highest courts is characterized by learning and talent, a spirit of independence and integrity, and a manliness of conduct, which give it great weight and popularity. Lawyers, more than any other class, are the favorite candidates for seats in the legislative and executive departments of the government. The foregoing sketch is necessarily imperfect; but it may give the common reader a general outline of the jurisprudence and organization of the national courts, as contradistinguished from the state courts. To treat the subject with the fulness which belongs to it, would require a volume.

Courts of the Several States in the United States

The limits of this work will not permit a particular account of all the courts of the several states in the Union. In some respects, their judicial systems correspond with each other. The office of justice of the peace is very similar in all, the general police of the counties being confided mostly to these magistrates. They generally have authority to cause offenders and criminals, and all disturbers of the peace, to be arrested, and, if the offence is small, to fix its punishment; if it falls without their jurisdiction, they commit the offenders to prison, to be detained for trial before the proper tribunals. But for all considerable offences, the parties are liable to be put upon trial only on a bill being found against them by a grand jury. In the county courts of sessions, the assembled justices, or a select number of them, in many of the states, have a pretty extensive jurisdiction in matters of police, in the regulation of the affairs of the county, such as building courthouses, assessing county taxes, laying out roads, licensing taverns and victualling houses, and, in some states, granting the right to erect mills, and settling the questions of damages thereby occasioned. In Virginia, the county sessions have a still more extensive jurisdiction, both civil and criminal, the civil jurisdiction extending to suits in which an amount not exceeding $300 is in dispute; and, though a vast amount of the business of both descriptions comes into these courts, the justices discharge all their duties without fees, and this paternal, friendly superintendence of the general interests of the county is supposed to have a very salutary influence upon the community. Besides this general superintendence of the police, and maintenance of the peace and good order of the community, exercised by the justices individually or collectively, they have, in most of the states, a jurisdiction of civil actions to amounts varying from $13 to $100, reserving to the parties a right to appeal, and have a new trial before the county sessions or county courts of common pleas, or some other superior tribunals, in cases where the sum in dispute exceeds a certain amount. In some states, there is a right of appeal in case the amount of $4 or more is in dispute: in others, the final jurisdiction of the justices extends to a greater sum; in Massachusetts, to $20; and there is a distinction, in some states, in the local extent of the civil and criminal jurisdiction of justices, the former extending only to the town in which the magistrate resides, the latter to the whole county. In some of the capitals and more considerable towns, special courts are established, to which is assigned the jurisdiction of many of the offences and suits, which, in the counties, generally come under the cognizance of the justices, individually or collectively. In all the states, another class of county courts is established, variously denominated, courts of common pleas, county, district or circuit courts, which have original jurisdiction of the great mass of civil actions at law, or indictments for crimes not capital; and over these are established the superior or supreme courts, or courts of errors or appeals. In some states, the county courts for trials by jury are held by one of the judges of the supreme court, and all questions of law are reserved for the determination of all the judges. In others, the judge of the supreme court, who presides in trials by jury, in the counties, is assisted by associate justices: this is the case in Maryland. In other states, trials by jury are held in the counties by a court of which the jurisdiction is limited to the county; and, in case of the amount in dispute exceeding a certain sum, varying, in the different states, from $100 to $300, or in cases involving land titles, and some others, either party may appeal, and have another trial of the same facts, by jury, before a judge of the superior court. This trial of the same facts a second time, by jury, without the allegation of any error or misdirection on the first trial, or any surprise on the part of either of the litigants, or any discovery of new evidence, or, indeed, any other reason than to give the parties opportunity for another contest, upon precisely the same footing as the first, is an anomaly. It is, in effect, an appeal from one jury to another, for which there might be more reason if juries were, like courts, differently constituted, so that one should be considered superior to the other; but this is not the case, the juries in both courts being selected upon the same principles. This is a feature of some of the state courts, by which they are distinguished from the English courts, and also from those of the U. States. A similar practice prevails, in some of the states, in criminal trials, except for felonies or the more heinous offences, of which the superior court has original and exclusive cognizance. This right to two trials of the same case, in the same state of it, though theoretically an irregularity not easily reconciled to any principle, is yet not the cause of any very serious inconvenience in practice, for very few of those actions in which the parties have a right to two trials are, in fact, tried more than once. The equity jurisdiction is in a distinct court in some of the states, as New York, Maryland, Virginia; in others, the same courts act as courts of law and equity, as in Massachusetts, Ohio, North Carolina; and there is a great diversity in the extent of equity jurisdiction possessed by the courts, those of Pennsylvania, for instance, having very circumscribed powers; and in the New England states, excepting Connecticut, the prejudices against equity courts and proceedings derived from some of the old common law writers, particularly lord Coke, have taken deep root, and are the more difficult to eradicate, as they have no definite foundation, but rest upon a vague notion of the delays supposed to be necessarily attendant upon chancery proceedings, and the still more groundless notion that a court of chancery proceeds, without any regard to the law or to principles, upon the mere arbitrary discretion of the judge. These prejudices are, however, gradually wearing away, and the remedies, which can only be obtained by proceedings in equity, are from time to time introduced by successive legislative acts.

In all the states in which the two species of courts are distinguished, the tribunal of final resort, as in England, is the same in appeals from courts, both of law and equity. There is established, in the city of New York, a tribunal called the *marine court*, having jurisdiction of marine torts and questions between masters of vessels and their crews; but, in general, all subjects of commercial and maritime jurisdiction, not belonging exclusively to the courts of the U. States, but remaining in the state tribunals, either exclusively or concurrently with the courts of the U. States—such as bills of exchange, bills of lading, charter-parties, policies of insurance, claims for seamen's wages, claims for contributions in general average, and maritime torts—are within the jurisdiction of the same courts which have cognizance of other contracts, and torts of similar amounts. In most of the states, the jurisdiction of the subject of wills, and granting administration, on the estates of persons deceased intestate, and the appointing of guardians to minors, is assigned to certain tribunals, denominated courts of *probate*, *orphans'* courts, sometimes the register's court; and, in one state, a part of this jurisdiction is vested in the court of the *ordinary*. These courts are held in the several counties. An appeal lies from them, generally, to the higher tribunals. In some states, the sessions of the tribunal of final resort are held only at the capital; in others, again, the sessions are held in the several counties, one session or more in the year being devoted, in each county, to the determination of questions of law, for which purpose all the judges make a circuit of the state in a body.

ENCYCLOPÆDIA AMERICANA.

A

POPULAR DICTIONARY

OF

ARTS, SCIENCES, LITERATURE, HISTORY, POLITICS AND BIOGRAPHY,

A NEW EDITION;

INCLUDING

A COPIOUS COLLECTION OF ORIGINAL ARTICLES

IN

AMERICAN BIOGRAPHY;

ON

THE BASIS OF THE SEVENTH EDITION OF THE GERMAN

CONVERSATIONS-LEXICON.

EDITED BY

FRANCIS LIEBER,

ASSISTED BY

E. WIGGLESWORTH

VOL. IV.

PHILADELPHIA:
LEA & BLANCHARD.
1844.

CRIMINAL LAW

[This article, to the paragraph on page 83, is from the *German Lexicon.*]

In no department of legal science do so many different views prevail among jurisconsults, and in none have these views exercised so great an influence upon the theory and practice, as in this. The doctrine of the criminal law is, that the individual committing an unlawful act, must not only make amends to the party injured, but also be punished by the supreme authority of the state. The first question is, whether and how far the state is authorized to inflict punishment. This question cannot be decided by positive rules of law, because the object of the inquiry is to reconcile these rules with natural justice. States have, indeed, at all times, exercised the power of punishment, without waiting for or regarding such theoretical investigations, because it is obvious that, without the right of punishing, no state could exist. The different systems, which have attempted to establish theoretically the right of punishment, may be brought under the following heads;

I. The System of *Vengeance.* From the opinion that he who has injured another, cannot complain of injustice, if a similar evil is inflicted upon himself, and the injured person, or, in case of murder, his family, would be disgraced, if they did not obtain satisfaction, arises the rude system of retaliation, which we meet with in so many nations; but, whilst those who take revenge must beware not to exceed the measure of the injury received, lest they

* This comparative statement of offences in France, Switzerland, the U. States and Spain, rests upon the authority of an article in the *Bulletin Universel*, for September. The precise year taken for Spain is not mentioned.

become aggressors in their turn, they will be obliged to adhere literally to the rule of "an eye for an eye, a tooth for a tooth;" and in this state we find the criminal law subsisting among nations for a considerable time, and bloody revenge and retaliation become a common right and duty. (See Michaelis, *On the Mosaic Law*.) In this state of things, the punishment of offences against the law belongs not to the community, but to the individual, and the public authority is active only in putting limits to the continual exercise of revenge, and in providing means for terminating the hostilities among families, which threaten the nation itself with destruction. From this arises the system of composition. Offences are estimated at certain rates in money; and not only is the offender forced to pay the sum fixed, but the offended party must also receive it in satisfaction. With this degree of progress is connected the idea of a national peace, which is developed in various forms and relations, as the peace of the king, the peace of the court, &c., involving, at the same time, the acknowledgment of a public power, whose duty it is to protect and judge. We find the law of composition among the old Germans, as well as the nations of the Indian archipelago, and the tribes of American savages. The next step is the acknowledgment of the principle, that the community is bound to prevent crimes. The right of revenge passes into the hands of the state, which does not wait for the complaint of the offended party, but takes upon itself the duty of the accuser. The theory which next succeeds is,

II. The System of *Deterring*. By the punishment of the offender, others are to be deterred from similar acts. The punishment is, therefore, inflicted publicly; and the more horrible the crime, the more effort is made to confirm the popular abhorrence of it by severe penalties. This system is liable to the most weighty objections. It cannot be allowable to torment or put to death a human being, simply with the view that others may receive from his sufferings such an impression; as to be proof against the temptation to commit crime. In point of fact, this end has never been attained, and would require a scale of punishments offensive to sound reason. The mere fear of punishment is of very little weight. Men are kept from crime principally by the natural abhorrence of wrong, heightened by a good education and good example. If the plan of deterring should be carried through consistently, it would compel us to proportion punishment rather to the temptation to commit crimes than to their magnitude. (See Feuerbach's *Revision der Grundsätze des peinl. Rechts*, Erfurt, 1799—Revision of the Principles of Penal Law.) With regard to capital punishments, more particularly, the system of deterring fell by degrees into disrepute, after the marquis Beccaria (*On Crimes and Punishments*, London, 1770), and a great many other learned men, had declared themselves for,

III. The System of *Prevention* which is ingeniously defended by the Hessian minister Von Grolman (*Grundsätze der Criminalrechtswissenschaften*, Giessen, 1798—*Principles of the Science of Criminal Law*). Every crime contains, if man is considered as a consistent being, the expression of a principle of conduct, and, accordingly, besides the present transgression of the law, a threat of a repetition of the offence. The community is, therefore, entitled to take measures of prevention against it, which, if the injury done is irreparable, may extend to the deprivation of life. This system may be said to afford the true reason for punishment in general. It may, however, be objected to it, that this provision against future crimes is not really punishment, and that the punishment must needs be omitted, if this presumption of the future offences is refuted by the particular circumstances of the case. This principle, moreover, admits of no scale of punishment, because the means of effectual prevention must always be the same—death or imprisonment for life. The direction which the science of natural law had taken, at this period, seeking for the foundation of every right in a contract, led to,

IV. The System of *Compact*, which asserts that, by becoming a member of the state, every individual has, by tacit compact, bound himself to submit to punishment, if the society choose to inflict it. As, however, no one can be bound by a contract to any thing which is not right in itself, the lawfulness of punishment cannot be shown in this manner. Fichte, therefore, in his original way, modified this theory. He proceeded upon the principle that, by trespassing upon the right of others, the criminal deprived himself of the claim to be treated as a rational being, since the rights of a free agent depend on his respect for those of others. Every crime, therefore, he says, justifies the expulsion of the offender from human society. The compact, by which the punishment is determined, is consequently in favor of those who receive a lighter punishment than such expulsion. They acquire a right, by suffering some determined evil, to be admitted again into civil society. Much of this theory is true, but the real existence of such a compact seems to be wanting.

V. At the same time, the theory of *atonement* was introduced by Klein and others. The criminal does injury in two ways; 1. to the person who is the immediate subject of the wrong, for which he has to make him amends according to the rules of private law; and, 2. by the bad example afforded by the diminished respect for the laws of the state, for which he is answerable to the community. This latter injury is compensated by the punishment, which vindicates the authority of the law in the minds of the people. This theory has, in later times, been further developed, with great ingenuity, by Schultz (*Entwickelung der philosoph. Principien des bürgerl. und peinl. Rechts*, 1813—*Development of the Philosophical Principles of Civil and Criminal Law*), and by Martin (*Lehrbuch des Criminalrechts*, 1819–1825—Compendium of Criminal Law).

VI. The Theory of *Psychological Constraint*, by Feuerbach, is founded upon the system of deterring, with the addition of this position—that the threatening of punishment, in general, is lawful, because it forbids no one to do any thing which he can have a right to do; and this menace renders punishment lawful in case of an offence occurring, because the individual knew beforehand what he had to expect. This theory is exposed to most of the objections against the theory of deterring, and the grounds on which it rests often fail in particular cases.

VII. The Principle of *Moral Correction*, has been little used as the basis of the right to punish. It has for its end to correct, by punishment, in the criminal himself, those unlawful propensities which impelled him to crime. It is undeniably correct, so far as this, that the punishment ought never to be such as to make the moral correction of the criminal impossible, by the annihilation of his sense of honor, by exposing him to corruption in the society of other criminals, and destroying his ability to support himself in an honest manner. But it is evident, on the other hand, that the sentiments of men, and their moral reformation, cannot be the direct object of legislation, from the very circumstance, that this effect is not of a kind to be ascertained; but to produce an outward habit (for instance, to dispose the idle to labor, the drunkard to sobriety, &c.), is practicable.

Finally, VIII. The Theory of *Retaliation* has been adopted, since the time of Kant, by almost all the German philosophers, but, at the same time, by very few lawyers. It is founded upon the principles, that the state ought to suffer no wrong within itself; that every unlawful action ought to be annihilated, and is annihilated when made to revert on the author; and that the latter suffers no injustice by being treated in the same way as he has treated others. This retaliation is not, however, a literal one. It inflicts not the same evil on the criminal which he has done to another; but it seeks for a generic notion of the offence, and applies, according to this, the principle of the criminal against himself. This affords, at the same time, a measure for punishment, which no other principle of penal law affords, though it still requires that the degree of punishment, in particular cases, should be fixed by positive law.

We have thus set forth the theories on the subject of criminal legislation. In no branch of law has legislation been at all times so active as in this. The influence of theory has extended even to the forms of process, and the civilization of nations always manifests itself early by the improvement of the criminal law. Criminal law was first treated scientifically in Italy, but remained in a very rude state till the middle of the 16th century. The dreadful abuses in the administration of criminal justice in Germany and France, gave occasion to the two great reforms introduced by the Penal code of Charles V, of 1532, and the criminal ordinance of Francis I, of 1539. This branch of jurisprudence now assumed a more systematic character. The ordinances of Charles V greatly improved the forms of process, but retained, according to the spirit of the times, cruel punishments, and even torture. Of the points of criminal law, which, in recent times, have given rise to much diversity of opinion, the following are of particular practical importance:

1. The right of punishing flagrant crimes without the authority of an express law. Those who acknowledge the authority of a natural law, affirm the existence of such a right, and divide criminal actions into those which are bad in themselves (*delicta juris naturalis*), or, as the English law terms them, *mala in se*, and actions which are of themselves indifferent, but are subjected to a penalty by

particular laws (*delicta juris positivi*), or, as the English law terms them, *mala prohibita*. Crimes of the first class, as murder, theft, &c., must be every where punished, even without a positive law; but those of the second, as contraband trade, are punishable only when made penal by express enactment. Feuerbach and others, however, acknowledge no right of punishment without an express law.

2. With the preceding is nearly connected the question—how far it is the right or duty of the state to punish crimes, which have been committed in foreign countries. On this point, in addition to the difficulties attending the main question, there exists a great difference of opinion; as to the laws by which such crimes are to be judged, whether by the laws of the foreign country, or of that to which the individual belongs.

3. What power should be given to the judge to vary the punishment according to the different circumstances attending the offence? The tendency, in modern times, is to define crimes and their punishments so exactly as to leave nothing to the discretion of the judge, and to enable every man to see what he has to expect from a violation of the law. It is doubtful whether so much precision is generally advantageous, since it almost necessarily produces an unequal distribution of punishment, the question whether it shall be light or severe frequently depending on a little difference in the age of the offender, the amount of property stolen, &c.; so that a penny more or less may make a difference of several years' confinement in a penitentiary; or the difference of a day, in the age of the culprit) may decide whether he shall be punished with a few stripes, or deprived of his liberty for years, or of his life. 4. One of the most difficult points is the just estimation of injuries done to the honor of another, which involves the great question of the liberty of the press. The most important differences of opinion, however, are those which prevail with regard to criminal process. From the representation given above of

the principles and the development of penal law, it is evident that criminal proceedings have always been founded at first upon private accusations, in regard to which almost the same principles prevail as those observed in civil actions. In the course of time, this mode is superseded by a public accusation on the part of the state, appearing by an attorney, to prosecute the offence. Upon this principle are founded the criminal proceedings of the English courts, and of the French courts since the revolution. With this may be united the public trial by jury, which has found so many adherents in modern times. Its fundamental character consists in this, that the party accused remains merely passive, and waits for the charge to be proved. The consequence is, that the sentence must be pronounced from a view of probabilities, and depends, therefore, more on a knowledge of men, and the deductions of a sound judgment, than on technical rules. It has been considered the safest mode of trying offences, in particular, as it prevents the dangers arising from the influence of the higher officers of the state over judges deriving their salaries from the sovereign, by referring the question of guilt or innocence to the verdict of men taken immediately from among the people, i.e. jurors. The German criminal proceedings are directed principally, it may be said solely, to the end of obtaining from the accused a confession of the deed, and of its circumstances, by inquisitory process. This admits neither of an accuser nor of a public trial, but the judge must inquire of the accused himself, and obtain from him, if possible, by a skilful combination of the circumstances, as well as by awakening the voice of conscience, complete truth. What is in Germany the chief business of the judge, belongs, in France, to the judge instructeur, and, in England, to justices of the peace, as police officers, whose investigations afford, in common cases, the materials for the final trial. The opponents of the trial by jury allege, as a chief reason for their opposition, that, when the preparatory process affords no certain results, the subsequent trial is attended by the same uncertainty.

To the preceding article, taken from the *German Lexicon*, we have to add a few suggestions growing out of the practice of the common law, which constitutes the basis of the institutions of the U. States, as well as of England. The general theory of the common law is, that all wrongs are divisible into two species; first, civil or private wrongs; secondly, criminal or public wrongs. The former are to be redressed by private suits, or remedies instituted by the parties injured. The latter are redressed by the state, acting in its sovereign capacity. The general description of private wrongs is, that they comprehend those injuries which affect the rights and property of the individual, and terminate there; that of public wrongs or offences is, that they comprehend such acts as injure, not merely individuals, but the community at large, by endangering the peace, the comfort, the good order, the policy, and even the existence of society. The exact boundaries between these classes are not, perhaps, always easy to be discerned, even in theory; for there are few private wrongs which may not and do not exert an influence beyond the individual whom they directly injure. In doubtful cases, the legislature usually interferes, and prescribes a positive rule. In clear cases, the right of punishment on the part of the state is assumed as a deduction from natural justice and the duty of the state to protect all its subjects. Hence, in the common law, two classes of offences are distinctly traced out. The first embraces those which rest upon legislative enactments. The second embraces those which, independently of any such enactment, are deemed, from their very nature, injuries to the public. The offences belonging to this last class are not, perhaps, capable of a perfect enumeration; and the test by which they are ascertained is left to the judgment of judges, as cases arise, to be fixed, not according to their own discretion, but by analogy and appreciation of the principles and cases already well settled by former adjudications. When, therefore, a non-enumerated wrong arises, which does not fall under any known former rule, the question which is discussed is, how far it falls under the principles already established respecting public crimes. If reasoning furnishes a strong analogy, it is deemed a public offence; if otherwise, it is left for the legislature to declare that it shall be such. Treason, murder, setting fire to a dwelling house in a large city, riots disturbing the general peace, poisoning public wells, &c., it will be readily admitted, naturally endanger the good order and safety of the state, and therefore are properly to be punished by the state. But it is not so easy to trace the same principle in mere secret thefts, or a private fight, and yet deny its existence in violent seizures of private property, and private quarrels producing defamation of character. The common law considers the great object of the public punishment of crimes to be the prevention of offences, by deterring both the offender and others from a repetition of the same. Its object is not so much an atonement for, or expiation of, the offences, as a precaution against their recurrence. This naturally includes, not as a primary motive, but as an incident, the reformation of the criminal himself; for, so far as that is effected, it prevents offences. That system of punishments is indeed most desirable, which attains its object by such a reformation. But it is obvious, that reformation cannot, always be relied upon as a sufficient security for society. Hence arises the necessity or policy of capital punishment, which, by cutting off the offender, not only operates as a terror to others, but secures society against the possible perpetration of the same offence by him. Undoubtedly it ought never to be resorted to except in cases of atrocious guilt, and where less punishments are manifestly inadequate to produce security. Some persons, indeed, doubt the lawfulness of capital punishment altogether; but the divine law has certainly sanctioned it. Others, who do not question its lawfulness, doubt or deny its policy. It is certain that the frequency of capital punishment has some tendency to abate its terrors; and it is by no means as certain that capital punishments have a tendency to prevent the occurrence of the crime, or to secure a conviction. There is a natural repugnance to punish, with so much severity, slight offences; and judges and juries, as well as the public, under such circumstances, lean against prosecutions and in favor of acquittals. Hence the probability of conviction is sometimes in proportion to the moderation of punishments. On the other hand, it is found by experience, that the punishment of death is not sufficient to deter men from the commission of offences to which they are strongly tempted by their passions or their wants.*

The tendency of modern legislation has, therefore, almost uniformly been in favor of relaxing the severity of the penal code. In England, capital punishments are very extensively provided for by statute. There are more than 160 capital offences in her code. (4 *Bl. Comm.* 18.) In the U. States, there has been a constant effort to diminish the number of capital offences. There are but 9 in the criminal code of the U. States; and the codes of the respective states do not generally embrace a larger number. Treason, murder, rape, arson or burning of a dwelling house, are generally punishable with death; and sometimes robbery, burglary or breaking into a dwelling house in the night time with intent to steal.

The code of the U. States also includes piracy, the slave-trade, fraudulently casting away ships on the sea, robbery of the mail, burning public ships of war, and the rescue of convicts capitally convicted when the sentence is about to be executed. The punishment of other offences is,

*Indeed, the severity of the punishment sometimes induces the offender to become more savage and atrocious. Thus, where robbery is punishable with death, it is often attended with murder.

for those of great enormity, solitary confinement or hard labor in a penitentiary or prison erected for that purpose; and for those of a lower degree, fine or imprisonment, or both, according to the nature and aggravation of the offence. In the U. States, no capital punishments are inflicted unless by the injunctions of some positive statute. In England, the same rule prevails to a limited extent. A few offences are punished by the common law with death, without any statute to direct it, founded either upon the notion of conformity to the divine law, or upon some positive law whose existence cannot now be traced. Such are murder, rape, robbery, burglary, and certain other felonies at the common law. In respect to other offences, for which no statute has prescribed any punishment, the general rule of the common law is, that they are punishable by fine or imprisonment, or by both. Considering the infinite variety of circumstances which may occur to extenuate or aggravate the offence, not only the common law, but the legislature has left much of the degree of punishment to the discretion of the judges who try the case. That discretion must be exercised in public; and experience has proved that it is, on the whole, wiser and safer to leave it to the natural operations of judicial responsibility, than, by any attempts to define and limit the exact degree of punishment, to run the hazard of introducing other mischiefs by excluding mercy where it might be most desirable. No code of laws could be sufficiently minute to embrace all circumstances; and none could, therefore, provide for a perfect uniformity of punishments, according to the absolute nature of the offence. Another inquiry is, Who are, in a legal sense, capable of committing crimes, so as to be amenable to punishment? The general rule of the common law is, that all persons are punishable for disobedience to, and infractions of the law. The exceptions are few, and are clearly defined. They are such as presuppose a defect of reason and understanding, or of intention. A defect of understanding exists in the case of injuries committed by persons in a state of infancy, lunacy, idiocy, or intoxication. A defect of intention exists in the case of offences committed by chance, mistake and ignorance, wholly without or against the intention of the party. In respect to want of capacity, idiots, mad-men, and other persons not at the time in possession of reason, such as somnambulists, are generally excused, whatever injuries they may commit. But the common law does not extend this indulgence to climes committed by persons who are in a state of voluntary intoxication. It considers this circumstance rather in the light of an aggravation of the offence. But a distinction is here to be made. If the party be, at the time of the offence, drunk by the use of strong liquors, he is punishable, though he may be thereby reduced, at the time, to a state of insanity. But if drunkenness be only the remote cause of the insanity, and the party be not, at the time, under the influence of intoxicating liquors, the law treats his case like that of any other insane person. It does not look back to the original and remote cause of the insanity, to ascertain whether it has been produced by criminal indulgence, or neglect of duty, but to the immediate and operating cause, at the time when the crime is committed. The exception, therefore, of the case of insanity by immediate intoxication, is carved out of the general exception in favor of insanity, and arises from, or at least is countenanced by, motives of public policy, to prevent the dangerous effects arising from indulgence in strong liquors. The common law is, in this particular, more severe than the civil law. The latter never punished capitally for an offence committed under such circumstances. (4 *Bl. Comm.* 26.)

As to crimes committed by infants. There are various ages of infancy, in the common law, for different purposes. The general age of majority for all proposes is, in our law, 21 years; in the civil law, 25 years. Children under 7 years of age are deemed without discretion, and are universally exempted, by our law, from punishment. Between 7 and 14 years, they are said to be in a dubious stage, in point of discretion. If they, in fact, possess it, if they appear to have judgment, and understanding, and a sense of crime, they are liable to punishment; otherwise not. Generally, the rule of presumption is in favor of mercy, that an infant under 14 is *doli incapax*; but this presumption may be removed by facts establishing a clear sense of the deterrence between good and evil, together with malice and superior cunning. (4 *Bl. Comm.* 22, 23.) However, it deserves consideration, whether this is a sufficient test of rational discernment of the nature of crime and duty; and judges may well lean against convictions in such cases, upon principles not merely of humanity, but of philosophical responsibility. After 14, the general presumption is in favor of an infant being *doli capax*, and therefore he generally stands upon grounds similar to those of adults, until his actual incapacity is proved.

As to crimes committed by lunatics and idiots, the exception on account of want of capacity obviously applies only to cases where it exists at the time of the commission of the offence. Hence it is no excuse, if a person who has been insane commits an offence in a lucid interval, or at a time when his reason is clearly restored. So, on the other hand, a person may not be an absolute idiot, so as to have no discernment whatsoever, and yet may be excusable from punishment if his capacity be so weak that he does not, though an adult, understand clearly the distinctions between right and wrong. Extreme old age sometimes reduces persons to a state almost of fatuity, and exposes them to be imposed upon, and even seduced to the commission of offences, under circumstances where they would be held no more liable to punishment than infants. Every thing depends upon soundness of mind and real discretion at the time of committing the offence. When a person becomes insane after the commission of an offence, and before trial, he is not, by the common law, ever allowed to be brought to trial, until he is restored to his reason. At whatever stage of a public prosecution the insanity occurs, it operates as a suspension of all further proceedings. Thus, if it occurs before arraignment, the party ought not to be arraigned for the offence; if after arraignment, he ought not to be required to plead; if after plea, he ought not to be put to trial; if after trial, he ought not to have judgment or sentence pronounced against him; if after judgment, execution of the sentence ought to be stayed. The ground upon which this rule of law is commonly supposed to stand is, that it ought never to be presumed that the party, if sane, might not suggest some defence that, in reason or justice, would entitle him to mercy, or to exemption from punishment. A reason quite as satisfactory is, that the punishment of an insane person can produce no good result, either to reform the offender or as a public example. It would shock all the feelings of humanity to inflict punishment on those who the visitation of Providence had already made objects of wretchedness and of compassion. In all cases where it is doubtful whether the party be insane or not, the fact is, by the common law, to be tried by a jury.

In respect to injuries committed without the intention of the party, as through misfortune or chance. Where an accidental mischief happens in the performance of a lawful act, in the doing of which the party uses reasonable care and diligence, he is wholly free from guilt, and it is deemed his misfortune; but if he does not use reasonable care and diligence, he is liable to punishment according to the nature and extent of his negligence. If guilty of gross negligence, he is sometimes punishable in the same manner as if the act were intentionally committed; if guilty of slight negligence only, he escapes with a more moderate punishment. If the mischief happens in the performance of an unlawful act, and a consequence ensues which was not intended or foreseen, the party is not free from guilt. But the degree of punishment ought to depend upon the nature of the unlawful act itself. A distinction is taken, in the common law, between cases where the original act is wrong and unlawful in itself (*malum per se*), and where it is merely prohibited by statute (*malum prohibitum*). In the former case, the party is responsible for all incidental consequences of the unlawful act; in the latter, not. An illustration of these principles may be found in cases commonly put in our treatises on criminal law: If a man be at work with a hatchet, and the head flies off, and kills a standerby, this is not any offence, for the party was doing a lawful act, without any intention of hurt. So a parent may moderately correct a child, and if, in so doing, death happens, against his intention, it is mere misadventure. But if he corrects the child immoderately, or uses an instrument which is dangerous to life, or is wanting in reasonable caution, he is guilty either of manslaughter or murder, according to the circumstances and the degree of the punishment. If a man, riding a horse with reasonable care, accidentally runs over a child and kills him, he is not guilty of any offence. If he rides him furiously in a street where there may be danger, and the like mischief happens, he is guilty of manslaughter at least. If he rides him furiously into a crowd, either from wantonness or thoughtlessness, and the like accident happens, it will be murder. If a person in England, duly qualified by law to kill game, accidentally kills another while so doing, he is guilty of no offence. If a person be prohibited by statute from killing game, and the like accident happens by his shooting, he is not answerable in any other manner than a person duly qualified. This last case illustrates the distinction as to cases of *malum prohibitum*. On the other hand, if a person, shooting at poultry belonging to another person, by accident kills a man, if his intention was to steal the poultry, it will be murder, by reason of the felonious intent: if his intention was not to steal, but it was an act of mere wantonness, it will be manslaughter only. In these last cases, the act is *malum in se*.

In respect to injuries committed through ignorance or mistake. This may arise when a man, intending to do a lawful act, does what is unlawful. An illustration commonly put is that of a man intending to kill a thief or housebreaker, in his own house, who, by mistake, kills one of his own family. In this case, if he acted under circumstances of reasonable belief that the party killed was the thief or housebreaker, there is no ground to impute criminality to him. His conduct was founded in a mistake of fact, that is, of the person; for it is sometimes lawful, by the common law, to kill a housebreaker found in your house. But a mistake, or ignorance of law will not justify an act of the like nature. If a person supposes he has a right to kill a trespasser or outlaw, or excommunicated person, and be does so, he is guilty of murder.

In respect to crimes committed by compulsion or force. The common law recognises but few cases in which the authority or command of a superior furnishes any excuse for the commission of an offence. In the case of children or servants, the commands of the master or parent furnish no excuse. In the case of a wife who commits a crime in company with her husband, she is deemed, by the benignity of our law, to act under compulsion, and therefore she is excused in all cases except murder, manslaughter and treason. These exceptions are founded upon the peculiar danger and atrocity of the offences, and the public policy of discouraging every motive to commit them. Where the wife commits the offence alone, without the company or compulsion of her husband, she is personally responsible in the same manner as if she were unmarried. There are other species of compulsion recognised in the common law, which may excuse the commission of offences. Thus where a person commits an offence in consequence of threats or menaces, which induce a fear of death or other bodily harm.

This is called *duress per minas*. But the fear which compels a man to do an illegal act must be just and well grounded, such as may intimidate a firm and resolute man, and not merely of such a nature as may operate upon the timid and irresolute, otherwise it will constitute no excuse. Thus, in time of war or rebellion, a man may be excused for doing treasonable acts, if they are caused by the compulsion of the enemy or rebels. But the compulsion must not be a mere threat to do injury to property, nor even slight injury to the person, but a just fear either of death or of great bodily injury; and even in such case, it is the duty of the party to avoid doing such acts as soon as he safely may, by escape or otherwise; for if he does not, he will be liable to punishment as a volunteer. But even this excuse is not allowed in all cases, but seems principally confined to crimes positively created by society; for no man can justify or excuse himself for murdering an innocent person, under the pretence of fear or necessity, though he certainly may kill another in necessary self-defence. Another case of compulsion or necessity often occurs in the reasoning of speculative writers, whether a person in extreme want of food is excusable for stealing to satisfy his hunger. Whatever may be the doctrine of foreign jurists, or the opinion of publicists, it is certain that no such excuse is now admitted in the common law. If the offence should be committed under circumstances of extraordinary suffering, the case would rarely be brought before any tribunal of justice; and if it should be, the power of pardon in the government, and the humanity of the court itself, would either annul or mitigate the punishment. There is another case often put, where two persons at sea are shipwrecked, and get on a single plank, and it cannot support both, but both must be drowned unless one is displaced: what is then to be done? In such a case, the law of self-preservation has been supposed to justify either party in a forcible dispossession of the other. The common law seems to recognise this principle, and, in such a deplorable calamity, imputes no blame to the survivor.

We now proceed to notice another important distinction, which the common law acts upon in relation to crimes. It is the distinction in guilt and punishment which is made between principals and accessories. Persons are called *principals in the first degree*, who are the actors or perpetrators of the offence. Persons who are present, aiding and abetting the perpetrator, are called *principals in the second degree*. This presence may be either in fact, as where the parties are immediately standing by, or are within sight and hearing; or constructive, as when the party, though not within sight or hearing, is on the watch at a convenient distance, ready to assist, and near enough to do so, if required. There are cases, too, in which a person may be the principal in construction of law, although he is absent, and the fact is done through the instrumentality of another; as, in case of murder by poisoning, a man may be the principal felon by preparing or laying the poison, with an intention that it should be taken, or by employing an innocent person to administer it, under false pretences, although he is not personally present when it is taken or administered. Many cases of the like nature may be easily put. An *accessory* is he who is not the chief actor in the offence, nor present at its perpetration, in the sense above stated, but who is in some manner concerned in it, either before or after the fact is committed. If he procures, counsels, abets or commands the crime, and is absent at its commission, he is deemed an accessory *before* the fact. If, without any such participation in it, he knows that the crime has been committed, and afterwards relieves, assists, comforts or receives, the offender, he is deemed an accessory *after* the fact. Thus, if he aids the offender to escape, or rescues him from arrest, or conceals or supports him, he is deemed an accessory after the fact; so if he buys or receives stolen goods, knowing them to be stolen. There are certain classes of offences at the common law which admit of no accessories. Thus, in treason, all the parties concerned are deemed principals *propter odium delicti*; and in offences which are under the degree of felony, and in trespasses, all persons concerned are deemed principals, for an opposite reason, because the law will not condescend, in petty crimes, to ascertain the different degrees of guilt. In all other offences, that is, in all except the highest and the lowest, there may be, technically speaking, accessories. It follows as a maxim, that, in such cases, the accessory cannot be guilty of a higher offence than this principal. In respect to punishment, the ancient common law did not make any distinction between accessories and principals; but by statute, many distinctions are now made, and especially regarding accessories after the fact. In the U. States, few of our criminal codes have failed to mark out very strong differences in the punishment. There are, in fact, many reasons which require the distinction between principals and accessories to be constantly kept in view. In the first place, in many instances, a man cannot be tried as accessory until after the trial and conviction of the principal. In the next place, if a man be indicted as accessory and acquitted, he may still be indicted as principal. In the third place, as a natural inference from the other considerations, the defence of the accused may, and often must, turn upon very different principles, where he is accused as accessory, from what might or could arise if he were accused as principal.

In respect to the mode of presentment and trial for offences. In England, no person can be brought to trial, for any capital offence or felony, except upon the presentment or indictment of a grand jury; but for inferior offences or misdemeanors, an information, in the nature of an indictment, may be filed by the king's attorney-general, or other proper officer, upon which the party may be put upon trial. Even in such cases, an indictment also lies. In the U. States, informations are rarely resorted to in any of the states in such cases; and the usual, and, in many cases, the only constitutional course is an indictment by a grand jury. All offences, whether charged by indictment or information, are, by the common law, to be tried by a jury composed of 12 men, and their verdict is conclusive upon the facts. In the U. States, this privilege of trial by jury is generally secured by the constitutions of the state and national governments. A privilege often quite as valuable to the accused, is that of being assisted by counsel in the management of his defence. It is a curious anomaly in the English jurisprudence, that counsel are admissible in the argument of facts to the jury only in the highest and lowest offences; in treason, by the express provision of statute, and in mere misdemeanors, by the common law. In all capital cases, except treason, the accused is denied this privilege; and, however important and useful such a privilege may be, the introduction of it has been hitherto successfully resisted in the British parliament. In the U. States, a far different, and, as we think, wiser and more humane rule prevails. In all criminal cases, the accused is entitled, as of right, to the assistance of counsel in his defence; and this right, also, is generally secured by the state and national constitutions of government. This is not the place for a discussion of the value of such a right, though to us it seems recommended by principles of policy as well as of justice and humanity. The mode of impanneling juries, the right of challenge, and other incidents of criminal trials, belong more appropriately to other heads. (See *Crime, Courts*, and *Jury*.)

Death, Punishment of

The questions most commonly discussed by philosophers and jurists, under this head are, 1. as to the right of governments to inflict the punishment of death; 2. as to the expediency of such punishment; 3. as to the crimes to which, if any, it may be most properly confined and limited; 4. as to the manner in which it should be inflicted. A few words will be said on each of these points.

1. As to the *right* of inflicting the punishment of death. This has been doubted by some distinguished persons; and the doubt is often the accompaniment of a highly cultivated mind, inclined to the indulgence of a romantic sensibility, and believing in human perfectibility. The right of society to punish offences against its safety and good order will scarcely be doubted by any considerate person. In a state of nature, individuals have a right to guard themselves from injury, and to repel all aggressions by a force or precaution adequate to the object. This results from the right of self preservation. If a person attempts to take away my life, I have, doubtless, a right to protect myself against the attempt by all reasonable means. If I cannot secure myself but by taking the life of the assailant, I have a right to take it. It would otherwise follow, that I must submit to a wrong, and lose my life, rather than preserve it by the means adequate to maintain it. It cannot, then, be denied that, in a state of nature, men may repel force by force, and may even justly take away life, if necessary to preserve their own. When men enter society, the right to protect themselves from injury and to redress wrongs is transferred, generally, from the individuals to the community. We say that it is generally so, because it must be obvious that, in many cases, the natural right of self defence must remain. If a robber attacks one on the highway, or attempts to murder him, it is clear

that he has a right to repel the assault, and to take the life of the assailant, if necessary for his safety; since society, in such a case, could not afford him any adequate and prompt redress. The necessity of instant relief, and of instant application of force, justifies the act, and is recognised in all civilized communities. When the right of society is once admitted to punish for offences, it seems difficult to assign any limits to the exercise of that right, short of what the exigencies of society require. If a state have a right to protect itself and its citizens in the enjoyment of its privileges and its peace, it must have a right to apply means adequate to this object. The object of human punishments is, or may be, three fold; first, to reform the offender; secondly, to deter others from offending; and, lastly, to secure the safety of the community, by depriving the offender of the power of doing mischief. The first consideration rarely enters into human legislation, because of the inadequacy of our means to produce great moral results by the infliction of punishment. The two latter considerations enter largely into the theory and practice of legislation. Who is to be the judge, in such cases, what is the adequate punishment for any offence? Certainly, punishments ought not to be inflicted, which are utterly disproportionate to the offence, and beyond the exigencies of society. No government has a right to punish cruelly and wantonly, and from mere revenge; but, still, the discretion must be vested somewhere, to say what shall be the degree of punishment to be assigned to a particular offence. That discretion must be, from its nature, justly a part of the legislative power, and to be exercised according to the actual state of society. It may, nay, it must be differently exercised in different ages, and in different countries; for the same punishment which, in one age or country, may be sufficient to suppress an offence, or render it comparatively harm less, may, in another age or country, wholly fail of the effect. If mild punishments fail of effect, more severe must be resorted to, if the offence be of a nature which affects society in its vital principles, or safety, or interests. The very frequency of a crime must often furnish a very strong ground for severe punishment, not only as it furnishes proof that the present punishment is insufficient to deter men from committing it, but from the increased necessity of protecting society against dangerous crimes. But it is often said, that life is the gift of God, and therefore it cannot justly be taken away, either by the party himself, or another. If he cannot take it away, he cannot confer that power on others. But the fallacy of this argument is obvious. Life is no more the gift of God than other personal endowments or rights. A man has, by the gift of God, a right to personal liberty and locomotion, as well as to life; to eat and drink and breathe at large, as well as to exist; yet no one doubts that, by way of punishment, he may be confined in a solitary cell; that he may be perpetually imprisoned or deprived of free air, or compelled to live on bread and water. In short, no one doubts that he may be restrained in the exercise of any privileges or natural rights short of taking his life. Yet the reasoning, if worth anything, extends to all these cases in an equal degree. If, by his crimes, a man may justly forfeit his personal rights, why not his life? But we have seen that it is not true, even in a state of nature, that a man's life may not be taken away by another, if the necessity of the case requires it. Why, then, may not society do the same, if its own safety requires it? Is the safety of one person more important than the safety of the whole community? Then, again, as to a man's inability to confer on others a right which he does not himself possess. Suppose it is so; the consequence which is deduced from this does not, in fact, arise. Blackstone, indeed, in his *Commentaries* (4 *Bl. Comment*. 8), seems to deduce the right of society to punish capital offences, in certain cases (that is, in cases of *mala prohibita*, and not *mala in se*), from the consent of the offenders. The marquis Beccaria, on the other hand, denies that any such consent can confer the right, and therefore objects to its existence. But the notion of consent is, in nearly all cases, a mere theory, having no foundation in fact. If a foreigner comes into a country, and commits a crime at his first entrance, it is a very forced construction to say that he consents to be bound by its laws. If a pirate commits piracy, it is almost absurd to say that he consents to the right of all nations to punish him for it. The true and rational ground on which the right rests, is not the consent of the offender, but the right of every society to protect its own peace, and interests, and property, and institutions, and the utter want of any right, in other persons, to disturb, or destroy, or subtract them. The right flows, not from consent, but from the legitimate institution of society. If men have a right to form a society for mutual benefit and security, they have a right to punish other persons who would overthrow it. There are many cases where a state authorizes life to be taken away, the lawfulness of which is not doubted. No reasonable man doubts the right of a nation, in a just war, especially of self-defence, to repel force by force, and to take away the lives of its enemies. And this right is not confined to repelling present force, but it extends to precautionary measures, which are necessary for the ultimate safety of the nation. In such a war, a nation may justly insist upon the sacrifice of the lives of its own citizens, however innocent, for the purpose of ensuring its own safety. Accordingly, we find that all nations enroll militia and employ troops for war, and require them to hazard their lives for the preservation of the state. In these cases, life is freely sacrificed by the nation; and the laws enacted for such purposes are deemed just exercises of power. If so, why may not life be taken away by way of punishment, if the safety of society requires it? If a nation may authorize, in war, the destruction of thousands, why may it not authorize the destruction of a single life, if self-preservation require it. The mistake, however, is in supposing that life cannot be taken away without the consent of the party. If the foregoing reasoning is correct, such consent is neither supposed nor necessary. In truth, the supposition of an original compact between all the persons who are subject to the regulations of a society, by their own free consent, as the necessary and proper basis on which all the rights of such society depend, is, at best, a gratuitous supposition; and it sometimes leads to very incorrect results. It may be added, that the Scriptures most clearly recognize and justify the infliction of capital punishments in certain cases.

2. As to the *expediency* of capital punishment. This opens a wide field for discussion. Some able men, who do not doubt the right, do still deny the expediency of inflicting it. It may be admitted, that a wise legislature ought to be slow in affixing such a punishment to any but very enormous and dangerous crimes. The frequency of a crime is not, of itself, a sufficient reason for resorting to such a punishment. It should be a crime of great atrocity and danger to society, and which cannot otherwise be effectually guarded against. In affixing punishments to any offence, we should consider what are the objects and ends of punishment. It is clear that capital punishment can have no effect to reform the offender himself. It may have, and ordinarily does have, the effect to deter others from committing a like offence; but, still, human experience shows that even this punishment, when inflicted for small offences, which are easily perpetrated, and to which there is great temptation, does not always operate as an effectual terror. Men sometimes are hardened by the frequent spectacles of capital punishments, and grow indifferent to them. Familiarity deprives them of their horror. The bloodiest codes are not those which have most effectually suppressed offences. Besides, public opinion has great weight in producing the acquittal or condemnation of offenders. If a

punishment be grossly disproportionate to the offence, if it shock human feelings, there arises, insensibly, a sympathy for the victim, and a desire to screen him from punishment; so that, as far as certainty of punishment operates to deter from crimes, the object of the legislature is often thus defeated. It may be added, that a reasonable doubt may fairly be entertained, whether any society can lawfully exercise the power of punishing, beyond what the just exigencies of that society require. On the other hand, a total abolition of capital punishments would, in some cases at least, expose society to the chances of deep and vital injuries. A man who has committed murder deliberately, has proved himself unfit for society, and regardless of all the duties which belong to it. In his case, the *lex talionis* can hardly be deemed unjust. The safety of society is most effectually guarded by cutting him off from the power of doing further mischief. If his life be not taken away, the only other means left are, confinement for life, or transportation and exile for life. Neither of these is a perfect security against the commission of other crimes, and may not always be within the power of a nation without great inconvenience and great expense to itself. It is true that the latter punishments leave open the chance of reform to the offender, which is, indeed, but too often a mere delusion; but, on the other hand, they greatly diminish the influence of another salutary principle, the deterring of others from committing like crimes. It seems to us, therefore, that it is difficult to maintain the proposition that capital punishments are, at all times and under all circumstances, inexpedient. It may rather be affirmed that, in some cases, they are absolutely indispensable to the safety and good order of society. We should incline to say that, as a general rule, every nation, in its legislation on this subject, must be governed very much by the manners, customs, habits of thinking, and state of opinion, among the people upon whom it is to operate. In a rude and barbarous state of society, summary and almost vindictive punishments seem more necessary than in a highly polished and civilized state of society.

3. As to the *crimes* to which capital punishments may, most properly, be limited. From what has been already said, this must depend upon the particular circumstances of every age and nation; and much must be left to the exercise of a sound discretion on the part of the legislature. As a general rule, humanity forbids such punishments to be applied to any but crimes of very great enormity, and danger to individuals or the state. If any crimes can be effectually suppressed by moderate means, these ought, certainly, to be first resorted to. The experience, however, of most nations, if we may judge from the nature and extent of their criminal legislation, seems to disprove the opinion so often indulged by philanthropists, that moderate punishments are sufficient to suppress crimes, and that capital punishments are rarely necessary. The codes of most civilized nations abound with capital punishments. That of Great Britain, a nation in which the public legislation has a deep infusion of popular opinion, is thought to be uncommonly sanguinary. Blackstone, in his *Commentaries* (vol. iv, 18), admits that, in his time, not less than one hundred and sixty crimes were, by the English law, punishable with death. In the code of the U. States, only nine crimes are so punishable, viz., treason, murder, arson, rape, robbery of the mail, fraudulent casting away ships, rescue of criminals capitally convicted during execution, and piracy, one species of which is the African slave trade. In the codes of the several states of the Union, still fewer crimes are generally punishable with death. It remains yet to be proved, whether the general mildness of our penal code has afforded us any greater security against crimes than exists in other nations. Hitherto, the temptations to commit them have been less here, than in other countries less abundantly and cheaply supplied with the necessaries

of life. It is still a question, fit to exercise the solicitude and ingenuity of our statesmen and philanthropists, whether we can safely carry on so mild a system in a more corrupt and dense state of society. If we can, it must be by a very sparing use of the power of pardoning; so that the certainty of absolute, unmitigated punishment shall follow upon the offence. Beccaria, with his characteristic humanity and sagacity, has strongly urged that the certainty of punishment is more important to deter from crimes than the severity of it. At present, there is great danger that the pardoning power, in our free forms of government, will, in a great measure, overthrow this salutary principle. Its exercise, therefore, ought to be watched with the greatest jealousy and care, lest the abuse of it should lead to the introduction either of absolute impunity for offences, or of more extensive capital punishments. It will probably be found, from the experience of most nations, that capital punishment ought not wholly to be dispensed with. On the other hand, it may be safely affirmed, that there is no positive necessity to apply it to a very large number of crimes. Treason, murder, arson, piracy, highway robbery, burglary, rape, and some other offences of great enormity, and of a kindred character, are not uncommonly punished in this manner; but beyond these, it is extremely questionable whether there is any necessity or expediency of applying so great a severity. Still, however, as has been already intimated, much must depend upon the opinion and character of the age, and the prevailing habits of the people, and upon the sound exercise of legislative discretion. What may be deemed uselessly severe in one age or country, may be positively required by the circumstances of another age or country.

4. As to the *manner* of inflicting the punishment of death. This has been different in different countries, and in different stages of civilization in the same countries.

Barbarous nations are generally inclined to severe and vindictive punishments, and, where they punish with death, to aggravate it by prolonging the sufferings of the victim with ingenious devices in cruelty. And even in civilized countries, in cases of a political nature, or of very great atrocity, the punishment has been sometimes inflicted with many horrible accompaniments. Tearing the criminal to pieces, piercing his breast with a pointed pole, pinching to death with red hot pincers, starving him to death, breaking his limbs upon the wheel, pressing him to death in a slow and lingering manner, burning him at the stake, crucifixion, sawing him to pieces, quartering him alive, exposing him to be torn to pieces by wild beasts, and other savage punishments, have been sometimes resorted to for the purposes of vengeance, or public example, or public terror. Compared with these, the infliction of death by drowning, by strangling, by poisoning, by bleeding, by beheading, by shooting, by hanging, is a moderate punishment. In modern times, the public opinion is strongly disposed to discountenance the punishment of death by any but simple means; and the infliction of torture is almost universally reprobated. Even in governments where it is still countenanced by the laws, it is rarely resorted to; and the sentence is remitted, by the policy of the prince, beyond the simple infliction of death. In Prussia, where atrocious criminals are required, by the penal code, to be broken upon the wheel, the king always issues an order to the executioner to strangle the criminal (which is done by a small cord not easily seen) before his limbs are broken. So, in the same country, where larceny, attended with destruction of life, is punished by burning alive, the fagots are so arranged as to form a kind of cell, in which the criminal is suffocated by the fumes of sulphur, or other means, before the flame can reach him. In England, in high treason, the criminal is sentenced to be drawn to the gallows, to be hanged by the neck, and cut down alive, to have his entrails taken out and burned while he is yet alive, to have his head cut off, and his body divided into four parts, and these to be at the king's disposal. But, generally, all the punishment is remitted by the crown, except the hanging and beheading; and when it is, not, by connivance of the officers, the criminal is drawn on a hurdle to the place of execution, and is not disembowelled until actually dead. In other cases, the punishment is now simply by hanging, or, in the military and naval service, by shooting. In France, formerly, the punishment of death was often inflicted by breaking the criminal on the wheel. (Damiens was torn to pieces by horses, after he had been tormented with red hot pincers, and had suffered other horrid tortures.) The usual punishment now is beheading by the guillotine. In cases of parricide, the criminal is conducted, barefooted, and covered with a black veil, to the place of execution, where his right hand is cut off just before he is beheaded. In Austria, the general mode of punishment is by hanging. In Prussia, hanging is rarely inflicted; but the usual punishment is beheading with a heavy axe, the criminal's head being first tied to a block. In other German states, the uncertain mode of execution by the sword still exists. Sand was executed in this manner. It should be remarked, however, that, in Germany, hanging has always been deemed the most infamous sort of punishment; and the sentence has often been commuted for beheading by the sword, as a milder mode of punishment. In the U. States of America, hanging is the universal mode of capital punishment; and, indeed, the constitution of the U. States contains a provision, declaring that "cruel and unusual punishments shall not be inflicted." In China, murderers are cut to pieces; robbers, not. In Russia, the punishment of death has been frequently inflicted by the knout. In Turkey, strangling, and sewing the criminal up in a bag, and throwing him into the sea, are common modes of punishment. In the Roman code, many severe and cruel punishments were prescribed. During the favored times of the republic, many of these were abolished or mitigated. But again, under the emperors, they were revived with full severity. In the ancient Grecian states, the modes of punishment were also severe, and often cruel. But the most general mode of punishment, in ordinary cases, seems, both in Greece and Rome, to have been by hanging. Whether the ancient Greek mode of capital punishment, by taking poison at such hour as the condemned party should choose, has ever been adopted in any modern nation, we are unable to say. As far as we have been able to learn, it is not in use among any Christian people; and the idea of suicide connected with it would probably prevent any such nation from adopting it.

Whether executions ought to be in public or in private, has been a question much discussed, and upon which a great diversity of opinion exists among intelligent statesmen. On the one hand, it is said that public spectacles of this sort have a tendency to brutalize and harden the people, or to make them indifferent to the punishment; and the courage and firmness, with which the criminal often meets death, have a tendency to awaken feelings of sympathy, and even of admiration, and to take away much of the horror of the offence, as well as of the punishment. On the other hand, it is said that the great influence of punishment, in deterring others from the like offence, cannot be obtained in any other way. It is the only means to bring home to the mass of the people a salutary dread and warning; and it is a public admonition of the certainty of punishment following upon crimes. It is also added, that all punishments ought to be subjected to the public scrutiny, so that it may be known that all the law requires, and no more, has been done. If punishments were inflicted in private, it could never be known whether they were justly and properly inflicted upon the persons condemned; or whether, indeed, innocent persons might not become the victims.

In England, the court before which the trial is had, declares the sentence, and directs the execution of it; and its warrant is a sufficient authority to the proper officer to execute it. In the courts of the U. States, there is a like authority; but in the laws of many of the states, there is a provision that the execution shall not take place except by a warrant from the governor, or other executive authority. In cases of murder and other atrocious crimes, the punishment in England is usually inflicted at a very short interval after the sentence. In America, there is usually allowed a very considerable interval, varying from one month to six months. In England and America, there lies no appeal from the verdict of a jury and the sentence of a court, in capital cases. In France, there may be a review of it in the court of cassation. (q. v.) In Germany, there is, in criminal as in civil cases, a right of appeal; hence, in that country, few innocent persons have suffered capitally since the 16th century; and in England and America, the very fact that the verdict and sentence are final, produces great caution and deliberation in the administration of criminal justice, and a strong leaning towards the prisoner on trial. Capital punishment cannot be inflicted, by the general humanity of the laws of modern nations, upon persons who are insane or who are pregnant, until the latter are delivered and the former become sane. It is said that Frederic the Great required all judgments of his courts, condemning persons to death, to be written on blue paper; thus he was constantly reminded of them as they lay on his table among other papers, from which they were readily distinguished. He usually took a long time to consider such cases, and thus set an excellent example to sovereigns of their duty.

Domicil

The dwelling had peculiar privileges among the Roman; it was regarded as inviolable; for example, no debtor could be arrested in his domicil; no officer of the police or court could pass the threshold of a private house, to arrest even a person who did not dwell there. These rights and privileges still belong to the dwelling-house in England, the Netherlands and the U. States of America. The name domicil implies, in general, a place of residence; in a narrower sense, the place where one lives, in opposition to that where he only remains for a time. (See *Appendix*.)

Appendix

Domicil, in Law

By the term *domicil*, in its ordinary acceptation, is meant the place where a person lives, or has his home. In this sense, the place where a person has his actual residence, inhabitancy or commorancy is sometimes called his *domicil*. In a strict and legal sense, that is properly the domicil of a person, where he has fixed his true, permanent home, and principal establishment, and to which, whenever he is absent, he has the intention of returning (*animus revertendi*). The Roman law stated it thus: *In eodem loco singulos habere domicilium non ambigitur, ubi quis larem rerumque ac fortunarum suarum summam constituit, unde cursus non sit discessurus si nihil avocet; unde, cum profectus est, peregrinari videtur; quod si rediit, peregrinari jam destitit*. (*Cod. Lib.* 10, *tit*. 39,1. 7.) In the French law, some of its best writers define it thus: *Le domicile est le lieu ou une personne jouissant de ses droits, établit sa demesne et le siege de sa fortune* (Denizart, article *Domicile*); or, as the *Encyclopedie Moderne* (article *Domicile*) expresses it, *C'est, à proprement parler, l'endroit ou l'on a placé le centre de ses affaires.* Vattel (B. I, *ch.* xix, § 22) seems to define it to be a fixed residence in any place, with an intention of always staying there. This is not quite accurate. It would be more correct to say, that that place is the home or domicil of a person, in which his habitation is fixed, without any present intention of removing therefrom (10 *Mass*. R. 488). The question of domicil is often one of great difficulty and nicety, and so dependent upon circumstances, that, as it has been observed by Lord Stowell (2 *Rob*. 322), it is hardly capable of being defined by any general, precise rules. It is compounded partly of matter of fact and partly of law. It is often a mere question of intention; sometimes of express intention, and sometimes of presumptive intention, from acts and conduct. The mere dwelling or residence in a place is not, of itself, sufficient to make it the domicil of the party. He must be there with the intention of remaining (*animo manendi*). The act of residence must be coupled with the intention of making it the real, substantial home of the party, excluding all others. If, therefore, a person, having his home in one place, go to another for temporary purposes, but with an intention to return, his domicil is not changed by such absence; nor does he acquire a new domicil in the place of such temporary residence. If a person go on a voyage to sea, or to a foreign country for health or pleasure, or business of a temporary nature, with an intention to return, no one supposes his domicil to be changed thereby. But, sometimes, where there has been a removal for temporary purposes at first, there may be engrafted on it, subsequently, an intention of permanent residence. And, in many instances, therefore, where we are called upon to decide upon questions of domicil, the length of time of the residence becomes a material ingredient. Lord Stowell has observed, that it is not unfrequently said, that if a person comes to a place for a special purpose, that shall not fix a domicil. "This," he adds, "is not to be taken in an unqualified latitude, and without some respect had to the time which such a purpose may occupy; for if the purpose be of a nature that may probably, or does actually, detain the person for a great length of time, a general residence might grow upon the special purpose. A special purpose may lead a man to a country, where it shall detain him the whole of his life." (2 *Rob. Rep*. 322, 324.) These remarks, again, require some qualification; for time is not absolutely decisive in such cases, if it is clear, from other circumstances, that the purpose was wholly temporary and positive. Suppose a man should go to a country in ill health, and remain there a number of years, and, during that whole period, were incapable of being removed, or of returning home, without danger to his life; if such residence were so constrained, it would not change his former domicil. The question of domicil is of very great importance, for it often regulates political and civil rights, and founds or destroys jurisdiction over the person or property. Thus, for instance, there is what is called a *political domicil*, which is that place where a party must exercise his political rights, duties and privileges, as his right to vote, his duty to pay taxes, &c. Then there is what is called a civil domicil, or that where he has fixed his habitual home or residence, which decides upon his civil rights, and power to acquire, alienate and dispose of property, to contract marriage, &c. Then, again, there is, or may be, a *forensic domicil* (*forum domicilii*), or place where he is to sue or be sued, and to be subjected to the exercise of the jurisdiction of judicial courts. It may, and it often does happen, that the political, civil and forensic domicil is the same; but this is a matter, not so much of general principle, as of positive legislation in different countries; and, therefore, it is often regulated, in different countries, by very different rules, sometimes by opposite rules. Some general principles, however, may assist to guide us, in cases where there is no positive legislation to govern the case.

1. The place of birth of a person is considered as his domicil, if it be at the time the home of his parents. *Patris originem unusquisque sequitur*. This is generally called *domicilium originis* (the domicil of nativity). But, if the parents were then on a visit or journey (*in itinere*), the home of the parents (at least if it were in the same country) would be deemed the domicil of nativity. A person born in a foreign country, while his parents are there under the allegiance of the government of the country, though they are there for temporary purposes only, is generally deemed a subject of such country, and owing allegiance to its sovereign.

2. The domicil of birth continues until a new domicil has been obtained. Infants are generally deemed incapable of changing their domicil during their minority, and, therefore, they always retain the domicil of their parents; and if their parents change their domicil, that of the infant follows; and if the father dies, his last domicil is that of the infant. A person who is of age to choose a domicil for himself, still retains the paternal domicil, while he continues to remain with his parents. But when he is emancipated, or has acquired a domicil of his own, he no longer follows the paternal domicil.

3. The domicil of birth, also, easily reverts; and it requires fewer circumstances to establish in proof, that a party has reverted to the domicil of his nativity, or family domicil, than to establish his foreign domicil. The reason is obvious. A residence in the place of one's birth, unexplained, gives rise to a general presumption, that it is of permanent choice;

because an affection for such a place, and a desire to abide there, are so commonly found among all classes of persons.

4. The domicil of a married woman follows that of her husband. This results from the general principle, that a person who is under the authority and power of another, possesses no right to choose a domicil.

5. By the civil law, minors retain, as we have seen, the domicil of their parents; and the same principle is said to apply, in that law, to the case of persons insane, or non *compos mentis*, whether they are under guardianship or not; for the guardian has no power to change their domicil, as it may change the order of succession to their estates. But it has been said that our law is different, and that a guardian may change the domicil of his ward, if he chooses. (9 *Mass*. 1R 543; 5 *Pick*. R. 20.) But this is a point which deserves very grave consideration, and does not seem universally settled, as a part of the common law. (See *Guier* v. *O'Daniel*, I Binney, 352, note; *Somerville* v. *Somerville*, 5 Vesey jr., *787; Pottinger* v. *Wightman*, 3 Meriv. R. 67.)

6. *Primâ facie*, the place where a person lives is taken to be the place of his domicil, until other facts establish the contrary.

7. Every person of full age having a right to change his domicil, it follows, that if he removes to another place, with the intention to remain (*animo manendi*), the latter instantaneously becomes his place of domicil. It is of no consequence, in such a case, how short his residence may have been; for it is the fact, coupled with the intention, that settles his domicil, and here both are unequivocal.

8. If a person has actually removed to another place, with an intention of remaining there for an indefinite time, and

as a place of present domicil, it becomes his place of domicil, notwithstanding he may have a floating intention to go back at some future period.

9. The place where the family of a married man resides is generally considered as his domicil. But this may be controlled by circumstances. For if the place be only a temporary establishment for his family, or for temporary objects, it may be different.

10. If a married man has his family fixed in one place, and does his business in another, the former is considered as the place of his domicil.

11. If a married man has two places of residence at different times of the year, that will be esteemed his domicil which he selects, considers or describes as his fixed home, or which appears to be the centre of his affairs, where he votes, or acts as a citizen.

12. If a man is unmarried, that is generally the place of his domicil where he transacts his business, exercises his profession, or assumes municipal duties or privileges.

13. Residence in a place by constraint, or involuntarily, will not give the party a domicil there; but his antecedent domicil remains.

14. Mere intention to acquire a new domicil, without the fact of removal, avails nothing; neither does the fact of removal, without the intention. Presumptions arising generally from circumstances, will not prevail against positive acts, which fix and determine domicil.

15. Widows retain the domicil which had been their husbands' until they have acquired a new one. *Vidua mulier amissi mariti domicilium retinet.*

There are some other considerations, of a general nature, which deserve enumeration, as they respect domicil in a foreign country. Those which have been already referred to, principally respect domicil in different parts of the same country.

1. We have already seen, that persons who are born in a country, are deemed inhabitants and citizens of that country. Foreigners, also, who reside there for permanent and indefinite purposes, or, as Vattel expresses it (B. I, *ch.* xix, § 213), who are permitted to settle and stay in a country, are deemed inhabitants. If they are there merely on a visit, or for temporary purposes, they are not deemed inhabitants.

2. A person who resides in a foreign country, for purposes of trade, is deemed an inhabitant of that country by foreign nations; and his character changes with that of the country. In peace he is deemed a neutral, in war an enemy; and his property is dealt with accordingly in prize courts. (*The Venus*, 8 Cranch R. 278.)

3. A person may have a national character of his trade, although his domicil be in a different country. Thus, if he be allowed to engage in the trade exclusively belonging to the subjects of an enemy's country, he will, so far as respects that trade, be deemed an enemy trader, and his property will be liable to condemnation as such, though his own domicil be neutral. So, if he is the owner of a plantation in an enemy's country, the produce thereof will be liable as prize in the same manner. So, if he be a partner in a house of trade in an enemy's country, his property in the partnership will be deemed the property of an enemy. (9

Cranch, 191; *The Vigilantia*, 1 Rob. R., 14, 15; *The Phœnix*, 5 Rob. R., 20; *The San Jose Indiano*, 2 Gallison's R., 268.)

4. A national character, acquired by residence in a foreign country, changes with a change of that residence; and if no other domicil be acquired by the party subsequently, his native domicil reverts; and, in such a case, it will revert as soon as he puts himself in motion to return to his native country, although he has not actually arrived there. But the mere return to his native country does not destroy his foreign domicil, unless there is an intention to abandon the latter. (*The Venus*, 8 Cranch R., 278, 281; *The France*, 8 Cranch R., 335.)

5. If a person quits his own country, for temporary purposes, or in public employment, and solely by reason of such employment, his native domicil is not changed thereby. If an Englishman, for instance, should go to Germany in the king's service, or for a temporary purpose, the domicil of his birth would not be changed. But if he entered into the German service, although with a general, indefinite intention to return to England, it would be otherwise.

6. The descent of real estate, such as lands, is according to the law of the place, *rei sitæ*. But the descent and distribution of personal estate is according to the law of the place of the owner's domicil. It has been recently doubted in England, whether a British subject can, by a foreign domicil, change the general law of succession, as to his personal estate, existing in his own country. But it is admitted he may change his domicil, in different parts of his own country, and thereby change the succession and distribution of his personal estate. (*Curling* v. *Thornton*, 2 Addam's Eccles. R., 17, 19.)

7. A will of personal estate, good by the law of the place where the party has his domicil, is sufficient to pass all personal estate in any other country. But, if not good by the law of the place of the party's domicil, it is said not to be good to pass personal property in any other country, although otherwise sufficient by the law of the country where the personal property is. (*Desesbats* v. *Berquier*, 1 Binney, 336. But see *Curling* v. *Thornton*, 2 Addam's Eccles. R. 6, 19 to 25.)

8. Ambassadors and other ministers still retain the domicil of the country which they represent, and to which they belong; and their children, born in the foreign country where they reside, are considered as natives of the country of their own sovereign. It is not so in relation to consuls and other commercial agents. They are considered as having, like other subjects, their domicil in the country where they reside. (*Vattel*, *B.* I, *ch.* xix, § 217; *The Indian Chief*, 3 Rob. 13, 27; *The Josephine*, 4 Rob. 26.)

9. Children born upon the sea are generally deemed to be natives of the country to which their parents belong. (See *Vattel*, *B.* I, *ch.* xix, § 216.) The reader who desires further information on the subject of domicil, is referred to the title *Domicile*, in Denizart, *Collection de Jurisprudence*. tom. 6; the same in *Encyclopédie Moderne*, tom. 10; in Merlin's *Répertoire de Jurisprudence*; in 2 Domat, 464, B. 1, title 16, s. 3, of Public Law; in Digest, lib. 50, title 1, 1. 1 et seq.; and Code, lib. 10, title 39, 1. 2, 4,5,7 ; *Code Civil de France*, tit. 3, art. 102, &c. ; Vdet ad Pand. lib. 5, tit. 1, sec. 90, 91, 92; Bynkershőck, *Quæst. Priv. Juris.*, lib. 1, ch. 16; Pothier, *Coutumes d'Orléans*, Introd. n. 16, 20. In the English and American law, the following references will be found most useful: *Bruce* v. *Bruce*, 2 Bosanquet & Puller, 229; *Somerville* v. *Somerville*, 5 Ves. jr., 786; *Bempde* v. *Johnstone*, 3 Ves. 195; *Curling* v. *Thornton*, 2 Addam's

Eccles. R. 5; *Pottinger* v. *Wightman*, 3 Merivale R. 67; Green's Admiralty Digest, *National Character*; *The Venus*, 8 Cranch, 278; Wheaton's Digest, title *Prize*, iv; *Holyoke* v. *Haskins*, 5 Pick. R. 20; *Cambridge* v. *Charlestown*, 13 Mass. Rep. 501; *Williams* v. *Whiting*, 11 Mass. Rep. 424; *Guier* v. *O'Daniel*, 1 Binney's Rep. 352, note; *Elbers* v. *U. Insurance Company*, 16 Johnson's Rep. 128.

EQUITY

We call that, in a moral sense, *equity*, which is founded in natural justice, in honesty, and in right, *ex æquo et bono*. So, in an enlarged view (as Mr. Justice Blackstone has observed, 3 *Comm.* 429), "equity, in its true and genuine meaning, is the soul and spirit of all law; positive law is construed, and rational law is made by it. In this, equity is synonymous with justice; in that, to the true and sound interpretation of the rule." Hence Grotius has defined it to be the correction of that, wherein the law, by reason of its generality, is deficient. It is applied to cases which the law does not exactly define, but which it submits to the sound judgment of the proper interpreter, *arbitrio boni vii permittit*. In this sense, equity must have a place in every rational system of jurisprudence; if not in name, at least in substance. It is impossible, that any code, however minute and particular, should embrace or provide for the infinite variety of human affairs, or should furnish rules applicable to all of them. Every system of laws must necessarily be defective; and cases must occur, to which the antecedent rules cannot be applied without injustice, or to which they cannot be applied at all. It is the office, therefore, of a judge, to consider whether the antecedent rule does apply, or ought, according to the intention of the lawgiver, to apply to a given case; and, if there be two rules, nearly approaching to it, but of opposite tendency, which ought to govern; and, if there exist no exact rule applicable to all the circumstances, whether the party is remediless, or the rule furnishing the closest analogy ought to be followed. The general words of a law may embrace all cases; and yet it may be clear that all could not have been intentionally embraced; for, if they were, it would defeat the obvious objects of the legislation. So words of doubtful import may be employed, and of a more or less extensive meaning. The question, in such cases, must be, in what sense the words were used; and it is the part of a judge to look to the objects of the legislature, and to give such a construction of the words as will further those objects. He is not at liberty to set aside the law, but to expound it. *Custos non conditor juris, juvare, supplere, interpretari, mitigare jus civile potuit; mutare vel tollere non potuit* (Taylor's *Elements of Civil Law*, 214). This is an exercise of equitable construction. It is the administration of equity. Hence arises a variety of rules of interpretation of laws according to their nature and operation, whether they are remedial or penal, or restrictive of general right, or in advancement of public justice. But this is not the place to consider those rules, or the application of them in different systems of law. In the law of England and the U. States, equity has a different and more restrained meaning. We distinguish our remedies for wrongs, or for the enforcement of rights, into two classes those which are administered in courts of law, and those which are administered in courts of equity. The rights secured by the former are called *legal*; those secured by the latter are called *equitable*. The former are said to be rights and remedies at common law, because recognised and enforced in courts of common law. The latter are said to be rights and remedies in *equity*, because they are administered in courts of equity or chancery, or by proceedings in other courts analogous to those in courts of equity or chancery. Now, in England and America, courts of common law proceed by certain prescribed forms, and give a general judgment for or against the defendant. They entertain jurisdiction only in certain actions, and give remedies according to the particular exigency of such actions. But there are many cases in which a simple judgment for either party, without qualifications and conditions, and particular arrangements, will not do entire justice, *ex æquo et bono*, to either party. Some modification of the rights of both parties are required; some restraints on one side or the other; and some peculiar adjustments, either present or future, temporary or perpetual. Now, in all these cases, courts of common law have no methods of proceeding, which can accomplish such objects. Their forms of actions and judgment are not adapted to them. The proper remedy cannot be found, or cannot be administered to the full extent of the relative rights of all parties. Such prescribed forms of actions are not confined to our law. They were known in the civil law; and the party could apply them only to their original purposes. In other cases, he had a special remedy. In such cases, where the courts of common law cannot grant the proper remedy or relief, the law of England and of the U. States (in those states where equity is administered) authorizes an application to the courts of equity or chancery, which are not confined or limited in their, modes of relief by such narrow regulations, but which grant relief to all parties, in cases where they have rights, *ex æquo et bono*, and modify and fashion that relief according to circumstances. The most general description of a court of equity is, that it has jurisdiction in cases where a plain, adequate and complete remedy cannot be had at law; that is, in the common law courts. The remedy must be *plain*; for, if it be doubtful and obscure at law, equity will assert a jurisdiction. So it must be *adequate* at law; for, if it fall short of what the party is entitled to, that founds a jurisdiction in equity. And it must be *complete*; that is, it must attain its full end at law; it must reach the whole mischief and secure the whole right of the party, now and for the future; otherwise equity will interpose, and give relief. The jurisdiction of a court of equity is sometimes concurrent with that of courts of law; and sometimes it is exclusive. It exercises concurrent jurisdiction in cases where the rights are purely of a *legal* nature, but where other and more efficient aid is required than a court of law can afford, to meet the difficulties of the case, and ensure full redress. In some of these cases, courts of law formerly refused all redress; but now will grant it. But the jurisdiction having been once justly acquired at a time when there was no such redress at law, it is not now relinquished. The most common exercise of concurrent jurisdiction is in cases of account, accident, dower, fraud, mistake, partnership and partition. The remedy is here often more complete and effectual than it can be at law. In many cases falling under these heads, and especially in some cases of fraud, mistake and accident, courts of law cannot and do not afford any redress; in others they do, but not always in so perfect a manner. A court of equity also is assistant to the jurisdiction of courts of law, in many cases, where the latter have no like authority. It will remove legal impediments to the fair decision of a question depending at law. It will prevent a party from improperly setting up, at a trial, some title or claim, which would be inequitable. It will compel him to discover, on his own oath, facts which he knows are material to the right of the other party, but which a court of law cannot compel the party to discover. It will perpetuate the testimony of witnesses to rights and titles, which are in danger of being lost before the matter can be tried. It will provide for the safety of property in dispute pending litigation. It will counteract and control, or set aside, fraudulent judgments. It will exercise, in many cases, an *exclusive* jurisdiction. This it does in all cases of merely *equitable rights*, that is, such rights as are not recognised in courts of law. Most cases of trust and confidence fall under this head. Its exclusive jurisdiction is also extensively exercised in granting special relief beyond the reach of the common law. It will grant injunctions to prevent waste, or irreparable injury, or to secure a settled right, or to prevent vexatious litigations, or to compel the restitution of title deeds; it will appoint receivers of property, where it is in danger of misapplication; it will compel the surrender of securities improperly obtained; it will prohibit a party from leaving the country in order to avoid a suit; it will restrain any undue exercise of a legal right, against conscience and equity; it will decree a specific performance of contracts respecting real estates; it will, in many cases, supply the imperfect execution of instruments, and reform and alter them according to the real intention of the parties; it will grant relief in cases of lost deeds or securities; and, in all cases in which its interference is asked, its general rule is, that he who asks equity must do equity. If a party, therefore, should ask to have a bond for a usurious debt given up, equity could not decree it unless he could bring into court the money honestly due without usury. This is a very general and imperfect outline of the jurisdiction of a court of equity; in respect to which it has been justly remarked, that, in matters within its exclusive jurisdiction, where substantial justice entitles the party to relief, but the positive law is silent, it is impossible to define the boundaries of that jurisdiction, or to enumerate, with precision, its various principles. (Those who wish for more information on the subject may consult the elementary treatises of Fonblanque on Equity, lord Redesdale's *Treatise on Equity Pleadings*, and Cooper's *Equity Pleadings*; and the *Practical Treatises of Equity* by Maddock and Jeremy.)

Equity, Courts of

The equity jurisdiction, in England, is vested, principally, in the high court of chancery. (See *Chancellor*.) The court is distinct from the courts of law. American courts of equity are, in some instances, distinct from those of law; in others, the same tribunals exercise the jurisdiction both of courts of law and equity, though their forms of proceeding are different in their two capacities. The supreme court of the U. States, and the circuit courts, are invested with general equity powers, and act either as courts of law or equity, according to the form of the process and the subject of adjudication. In some of the states, as New York, Virginia and South Carolina, the equity court is a distinct tribunal, having its appropriate judge, or chancellor, and officers. In most of the states, the two jurisdictions centre in the same judicial officers, as in the courts of the U. States; and the extent of equity jurisdiction and proceedings is very various in the different states, being very ample in Connecticut, New York, New Jersey, Maryland, Virginia and South Carolina, and more restricted in Maine, Massachusetts, Rhode Island and Pennsylvania. But the salutary influence of these powers on the judicial administration generally, by the adaptation of chancery forms and modes of proceeding to many cases in which a court of law affords but an imperfect remedy, or no remedy at all, is producing a gradual extension of them in those states where they have been heretofore very limited. (See *Chancellor*, *Common Law*, and *Courts*.)

ENCYCLOPÆDIA AMERICANA.

A

POPULAR DICTIONARY

OF

ARTS, SCIENCES, LITERATURE, HISTORY, POLITICS AND BIOGRAPHY,

A NEW EDITION;

INCLUDING

A COPIOUS COLLECTION OF ORIGINAL ARTICLES

IN

AMERICAN BIOGRAPHY;

ON

THE BASIS OF THE SEVENTH EDITION OF THE GERMAN

CONVERSATIONS-LEXICON.

EDITED BY

FRANCIS LIEBER,

ASSISTED BY

E. WIGGLESWORTH.

VOL. V.

PHILADELPHIA:
LEA & BLANCHARD.
1843.

EVIDENCE

EVIDENCE, in its most general sense, means the proofs which establish, or have a tendency to establish, any facts or conclusions. It may be divided into three sorts, mathematical, moral and legal. The first is employed in the demonstrations which belong to pure mathematics; the second is employed in the general affairs of life, and in those reasonings which are applied to convince the understanding, in cases not admitting of strict demonstration; the third is that which is employed in judicial tribunals for the purpose of deciding upon the rights and wrongs of litigant parties.

Probably in every system of jurisprudence aiming at exactness, some rules are introduced, and some restrictions are allowed, in respect to evidence, different from those which belong to mere moral reasoning upon probabilities. In our discussions on this head, we shall confine ourselves altogether to the consideration of evidence in a legal view, and principally with reference to the existing rules of the common law, recognised in England and America. According to our system of jurisprudence in common law trials, it is the peculiar province of a jury to decide all matters of fact. The verdict of the jury is, however, to be given, and the trial is to be had, in the presence of a judge or judges, who preside at the trial, and are bound to decide matters of law, arising in the course of the trial. Whenever, therefore, a question arises, whether any thing offered as proof at such trial is or is not proper to go before the jury as evidence, that question is to be decided by the court, and, unless permitted by the court, it can never legally come to the consideration of the jury. Hence, whatever is so permitted to be brought before the jury, for the purpose of enabling them to decide any matter of fact in dispute between the parties, is, in a legal sense, evidence, and is so called, in contradistinction to mere argument and comment. This gives rise to a very important distinction, at the common law, as to the *competency* and the *credibility* of evidence. It is *competent*, when, by the principles of law, it is admissible to establish any fact, or has any tendency to prove it. It is *credible*, when, being introduced, it affords satisfactory proof of the fact. It follows, therefore, that evidence may be *competent* to be produced before a jury, when it may, nevertheless, not amount to *credible* proof, so as to satisfy the minds of the jury; and, on the other hand, it may be such, as, if before them, would satisfy their minds of the truth of the fact, but yet, by the rules of law, it is not admissible. Whether there is *any evidence* of a fact, is a question for the court; whether it is *sufficient*, is a question for the jury, when the cause is tried by a jury.

Evidence is, in its nature, divisible into two sorts:—first, that which is *direct* and *positive* proof of any fact; and, secondly, that which is *presumptive* and *circumstantial*. It is again divisible, in respect to the mode or instruments of proof, into two sorts:—first, *written* evidence; and, secondly, *unwritten* or *oral* evidence. We are accustomed to consider that as *direct* and *positive* evidence, which is proved by some writing containing a positive statement of the facts and binding the party whom it affects; or that which is proved by some witness, who has, and avers himself to have, positive knowledge thereof, by means of his senses. Whenever the fact is not so directly and positively established, but is deduced from other facts in evidence, it is *presumptive* and *circumstantial* only. Perhaps, in a strictly philosophical sense, much of the evidence usually denominated *positive* is but *presumptive*; for there is an admixture in it of some circumstances of presumption, though the presumption may usually be deemed irresistible proof. For instance, a, promissory note is offered in evidence, as signed by the defendant; a witness, who attested it, swears to the execution and signature of the defendant. This is usually deemed positive proof; and yet it will be at once perceived, that it rests on the *credibility* of the witness, and the presumption that he has sworn what is true, which is a fact, that, in its nature, is not capable of absolute proof. But, however this may be, in a practical sense, the distinction above stated is sufficiently intelligible and well-settled for all the purposes of human life.

I. *As to* Presumptive Evidence

It must be obvious that in a very great proportion of the questions of fact arising in the litigations before judicial tribunals, the proofs must be of a merely presumptive nature. The want of written proofs; the death, or defect of memory, or treachery, of witnesses; the temptations to suppress evidence; the very nature of the transaction itself, founded in fraud, or in secret contrivances, or in personal confidence; all these, and many other considerations, require us to recur perpetually to presumptive evidence. And especially is this true in respect to public crimes; for these are rarely committed under such circumstances as lead to positive, unequivocal evidence of them. All presumptions are necessarily founded upon the connexion which human experience demonstrates usually to exist between a certain fact or circumstance, and other facts and circumstances. When the one occurs, the others are presumed to accompany them. Some presumptions of this nature are so strong and irresistible, that the law adopts them as *presumptiones juris et de jure*. Others, again, are left to be judged of according to the weight, which the court and jury may think them entitled to, taken in connexion with all the other circumstances of the particular case. There are other presumptions, or rather circumstances of presumption, which are so uncertain and unsatisfactory in their own nature, that the law rejects them, as unworthy of any credit, and too unsafe to found any judgment upon. And presumptions, favorable or unfavorable, often arise from the conduct, or motives, or want of motives, or character, or habits of a party, and may justly influence the decision of a case. But it would lead us too far to enter upon a full illustration of these remarks.

The common law has laid down many rules on the subject of presumptions, a few of which it may not be improper to enumerate. One is, that a man naturally intends the end and result, which must be the immediate consequence of his act. This is often applied to criminal cases. If a man strikes another with a dangerous weapon, and the effect of the blow would naturally produce death, he is deemed to intend to kill; and, under such circumstances, he will not be permitted to set up as a defence, that it was beside his intention. If a man strike another on the head with a heavy axe, so that his head is split open, and he instantly dies, the offender will not be permitted to excuse himself by pretending that he had no intention to kill. In our law, malice is a necessary ingredient in the crime of murder; and if a man kill another upon slight provocation, or use weapons, which are necessarily dangerous to life or conduct himself in a very cruel and brutal manner, the presumption of the law is, that the act is malicious, and this presumption will prevail against any evidence of mere private intention to the contrary.

Another presumption of law is that a man is innocent, until some proof is offered, that he is guilty of a crime. He is not bound, in the first instance, to show his innocence, for the law imputes no wrong to him without some proof. But as soon as such proof is offered against him, the presumption disappears, and, under particular circumstances, the burden of proof is on him to establish his innocence. For instance, if one man is proved to have killed another, the law presumes the act malicious, unless circumstances arising from the evidence produced against him repel that conclusion; and therefore he is required satisfactorily to establish all the circumstances of accident, necessity or infirmity, on which he relies for his defence.

These are instances in criminal cases. And there are many rules of presumption of a like nature in civil cases; some of which are conclusive, and others, again, which are liable to be rebutted by counter evidence; some founded on natural reasoning, and others, again, upon artificial grounds. Among these are the following: Every person is presumed to have done an act, the omission of which would be criminal in him, until the contrary is shown. Fraud is not to be presumed. A party is to be presumed to continue in life until the contrary is made probable. Where the principal act or title is proved, all the collateral circumstances to give it effect will also be presumed. A debt will be presumed paid after a long, unexplained lapse of time. Some presumptions of this nature are artificial. Thus, in our law, a bond will be presumed to be wholly paid after 20 years, where there have been no intermediate payments or recognitions of the debt. A man will be presumed to be dead after an absence of 7 years, unexplained. An heir will be presumed to be in possession of land, of which his ancestor died seized. After 20 years enjoyment of an easement or servitude, a title will be presumed.

On the other hand, there are certain presumptions, which the law rejects (as has been already stated), because of their unsatisfactory nature and tendency. Thus, it is a general rule, that hearsay, or mere report and reputation of a fact, is not evidence, for this amounts to no more than the mere declarations of third persons, not under oath, and of facts of which they may have no certain knowledge. Our law generally requires, that every fact to be substantiated against a person, should be proved by the testimony of a witness (when it is to be proved orally), who is sworn to speak the truth; or, if it is dependent upon written evidence, it must be proved by evidence that is sanctioned by him, or by which he ought to be bound, as importing truth. There are, however, some exceptions to this rule. Whenever the hearsay or declaration accompanies a fact, or, as it is often expressed, is a part of the *res gestæ*, it may be evidence. So in cases of pedigrees, and of prescriptions, customs and boundaries, where, from the nature of the title, the facts are of great antiquity, or, ordinarily, other proofs could not be presumed to exist, hearsay or reputation is admitted as evidence. A monument, or tomb-stone, or family bible, stating a relationship, is, upon this ground, admitted as evidence of the relationship, as it would be of the death of a party. So declarations of parents, either written or oral, of the legitimacy and births of their children, especially if such declarations be before any litigation has arisen (*lis mota*), are admissible, after their decease, in proof of the fact. But it has been lately said, that such declarations, made *post litem motam*, are not admissible. The admission of hearsay, too, is limited in extent, even in these classes of cases. It is admitted only to prove public or general rights, and matters of general reputation. But it is said to be inadmissible to prove mere private rights, or particular facts; as, for instance, upon a question of boundary, that a post was put down in a particular spot; or in a case of birth, that the birth was in a particular place; or that a party has a private right of way.

There are other cases, where the solemn declarations of parties, under whom the party to be affected by them claims, or with whom (as it is technically expressed) he is in *privity* of title, or estate, or blood, are good evidence; as, for example, the recital of a fact in a deed, under which the party claims title, binds him. So the testimony of a deceased witness, given upon a former trial, where the same point was in issue between the same parties. So dying declarations of a party, who has received a mortal wound, are evidence against the party accused of the crime. To go at large into this subject would require a treatise.

II. *As to* Oral *or* Unwritten Evidence

Having considered the nature and operation of presumptive evidence, we may now pass to a consideration of some of the rules of evidence, as to witnesses—when they are, and when they are not competent to give testimony. In general, it may be said that all persons, not under any known disability, are competent witnesses. Several grounds of incompetency exist, in the common law of England and America.

1. The first is, want of reason or understanding. Persons insane, lunatics and idiots, are incompetent to be witnesses. But lunatics and persons temporarily insane, are, in their lucid intervals, or returns of reason, restored to their competency. A person deaf and dumb, if he has sufficient understanding, and can, by signs, make known his thoughts through an interpreter, or otherwise, is competent. But a person deaf, dumb and blind, would be deemed incompetent. Children are admissible as witnesses as soon as they have a competent share of understanding, and know and feel the nature of an oath, and of the obligation to speak the truth. There can, therefore, scarcely be assigned any precise age fixed for the admission of them as witnesses. A child of five years of age is not necessarily incompetent, if he or she has sufficient reason, and a knowledge of the obligation and nature of an oath; although, certainly, at such an age, there ought to be great hesitation in admitting or relying on such testimony, and it ought to have little weight, if uncorroborated by other proof. And the like circumstances would govern the case of persons, whose memory and understanding are greatly impaired by age. If they have too little mind to know the value of truth, or to understand or remember facts, they are incompetent. But if they are not thus deficient, they are admissible, and their credit is to be left to the jury.

2. A second ground of incompetency is the want of religious belief. The law, in order to justify the administration of an oath, or a solemn equivalent affirmation, requires that the party should believe, that it is obligatory upon his conscience, and that lie becomes thus bound to tell the truth. But there is no certain sanction or obligatory force upon the conscience of a man, unless he believes, that his telling or not telling the truth, will, at all events, make him accountable to a Supreme Being for his conduct; and that, if he tells a falsehood, the Supreme Being will punish him accordingly. It is not sufficient, by the common law, that a witness believes himself bound to speak the truth from a regard to his own character and the opinion of the public, or his own permanent interests, or the civil punishments annexed to perjury. Such motives (as has been justly said) have their influence, and may be brought in aid of religious obligation; but they do not supply its place. Indeed, they are of so uncertain a nature, so liable to be perverted to wrong purposes, so infirm in their operation, and so mixed up with other motives, of present reward, of future favor, of hatred, or kindness, or prejudice, that they do not afford a solid foundation upon which to rest our confidence. But if a man does believe in a superintending Providence, and in his responsibleness to that Providence for all his conduct; if he feels that the eye of God can search his thoughts, and that he cannot escape his notice or his power, but will receive at his hands according to his deeds, there is a most solemn and affecting influence upon his mind. He may not always, with this belief; avoid falsehood; but he has the highest motives to do so. Our law, therefore, requires that a person, to be a witness, should believe in the existence of a Supreme God, to whom he is accountable for his actions. The rule is usually laid down, in our books, with this addition that he should also believe in a future state of rewards and punishments. And it has been accordingly held by some judges, that if he does not believe in a state of punishment, but only

of reward, in a future world, he is not a competent witness, although he may believe in punishment in the present world, for all crimes, by the order of Providence. But this doctrine has been doubted and denied by other judges, who think, that if a witness believes in a God, and that he will punish him in this world, if he swears falsely, he is admissible, notwithstanding he may not believe in a future state, or if he does believe in a future state, that he will be liable to any punishment in such state. This latter opinion was held by lord chief justice Willes, in the case of Omichund *vs*. Barker (Willes R. 538), and he is himself of very high authority. But upon such a question, where very able judges have differed, it becomes us to say no more than that the question may still be deemed unsettled. It was formerly a rule, that infidels, or disbelievers in Christianity, such as Jews, Mohammedans, and the various kinds of heathen, were not competent witnesses. But that rule has been abrogated for a considerable length of time; and it now matters not whether a person be a Jew or a Christian, a Mohammedan or a Hindoo, if he believes in a God, and in his responsibleness to him for his conduct, and that he will be rewarded or punished according to his conduct, he is a competent witness. This has been firmly settled in our law, at least since the great case of Omichund *vs*. Barker (Willes R. 538), in 1744–1745. But atheists, and such infidels as profess no religion, or do not believe in any responsibleness to any Supreme Being for their actions, are incompetent witnesses.

3. A third ground of incompetency is infamy of character. But this infamy is not that, which is morally attached to a man for his private profligacy and dissoluteness. That is not sufficient to exclude him as a witness, though it may go far to diminish his credibility. But the infamy, of which we speak, is that which results from a conviction of some crime deemed, in the law, infamous. It is not sufficient that a party

has been convicted and punished for a crime; nor that the punishment itself is deemed by the public degrading and infamous. But the offence must, in its own nature, be infamous. All capital offences and felonies are deemed infamous; all offences importing fraud and gross moral depravity; every species of the *crimen falsi*, such as forgery, perjury, subornation of perjury, piracy, bribery, conspiracy to accuse another of a crime or to commit a fraud, swindling, cheating, grand larceny, and uttering counterfeit paper. Many other offences, though very reprehensible in law, as well as in morals, do not carry with them this disqualification; such as libels, riots, assaults and batteries, and other subordinate misdemeanors. A pardon will, in cases where incompetency is thus a consequence of the conviction, restore the party to his competency, at whatever time it may be granted; and even though the party has suffered under it an infamous punishment. And it seems that our courts will not exclude a party as a witness upon a mere conviction of an infamous crime in another state or, country, though it will form a strong objection to his credit. Accomplices in an infamous crime, who have not been convicted, but who confess their own guilt, are not on that account disabled from giving testimony; but of course it is received with great distrust and caution, and it rarely happens, that any conviction takes place upon such testimony standing alone and uncorroborated.

4. A fourth ground of incompetency is on account of interest. It is, in our law, a general rule, that all witnesses, interested in the event of a cause, that is, such persons as must gain or lose by the event, are incompetent to give testimony in favor of the party, to whom their interest inclines them, but not incompetent to give testimony for the other party. The interest, however, required to exclude a witness, must be a *legal* interest (that is, a fixed interest, which is recognised in our jurisprudence as such), and not

merely a prejudice, affection or bias, or relationship, though these may go to his credit. In respect to relationship, a husband and wife cannot be witnesses for or against each other. They cannot be witnesses for each other, because their interests are, in legal contemplation, one and the same; nor, generally, against each other, because it would destroy the necessary confidence between them, which the law deems of primary and fundamental importance to social life. But all other relations may be witnesses, for or against each other, such as father and child, master and servant, guardian and ward. But an attorney or counsellor cannot be a witness against his client as to any matter of fact, which he derived from his client in professional confidence. This proceeds upon a large ground of public policy. If the interest be strictly a legal interest, it is immaterial whether it is great or small. If it be not a legal interest, it matters not how strong the bias of the party may be, for that goes to his credit only. It is not sufficient, that he has an interest in the question, or has a case of a like nature; he must have an interest in the event of the cause, or it must be such that the verdict may be given in evidence, for or against him. The interest, also, required to exclude a witness, must be a fixed, present interest, and not a remote, possible, or contingent interest. Whenever, therefore, the interest of the witness is doubtful, he is of course admitted. If a witness is really interested in the event of the suit, he is incompetent, although he supposes himself not to be. It would seem to follow, that if he believed himself interested, and he were, in fact, not so, he ought to be admitted as a witness. This is the English rule; but, in some of the American courts, it has been otherwise adjudged. A mere honorary engagement will not exclude a witness. If the verdict or record would secure any advantage to the witness, or repel a charge against him, or a claim upon him, in a future proceeding, he is incompetent. A party to the record is generally incompetent. So a person liable to costs; so bail in a suit; so a servant, in an action against his master for negligence or misconduct of the servant; so a tenant, to establish his landlord's title; so a devisee in a will, to prove the will; so a creditor, to increase the fund of a bankrupt's estate. These are merely put by way of example. If a witness have an interest on both sides, so, that, on the whole, he stands indifferent he is admissible. So, although he is interested, if that interest is released or extinguished in any manner, his competency is restored. So where the witness offers to release his interest and the other party refuses. A member of a corporation is, generally, incompetent to testify in a suit, brought by the corporation. But this rule has been, in many of the American states, abolished by express legislation.

There are certain exceptions to the rule, as to the incompetency of witnesses on account of interest, which have been recognised in our law, and which seem justified by a moral necessity. Thus, agents, factors and servants are, generally, if not universally, admissible as witnesses for their principals, as to things within the scope of their agency. So persons entitled to a reward for conviction of other persons of a crime. So informers entitled to share in a penalty; but this is provided for by positive law. So a party robbed, in an action against the hundred (q. v.) for his loss; for otherwise he might not be able to prove the robbery, which is usually a secret thing. So in America the party, whose name is forged, on an indictment for forgery; but the rule is otherwise in England. The rule of allowing interested testimony, *ex necessitate*, is to be understood not of a necessity in the particular case, but of a general necessity in cases belonging to that class.

If a witness be not interested at the time when the fact occurred, he cannot, by creating a subsequent interest voluntarily on his own part, deprive the party of his testimony, as by making a bet, or wager on the event; but it is otherwise if the interest be created by act of law, or the act of the party by whom he is called.

This may suffice as a general outline, of the law, as to incompetency on account of interest. And cases often arise on this subject, of extreme nicety and subtlety, where the application of the rule is full of doubt and difficulty. But the consideration of such points properly belongs to a full treatise on evidence.

In concluding this head, as to witnesses, we may advert to another exception, which has been extensively, but not universally, adopted in America. It is, that a party, to *negotiable* paper shall not be allowed as a witness to prove its *original invalidity*, although he may be a witness to establish any subsequent fact. The same rule formerly prevailed in England; but it is now abrogated there.

In respect to oral or unwritten evidence, there are some other rules, which it may not be without use to state. And,

1. First, as to *admissions*. These, when made by the party himself, or by his agent in the particular transaction, are evidence against him, though not for him. If there are several persons having a joint interest, an admission of one of them in respect to the joint interest is evidence against all. So an admission of one partner, as to partnership transactions, is evidence against all the partners. But in cases of crimes and torts (q. v.), the rule is more limited. There, the admission of one defendant does not affect the others, unless it be a part of the *res gestæ*; or there be proof of a common conspiracy or design, and the declarations of the party respect that design, and are a part of it, or are made in the course of executing it. But the admissions or declarations of an agent are not evidence against the principal, unless they are made in a case within the scope of his employment, or are a part of the *res gestæ*. His admissions at another time, or in another employment, are not so. What he states while he is doing an act, as agent, is evidence; what he states historically, afterwards, as to the acts

and proceedings under his agency, is not, because better proof may be obtained, for he may be called to appear personally as a witness. There is a distinction in respect to the effect of admissions. In some cases, they are conclusive; in some, not. They are often conclusive, when the party has thereby induced another to act, or give credit. In many other cases they may be contradicted, where they do not operate as a fraud on other persons.

2. Secondly; in respect to *confessions*. The common law seems to have taken a distinction as to the effect of confessions in civil cases and in criminal cases. Generally speaking, they are evidence in civil cases as admissions. In criminal cases, a free, voluntary confession by a party, of his guilt, is also evidence, and is sufficient, per se, to found a conviction; but where a confession has been obtained by duress, or threats, or by a promise of pardon by an agent of the government or the prosecutor, and the promise is not complied with, the confession cannot be given in evidence. These cases seem clear. But where a party has made a confession by the advice of a friend, or upon the suggestion of a stranger, who had no authority to promise any indulgence or pardon, there seems some contrariety of opinion, whether such a confession is, or is not admissible as evidence. However this may be (upon which it is unnecessary for us to express any opinion), it is certain, that any facts ascertained in consequence of any confession are, in all cases, evidence; as if a party confess, that he has stolen goods, and tells where they are hidden, and they are found, his statement, that they were there, would be evidence against him, coupled with the fact of finding them.

And if a prisoner has been admitted as a witness for the government, and has confessed, and afterwards, upon the trial of his accomplices, he has refused to give evidence, it has been decided, that, under such circumstances, he may be convicted upon his own confession.

3. Thirdly, as to the number of witnesses. Generally speaking, by the common law, the testimony of a single witness, if believed, is sufficient to establish any fact. There are, however, certain exceptions: First. On an indictment for perjury, the evidence of one witness is not sufficient to convict, for that would be only oath against oath. There must be either two witnesses, or strong independent evidence by circumstances, to corroborate the testimony of one. Secondly. In cases of treason, by statute, in England, there must be two witnesses to the *same overt* act of treason, or one witness to one, and another witness to, another overt act of the same treason. By the constitution of the U. States, no person can be convicted of treason unless on the testimony of two witnesses to the *same* overt act, or on confession in open court. In England, any confession would be sufficient, even when made out of court, if proved by two witnesses. But in regard to collateral facts, a single witness is sufficient, even in cases of treason. Thirdly, in courts of equity, the answer of the defendant (being under oath), as to facts which it positively and clearly denies, will prevail, unless disproved by two witnesses or one witness and corroborative circumstances. A single witness, without such circumstances, is insufficient. In suits at law, the rule is otherwise; and a single witness here suffices in ordinary cases. The practice in courts of ecclesiastical jurisdiction is, in this respect, like that of the courts of equity.

III. *In Respect to* Written Evidence

This is divisible into various sorts:

1. Statutes or acts of the legislature. These, if of a *public* nature, are evidence without any particular proof, for the judges are bound to take notice of them as the law of the land. They are deemed records, and of such a high nature, that they cannot be contradicted; for it is a general rule, that

a record is conclusive proof, that the judgment or decision was made as is therein stated. But judicial tribunals will not take notice of *private* acts of the legislature; and therefore, unless made evidence by some special law, they are admissible in proof only by a properly authenticated copy. But when so proved, they, as matters of record, cannot be contradicted.

2. Judgments. Those of the superior courts of law are matters of record, and are also conclusive. Generally speaking, verdicts and judgments are evidence in cases between the parties to the suit and privies; but they are not evidence in cases between strangers. When the judgment is directly upon the point, it is a bar between the same parties, and their privies, and may be pleaded as an estoppel. And in cases, where it need not be so pleaded., it is, as evidence, conclusive between the same parties and their privies. But it is not evidence of any matter, which came collaterally in question in the suit, nor of any matter incidentally cognizable, nor of any matter of inference from the judgment. There are some exceptions to the general rule.

a. The judgment in a suit between strangers is sometimes admissible, as the record of a judgment against a principal, who has been convicted of a felony, may be given in evidence against an accessory.

b. Judgments of courts of a peculiar and exclusive jurisdiction are sometimes conclusive upon all persons. Thus judgments *in remn*, in cases of seizures by the exchequer and other courts having exclusive jurisdiction, are conclusive. So sentences of courts of admiralty in matters of prize, and *in rem*, at least as to the direct effect of such sentences in changing the property. So sentences of ecclesiastical courts in cases of which they have exclusive jurisdiction.

c. Judgments in cases of *general rights*, as of a right of common, a public right of way, a custom, a pedigree, &c.,

are admissible as evidence of such right, custom, &c., in suit between third persons.

3. There are other judicial proceedings, which are not strictly matters of record, as decrees in chancery, and judgments in inferior courts, to which, however, the same general principles apply, as matters of evidence, as to judgments of record.

4. Depositions also, awards, and examinations by magistrates, are often evidence in cases between the same parties. There are also cases, in which public writings not judicial, such as journals of parliament, public gazettes, rate or tax books, ship's registers, rolls of manor courts, corporation books, and books of public entries, &c. &c., are evidence. But to go at large into the distinctions applicable to them would occupy too much space.

V. In respect to *private* writings, the rules applied to oral testimony are generally applicable here. Such writings are evidence between parties and privies, but not between strangers, except under the limitations already stated. There are some few cases, in which the written statements of the party himself may be given in evidence, in his own favor, such as, for instance, his account books, to verify charges made by him in respect to debts and charges, which are properly matters of account, such as debits and charges for goods sold, for labor and services, and for materials furnished. But the most common question, that arises in respect to written instruments relates to the mode of proving them to be genuine, or what they purport to be. When the original instrument is produced, if it is objected to, and there is a witness, who subscribed it, he must be called to prove the due execution of it by the party, whom it purports to bind. If the witness be dead, or out of the country, the handwriting of the witness must be proved by some person acquainted with it, and then it will be presumed, that the witness saw the due execution of it; and it is evidence without further proof. If there is no witness who subscribed it, the handwriting of the party who executed it may be proved by some person who is acquainted with it. But it is not sufficient to prove it by comparison of the handwriting with the known handwriting of the party, though such evidence may be admitted in some cases as corroborative evidence. And it has been held, that in case of deeds, even the *admission* of the party, that it is his deed, or that he executed it, is not, at least where there is a subscribing witness, proof of the due execution of it. If the instrument is lost, upon proof of the loss (and the party to whom it belongs may be sworn to prove the loss), the contents of it may be established by a copy or other proper proof. After an instrument has been executed thirty years, and any possession has followed, or right been exercised in conformity to it, it is admissible without any proof by witnesses.

In respect to *written* evidence, a question often occurs, how far parole (oral) evidence is admissible to control or affect it. There are two sorts of ambiguities affecting written instruments. One is called *latent* ambiguity, and the other *patent* ambiguity. The latter is such as appears upon the face of the instrument itself, from the doubtful nature of the terms used. The former is where the terms of the instrument are of themselves certain and free from doubt; but the ambiguity arises from some extrinsic matter or fact, collateral to the instrument. As, for instance, if A grant his manor in B to C; and he has two manors in B, the whole difficulty arises, not from the instrument itself, but from the extrinsic fact that he has two manors; for if he had but one, that would surely pass.

If A devise an estate to his nephew B, and he has no such nephew, but he has a nephew C, there is the same latent ambiguity. In each of these cases, and indeed in all cases of *latent* ambiguity, parole evidence is admissible to show what or who was intended; for as the difficulty arises from parole evidence, that may also be resorted to in order to remove it. But in cases of *patent* ambiguity, it is otherwise. Parole evidence cannot be admitted to supply a meaning which the words do not, of themselves, import, or to give certainty, where the words are uncertain. Indeed, the general rule in our law is, that no parole evidence is admissible to vary, explain or control written instruments, to add new terms to them, or to limit or restrain the import of the words used in them. The ground of this rule is the general insecurity, which would arise from allowing the deliberate acts of parties in writing to be controlled by evidence so variable, and subject to so much doubt, as that is, which depends upon the recollection of witnesses. Written instruments are presumed to be prepared with caution and deliberation, and to contain the best evidence of what the parties intend, and of all which they intend. There are, however, some exceptions to the rule, founded on general convenience, which illustrate rather than weaken its original propriety. Parole evidence may be admitted to show fraud or illegality in an instrument. So to show, that a deed, though dated on one day, was actually delivered on another; for this does not vary its legal effect, but only shows, when it began to operate. So a custom may be shown, bearing upon the subject matter of a contract and creating an obligation, though not provided for in it, because contracts are presumed to be made with a tacit reference to the known customs of the place, and to include the customary obligations and rights, if there is nothing in. the contract, which controls the operation of the custom. So the usages of trade are, for a like reason, admissible, not to supersede, but, in effect, to expound the real intention of the parties, So, in certain cases, courts of equity will allow parole evidence to establish a mistake in a written instrument; but this they do only upon the clearest proofs in an adverse case, where the mistake operates in fact as a fraud upon the party. So in relation to ancient instruments, such as charters, where there is some ambiguity in the words, a long course of practice under them is considered as good proof of the true original exposition of them; and parole evidence for this purpose is admissible; for though the words are now uncertain, they may have been certain in the age when they were used; and the parties, by their long acquiescence, are presumed to have put the proper construction on them. In all such cases it is the object of judicial tribunals, as far as they may, to uphold rather than defeat instruments.

There are, also, certain cases, in which express statute provisions exist, prohibiting any but written proofs of certain contracts. In our law, the principal statute on this subject is commonly called the statute of frauds, from its object being to suppress frauds. Among the contracts embraced in this statute are contracts for the sale of lands or interests in lands; contracts for the sale of goods above a certain value as in England above £10; contracts to become answerable for the debt, default or miscarriage of, another person; contracts to bind executors and administrators to answer damages out of their own estate; and contracts, which are not to be performed within the space of a year after they are made probably, in most countries, the civil policy has pointed out some express provisions of a like nature, by which a written contract is made indispensable to create a legal obligation. We will close this outline of some of the leading principles of our law on this Subject with an enumeration of a few rules, which did not properly fall under any former head.

1. On who the burden of proof (*onus probatndi*) lies. Generally it rests on the party, who alleges the affirmative of any proposition, to establish it by suitable proof. But sometimes even he, who alleges a negative, must prove it; as, in all cases where the party sets up a criminal neglect or

omission, he must establish such neglect or omission by suitable proof; and it is not the duty of the party charged to establish his innocence, for the law will presume it in his favor, until there is some proof to the contrary.

2. The best evidence that the nature of the case admits, is to be produced. The meaning of this rule is not, that, in all cases, the highest possible evidence is to be adduced; but such evidence as presupposes that no better is behind, and in the power of the party. The evidence, for instance, of a written contract is the original instrument; and, therefore, a copy is not generally admissible. But if the original is proved to be lost, then a copy is evidence; for that is the next best proof. In such case, the copy must be proved to be such. Again, oral evidence will not be admitted if there is a copy in existence; but if there is no copy, then it is admissible. But where the best evidence is given, it is not necessary to fortify it by producing all that exists of the same kind. As if there be two witnesses to a deed, it is sufficient to prove it by one. There are certain exceptions to this rule, founded on public considerations. As, for instance, the original of a public record need not be produced; but a copy is sufficient; for the public records ought, for general convenience and preservation, to remain always in one place. So public officers, acting under written commissions, need not show them; but their acting as officers publicly is evidence, *primâ facie*, of their authority; for it would be criminal so to act without authority. So, where the fact lies more immediately in the power of the other party, or his acts conclude him—as if a person act as collector of taxes, or as a clergyman in orders—that is sufficient evidence for third persons to establish his official character.

3. Generally, facts only are evidence, and not the mere opinions of witnesses. But there are certain exceptions; as, in questions of science or trade, persons of skill may be asked

their opinions. A physician may be asked if a particular wound or injury would, in his opinion, produce death and a shipwright, his opinion as to the sea-worthiness of a ship.

4. The substance only of any particular point or issue of fact need be proved. This gives rise to a great variety of questions, as to the materiality or immateriality of particular circumstances, included in the point at issue; and upon these questions depends the doctrine of variance in our law. What variance is, or is not material, is often matter of great nicety. There may be a variance in the proof of a date, or of some words of a contract, or of the time and place of making it, or, some of other circumstance. But a discussion of this subject cannot be had here without occupying too much space.

5. There are certain things, which courts and judges will judicially take notice of without any proof. They will take notice of all public and general laws; of all general customs of the realm; of the commencement and prorogation of the sessions of the legislature; of the king, president, governor, &c., of the state; of all the courts of general jurisdiction in the same state; of the general customs of merchants and trade; of the ordinary computations of time by the calendar; of the known civil divisions of the country into counties; of public holydays and festivals; of public proclamations, and other public documents of the executive and legislative departments; of the nations with which we are at peace or at war; of the nations and sovereigns acknowledged by our government; and of many other facts, which belong to the public proceedings and interests of the country. But of inferior courts of limited jurisdiction, not recognised in public statutes, of local customs and usages, of foreign laws, of peculiar tenures, and, in many instances, of local, geographical divisions, not necessarily involved in the discharge of public duties, judges and courts will not take

notice. We here finish our sketch, and refer the reader, for more full information on the common law doctrine of evidence, to *Peake on Evidence*; *Phillips on Evidence*, and *Starkie on Evidence*, whose treatises are full of practical illustrations upon all the leading questions.

ENCYCLOPÆDIA AMERICANA.

A

POPULAR DICTIONARY

OF

ARTS, SCIENCES, LITERATURE, HISTORY, POLITICS AND BIOGRAPHY,

A NEW EDITION;

INCLUDING

A COPIOUS COLLECTION OF ORIGINAL ARTICLES

IN

AMERICAN BIOGRAPHY;

ON

THE BASIS OF THE SEVENTH EDITION OF THE GERMAN

CONVERSATIONS-LEXICON.

EDITED BY

FRANCIS LIEBER,

ASSISTED BY

E. WIGGLESWORTH AND T. G. BRADFORD.

VOL. VII.

PHILADELPHIA:
LEA & BLANCHARD.
1844.

JURY

[Written by a civilian.*] The right of punishing is inseparable from the executive power in a state; but, since the penal authority has to decide respecting the property, freedom and life of citizens, the executive or highest power may easily degenerate into despotism, and the relation of the citizen to the government into slavery, if it can punish at will. It consequently becomes an object to deprive the government of the will and power to punish unjustly. Now, since, in every case of punishment, a double question is to be answered—first, whether the accused committed the act with which he is charged, and, secondly, if he is guilty, what consequences do the laws attach to the deed, and what punishment must be inflicted—the executive power will be sufficiently restricted, if we leave it to answer merely the last question, and leave the decision of the first to a separate, independent authority. This can neither be limited to single individuals, nor to a permanent college. Both are too much subject to the influences of the supreme power. The mass of the people, alone, is not to be corrupted. But, since the mass of the people cannot sit in judgment, and it is also known how little impartial justice is to be expected from the multitude, when their own interest is concerned, this agency must be committed to sworn substitutes, chosen

* This article, as far as the break on page 165, is translated from the German *Conversations-Lexicon*, and was written by a German civilian accustomed to the juridical practice of countries where the civil law prevails, and where the trial by jury is imperfectly understood, and, if introduced at all, has been imperfectly administered. It has been retained, because it has been thought that the views of the continental jurists on this subject would be curious and instructive. The writer, it will be seen, considers the trial by jury almost solely with reference to criminal cases.—The remainder of the article was written by an eminent American jurist.

for single cases, or only for short periods, in order that the popular tribunal may not degenerate into an established office. These substitutes, as they are not determined beforehand, cannot become the object of corrupting influences, which, though they may find access with some, hardly can with all. In these views lie the foundation and essence of juries; namely, of the petty jury in England, and of the *iury de jugement*, in imitation of it, among the French. In the former country, the love of freedom proceeded still farther, and on account of the mischief that may be produced by complaints, invented the grand jury, consisting, likewise, of sworn representatives of the people, whose function it is to decide respecting the admissibility of complaints, and whether, in conformity with them, a criminal prosecution is to be instituted against any one. Its counterpart existed in France till 1809, under the name of *jury d'accusation.* To this essential character of a jury are united several properties necessary to its perfection.

(a.) Not only must citizens sit in judgment on citizens, but the greatest possible equality of rank is to be sought, between the judges and the party to be judged, in order that the interests of different ranks may not give rise to injustice, partiality, or false decisions. In England, where all ranks, below the hereditary peers, are by law equal; and without exclusive prerogatives of rank or birth, all persons not born peers of the land (for they, as an intermediate part of the hereditary government, between king and people, have their equals, and, consequently, their jury, only in the house of lords) are tried by the same jury. In the ancient German courts, which, in substance, were juries, the equality of birth between the judge and criminal was most strictly observed; not, however, so much that no inferior person could be judged by a higher, as that no higher could be judged by an inferior.

(b.) The jurors cannot well be chosen otherwise than by a public officer, in England, by the sheriff. To guard against all danger of partiality and undue influence, the person arraigned has the right of rejecting a portion of the jurors empanneled. The right allowed to the prosecutor is more limited. In England, the former may [in capital cases] reject 20, and in crimes of high treason, 35. The public prosecutor cannot challenge any one without declared cause.

(c.) A jury, which, in most cases, must consist of men of little education, cannot be guided in their conclusions by legal rules of evidence, but only by their general impressions from the whole train of circumstances; and, on this account, its verdicts are not proper subjects of revision. In England, trial by jury is extended even to civil cases, especially for settling certain matters of fact; for instance, of possession, of estimating the amount of damage, &c.

(d.) All the operations, examinations, and other processes necessary in a criminal trial, are to be performed in the presence of the jury. To refer them for information to a protocol, or to the reports of an officer, would involve difficulties, and, at all events, leave them exposed to the errors which might arise from the subjection of the reporting officer to foreign influences, and thus defeat the essential object of trial by jury. With the French constitution, the trial by jury was spread on the continent and excited, in many persons, high admiration. It has been proved by Feuerbach, in his classical work on this subject (Landshut, 1813), that, in a political view, trial by jury has a value only in particular constitutions, in which its political advantages may induce us to overlook its defects, when considered merely in reference to criminal jurisdiction. Political objects make the trial by jury necessary in democracies. Intrusted to a single magistrate, or to a permanent authority, the criminal power would open an immediate avenue to sole dominion, or to aristocracy. Equally indispensable is it to a mixed constitution, like the English; for it would become either a pure monarchy, democracy or aristocracy, if the immense preponderance of the penal power should be committed solely to the monarch, or to one of the powers counteracting and restricting him, the people or the body representing the national sovereignty. On the other hand, it is apparent, that in a constitution where the monarch is absolute, the political advantage of a jury disappears. No constitution, no personal freedom of individuals can, in such case, be defended by juries, since the ruler can abolish it at any moment, or, in particular cases, render it inefficacious by a special commission. The most eloquent example is that of France in late years. The establishment, moreover, of trial by jury in a pure monarchy, already confirmed by long permanence, is not only null, but superfluous, inasmuch as the ruler can gain nothing more by injustice, but may lose every thing. But how far does the trial by jury satisfy the demands which are made of criminal jurisdiction? How far is a certain determination of guilt or innocence to be expected of it?

1. Can we believe the juryman, who is accustomed to move only in the circle of common intercourse, can we believe him possessed of sufficient sagacity to look through the most complicated relations, which often occur in criminal trials, permitting neither aversion nor predilection to influence his verdict? Certainly not. But to attempt to abolish the evil by means of permanent jurors, who should acquire ability by practice, would be to destroy the essential character of juries. Add to this, that in the oral proceedings in the presence of the jurors, every means is afforded for the operation of sophistry, and the excitement of the passions, and that the various grounds of defence or accusation, often infinitely numerous, can in no wise be fairly examined and compared with each other—a process possible only when the judge forms his opinion for written documents. In every case, the last impression of a jury will be the decisive one. The charge, by which, after the termination of the debates, the presiding judge, versed in the law, seeks to guide the deliberations of the jury, and aid their untaught judgment,

may contribute, indeed, to remove this and the deficiencies remarked below, but the effect of it is very inconsistent with the object of jury trials; for it makes him, in most cases, master of the judgment. One may generally foretell, in England, the verdict of the jury from the charge of the judge.

2. Experience confirms it, and it lies in the nature of things, that the jury regularly hesitate, even against their conviction, to give a verdict of guilty, when it exposes the party to a punishment, in the public opinion, more severe than just. To common penetration, it is extremely difficult to separate the fact from its legal consequences. This evil is seen to be in some degree necessary, especially in England, where the criminal code has not kept pace with the times, and a very slight theft is punished with the halter.

3. The question of guilt or innocence is not one of pure fact, but also a legal question, and presupposes, in every case, a knowledge of criminal law. To be able to say whether any one has committed a violent robbery, it must first be known whether he has done the act which the accuser asserts, and, secondly, whether this act had those characteristics, which the laws require to constitute the crime. But if, to remedy this evil, the jury should be restricted to the question whether a certain act had been committed or not, its object would be destroyed, and the authority to which is committed the decision of the point of law would be left to its free will, since it might make that act any crime it pleased. In England, recourse has been had to the dangerous practice of allowing the jury, when they find the accusation in a legal view but partially founded, or regard the crime committed as less heinous than the one charged, to give a verdict partly of acquittal, partly of condemnation, such as guilty of manslaughter, but not of murder. If the jury agrees on the point of fact, but cannot remove their doubts respecting its legal character, they have

to leave the decision to the judge. But will not the jury trust to their penetration more than is just? Does not the presiding judge become absolute? Some might, indeed, be inclined to make it a decided advantage of juries, that the accused is tried by judges who are his equals, and from whom, it would seem, may be expected a juster decision, more conformable to his peculiar situation, than from others. But, in the first place, the poorer class of people, who, above all others, fill the annals of criminal trials, must be excluded from the jury by reason of their want of information and comparatively small interest in the public welfare, by which means that equality is, in most cases, destroyed (thus, in England, to be a juror, a person must have a certain income; the same is the case in France, where attention is also paid to particular circumstances of rank); so that, from the infinite gradations and varieties of property, education, opinions, and innumerable outward circumstances, instead of full equality, the greatest inequality often subsists between the jurors and the accused. The various means by which it has been attempted, in France, to remedy the defects of the jury, and which, nevertheless, have produced no better criminal jurisdiction, satisfactorily prove their entire insufficiency in this respect. (See *Assizes*, and *Appeal.*)

I. *History of the Institution*

It has evidently been, from the beginning, a truly popular trial, and not, as Rogge has lately asserted (*Gerichtswesen der Germnanen*, 1820), a modification of the ancient process of compurgation. These institutions—compurgation and jury—have, indeed, many external similarities, and may, in some cases, have become blended with each other; but, in their nature, they are entirely separate. This appears evident from the circumstance that, in England, juries and compurgations occur at the same time. Criminal actions against the clergy were prosecuted under the direction of the bishop, with 12 of the clergy as jurors, but were begun by the accused, with 12 compurgators swearing to his innocence, and commonly ended in his acquittal, till an end was put to this disorder by law, in 1576. (See Blackstone's *Comment. on the Laws of England*, vol. iv.) It has long been known in Germany, and has lately been proved by Fenerbach (*Betrachtungen über die Mundlichkeit und Oeffentlichkeit der Gerichtigkeitspflege*, 1825), that the most ancient constitution of the German laws, and in Bavaria as late as the fifteenth century, consisted in the men of the communes finding judgment under the guidance and protection of an officer. As there must be some fixed number, that of 12 is as good as any other, and has been preferred from time immemorial; but the agreement of the 12 jurors consisted, at first, in many cases and places, in the circumstance, that the votes of all the men present and capable of giving an opinion, were asked, and the matter decided as soon as a majority of 12 votes was obtained for an opinion. One person could, therefore, cancel the vote of another juror, by declaring himself of another opinion, and commanding the juror to leave his seat. Some traces of this regulation are still to be found in England. In the house of lords, the whole body of nobles votes; but a valid condemnation is obtained only when a majority of 12 votes is declared for conviction. But in the courts of assizes, the place of absent jurors is immediately supplied from the people present, and if these 12 cannot agree, according to the original constitution, the trial must be by new jurors, who are chosen from time to time till a unanimous vote of 12 is obtained. In important cases in the county courts, all the freemen of the county were, in former days, summoned, which is termed judgment *per omnes comitatus probos homines*. (Reeves' *History of the English Law*, 1814, vol. i, 84.) But it was very naturally soon found better to summon only a fixed number of men to this service, and thus arose the number of 12, who could only unanimously give a valid decision. The oldest vestige of this change is found under Henry II, in the constitutions of Clarendon, in 1164, and of Northampton, in 1174. Contests about landed property, as well as criminal accusations, were to be decided by the oath of 12 respectable men of the neighborhood (*per sacramentum duodecim militum de hundredo*, or *liberorum legalium hominum de vicineto*). From this time, the trial by jury has remained essentially unaltered in England, and has gradually become the only form of process, partly by the abolition of the criminal courts which judged without jury, partly by the abrogation of the methods of criminal prosecution in which no trial by jury existed. Of the last, there remains only the pronouncing of punishment in the way of legislation, termed an attainder (*attinctura*), or *bill of pains and penalties*. There were, besides, several other ways of terminating a criminal trial without jury, but between which, not the accuser, but the accused, was entitled to choose. In the times of the Anglo-Saxons, the ordeals of red hot iron and boiling water were in vogue, besides which there was the consecrated bread. The clergy prepared a piece of bread or cheese, an ounce in weight, which was easily swallowed by the innocent, but which stuck in the throat of the guilty, and choked him. Of such a morsel, Godwin, earl of Kent, died in the reign of Edward the Confessor; and, according as the accused was suspected or hated, it was well known how to prepare the morsel. Under the Norman dominion, this ordeal was supplanted by the wager of battle. The wager of battle (*vadiatio duelli*) was used even in civil cases, and, according to the most ancient custom, it depended on the accused, if the accusor had supported his accusation by witnesses, to choose whether he would have recourse to this means, or swear to his innocence with twice as many compurgators as the accuser had produced, though not above twelve. This was called *vadiatio legis* (wager of law). In civil causes, the wager of battle disappeared in the thirteenth century, when Henry II introduced into the assizes a trial by jury. But in penal prosecutions, on the contrary, it continued much longer. The accused is still asked how he will be tried; and, though the answer—"by the law of the land," or "by the country" (*per legem terræ*, or *per patriam*)—has become a mere formality, yet, as late as 1819, a singular trial for murder took place, in which it stood at the option of the accused to challenge the accuser to the wager of battle. (See Kendall's *Appeal of Murder*, London, 1819, and *Appeal*.) A court of justice, moreover, formerly existed in England, which judged without jury, called the *star-chamber* (*camera stellata*)—a name respecting the derivation of which antiquarians are not agreed. It consisted of some lords, both temporal and spiritual, members of the privy council, and two judges of the supreme court of Westminster, and had properly jurisdiction only of some particular cases, rebellion, perjury, the official misconduct of sheriffs, &c., but extended its jurisdiction farther and farther, and became, especially under Henry VII and Henry VIII, an instrument of the most arbitrary power. After it had long been a subject of terror and hatred, it was entirely abolished under Charles I, in 1641. The trial by jury has since been regarded in England as one of the fundamental pillars of the constitution. By the Habeas Corpus act (see *Habeas Corpus Act*) of the reign of Charles II, greater security has been provided, that the trial by jury shall be withheld from no one; it is only to be lamented, that the petition for such an order is attended with extraordinary expense.

II. *History of the Jury in France*

In the article *France*, some of the cruelties are mentioned, which, are chargeable to the administration of penal justice in France before the revolution. Judicial despotism, united with ignorance and corruption, was exhibited in horrid forms. The laws were severe. The ordinance of criminal procedure of 1670 was written in blood, giving up the accused to the arbitrary will of the judge, and denying him the aid of counsel excepting in a flew cases (Tit. 14. § 8); admitting a double application of the torture (the *question préparatoire*, to extort from the accused a confession of his own guilt, and the *question préalable* before execution, to compel him to reveal his accomplices); and allowing any judge, even the patrimonial courts, to institute a process without any statement of the ground of suspicion. The judges were even more severe than the laws. Their ignorance and carelessness occasioned mistakes and abuses, which their pride and the clannish spirit of the higher classes prevented from being rectified, and under the operation of which crowds of innocent persons lost liberty, property, reputation, and even life. Even the most atrocious criminals, Damiens, for instance, could not be legally sentenced to such cruel torments as this offender actually underwent, when torn to pieces by wild horses. All the districts, therefore, in 1789, were unanimous in desiring that the judgment in criminal cases should be made dependent on the verdict of a jury. In fact, such a provision was introduced into the constitution of September, 1791, and on this subject there was hardly any difference of opinion. The form of the English institution was followed,—a grand jury being appointed to find bills of accusation, and, after the conclusion of the process, which was to be public and oral, the question of fact was to be determined by a jury of twelve persons. There were to be, also, as at present, justices of the peace, clothed with proper judicial authority only in cases of minor importance and disputes respecting the right of possession; and likewise district courts, who should exercise a mutual appellate jurisdiction in regard to each other's decisions. The judges were to be chosen by the people, to remain six years in office, were to be reëligible at the end of this period, and to be paid, scantily indeed, by the state, being prohibited from receiving any fees. These provisions were made by the law of Aug. 24, 1790, respecting the organization of the courts. An ordinance respecting criminal jurisdiction of Sept. 29, 1791, a penal code of Oct. 6, 1791 and the regulations for the conduct of criminal prosecutions, Oct. 21, 1791, completed this new system, which has been subsequently retained in its fundamental principles, though not without undergoing essential alterations, by which a portion of the benefits, that are ascribed to the constitution of English criminal courts, was lost again, and the influence of the officers of the government on the administration of justice (it is said) improperly enlarged. The criminal courts were at first derived from the district courts, the judges sitting alternately in the criminal courts of the department. One of the judges was director of the jury, drew up the indictment, and assembled the jurors. The jury of accusation (*d'accusation*) consisted of eight members, three voices for the accused being sufficient to reject the complaint. This jury of accusation is now entirely abolished in the new criminal ordinance of Nov. 17, 1808. (See *Codes les Cinq*.) The criminal courts for more important causes (*cours d'assises*) are now deputations of the king's court (*cour royale* or *cour d'appel*), and the decision respecting complaints is committed to a division of the *cour royale*. The liberty of the accused to hold consultation with counsel is less restricted by the new laws than by late practice. According to a very doubtful interpretation of the article 302 of the act of 1808, to regulate criminal process, the counsel is allowed access to the accused only a few days before the beginning of the public prosecution. And, in some cases, as in libels, the definitive decision is taken from the jury, and given to the police courts. To require the unanimous agreement of the jurors to a verdict, which, even in England, is often attended with great difficulties, and leads to striking inconsistencies, was soon found entirely impossible in France. The simplicity of the English process, which, at the end of the proceedings, leaves to the jury the verdict of guilty or not guilty, it was found in France impracticable to imitate. In England, only the most important witnesses are brought forward, and a day, or, in very complicated cases, three or four days are sufficient to complete a trial, and consequently no uncommon powers of mind are required to retain time testimony in the memory. But, in France, even the most unimportant testimony is admitted. Hence several hundred witnesses are sometimes brought forward, and more weeks spent in a case than there would be days employed in England. It having been found absolutely impracticable to insist on unanimity in the jury, it has been resolved to assume the simple majority of seven against five, as decisive. But in that case the court itself is obliged to deliberate on the same points, and an acquittal takes place, if the majority of the judges coincide with the minority of the jurors, so as to make the numbers of voices in favor of the acquittal equal to those for condemnation. The courts have also the right to set aside the verdict of the jury, if it appears to them to rest entirely on an error; but this must be their own free act, and cannot be proposed by any one. A simple majority of jurors decided the case of Fonk, and, at Paris, in 1823, that of doctor Castaing, indicted on a charge of poisoning. Among the objections made to the new French criminal process is the excessive power committed to the president. In England, the examination of witnesses is carried on by the prosecutor, and the counsel for the defendant, but in France, by the president alone. And there is frequently seen a very striking exercise of this privilege, as well as a hostility to the defendant, which ill comports with the judicial office. But the loudest complaints that at present are made, are of the selection of jurors (which belongs to the prefect alone), and the restriction of the right of challenging. The prefect draws up a list of sixty jurors, of which the president of the assizes strikes out twenty: the defendant (or defendants collectively, however many there may be of them) and the attorney-general, each, can strike out twelve, and the rest constitute the jury. In this way it is possible to collect a jury consisting of the enemies of the accused, and it is asserted that this is often done in the case of prosecutions for political offences. The best French jurists (Dupin, Berenger, Paillet, Bavoux, &c.) are therefore fully agreed, that the French jury contributes little towards a pure administration of justice. Even in England, its value is very doubtful. It may seem rash to attempt to assail the general conviction, not only of the English, but of the French also, and other nations that recognise, in this popular institution, the palladium of all genuine civil freedom, and place entire confidence in their trial by jury. But it is only the cases of political prosecutions, or those in which the innocent have been pursued by the revenge of the great, which give to the trial by jury its reputation; and there is still another question, not only whether the jury always merits this reputation, but whether the desired advantage cannot be attained equally well, and even better, by a proper organization of the judicial office.

But to return to what we were saying on the value of the jury: This body in England was not able to prevent the infamous judge Jeffreys (chief-justice under James II) from gratifying his private hatred, nor has the French jury been able to oppose any obstacles of importance to such an abuse of the judicial office. Algernon Sydney and Lord Russell were condemned to death by the verdict of a jury. For common criminal cases, there can hardly be any more uncertain, fluctuating form of decision than the trial by jurors, who, without imparting to others the grounds of their verdict, or even settling any just grounds in their own minds, decide on the honor, freedom and life of their fellow citizens. In the first place, the actual existence of a crime need not be proved according to fixed rules. Suppose the case of a man being missed, or of a corpse being found—the jury are persuaded that a murder must have been committed, and pronounce some suspected person guilty, when it is possible that the missing man still lives, or that the dead man perished without personal violence. Some years since, David Evans was executed in London as the murderer of his wife, because an apothecary, who had never practised as a surgeon, maintained that the woman died in consequence of a wound on her head, while a surgeon in actual practice asserted, on the contrary, that the wound had nothing to do with her death, and that this was occasioned by an inflammation of the bowels. (*Morning Chronicle*, 1818, Feb. 24.) In the second place, the jury give their verdict on the slightest and most remote evidence, when the offence in question is an injury to property, a theft, robbery, fraud, or the like. The instances in which the innocence of persons condemned for such offences subsequently appears are therefore constantly increasing, and the explanation of this circumstance is to be found in the character of the jury, who are taken mostly from men of business in the middle classes, who feel more hostility to a thief or a swindler than to a murderer. The jury act, in fact, the part of legislators: when the penalty imposed by the law appears to them too severe,—as, for instance, the punishment of death for stealing property to the amount of 40 shillings,—they settle at their own pleasure the degree of the offence, so as to avoid the strictness of the law; and it has happened that a jury has declared a man who had stolen 10 guineas (210 shillings) guilty of theft to the amount of 39 shillings. The personal feelings of the jury towards the accused, and the light in which they regard the offence often determine what the verdict will be, before the trial is begun. It has been proposed, in Germany, to make juries give their reasons for their verdicts; but this only proves that the nature of this institution is not understood. An exhibition of their reasons comports as little with their nature as a further examination by a different tribunal. The verdict of the jury comes like a decree of destiny, without being capable of justification, examination or amendment; for the whole of the decision rests on things which cannot be a second time exhibited in exactly the same modifications—the deportment of the accused and the witnesses, the individual and momentary dispositions of the jurors. Even in England, doubts of the importance of the trial by jury are by degrees excited, and there is an approximation to the fundamental views of the German criminal process, which aims at exciting the moral feelings of the criminal by solitude and examination, and producing a confession, which makes the accused his own judge. No criminal is so hardened as never to experience a state of mind when the burden of conscience is too heavy for him, and he desires to reconcile himself to the law and his inward judge. To produce this effect is the aim of the criminal judges of Germany; and certainly it is at least as conformable to the high dignity of the administration of justice as the trial by jury. The abridgment of the length of the process, and the publicity of the administration of penal justice, are different things, and, though they are commonly united with the trial by jury, are advantages which may be imbodied with any other system.

The views suggested in the previous part of this article, written, as has been already observed, by a civilian unaccustomed to the practical operation of the trial by jury, deserve the consideration of minds accustomed to a different course of jurisprudence, not only from their theoretical acuteness, but from their development of supposed practical defects in the trial by jury. It seems fit, therefore, to give another exposition of this subject, which is maintained by persons educated under the common law, and to suggest some of the reasons why it is deemed the bulwark of public liberty, and the best safeguard of private rights under our forms of free government. The remaining part of this article is to be considered as independent of the foregoing; not so much as presenting a counter view, but as presenting the true grounds on which the institution was established, and is still dear to the free inhabitants of England and America.

I. *The Origin of the Trial by Jury.* It has been traced back by antiquarians to a very early period in English history, and seems, indeed, in some form, if not coeval with the origin of the civil government in England, at least to have been used time out of mind in that kingdom. It is lost among the early Saxon colonies; and probably was derived from the mode of administering justice by the peers of the litigant parties in the feudal institutions of Italy, France and Germany. Mr. Justice Blackstone (3 *Comm.* 349, 350) considers that this tribunal was universally established among all the northern nations, and so interwoven with their very constitution, that the earliest accounts of the one give us also some traces of the other. Mr. Wynne (*Eunomus*, *Diag.* 3, *s.* 50) seems to entertain a different opinion, and, after stating that its origin is obscure (*caput inter nubila condit*), he asserts, that it is the noblest form of policy that was ever invented on earth, and comes nearest the impartiality of heaven. But, whatever may be the origin of the trial, it is of very high antiquity. And *Magna Charta* (ch. 29) referred to it as an existing institution, and provided that no person should be hurt, either in his person or property, unless by the judgment of his peers or the laws of the realm (*nisi per legale judicium parium suorum vel per legem terræ*).

II. *The Different Kinds of Juries*. Juries are of two sorts, viz. grand juries and petty juries. The former may consist of any number more than twelve, and less than twenty-four persons. The office of the grand jury is to accuse persons who are supposed to be guilty of an offence. It may, therefore, properly be called the *jury of accusation*. The petty or petit jury consists of twelve persons only, and may properly be called the *jury of trials*, both in civil and criminal cases.

III. We shall first consider the organization, functions and proceedings of the grand jury. The mode of accusation is by a written statement in solemn form, describing the offence, with all the proper accompaniments of time and circumstances, and certainty of act and person, which is called an *indictment*, or by a mode less formal (which is usually the spontaneous act of the grand jury), called a *presentment*, and which is afterwards put into solemn form by some proper officer. No indictment or presentment can be made except by the concurrence of at least twelve of the jurors. The grand jury may accuse upon their own knowledge; but it is generally done upon the testimony of witnesses under oath, and other evidence produced and heard before them. The proceedings of the grand jury are, in the first instance, at the instigation of the government or other prosecutor, and are *ex parte*, and in secret deliberation. The accused has no knowledge of, nor right to interfere with their proceedings. If they find the accusation true (which is usually drawn up in form by the public prosecutor), they write upon the indictment the words "a true bill," which is signed by the foreman, or chief of the grand jury, and is presented to the court publicly, and in the presence of all the jurors. If the indictment is not proved to the satisfaction of the grand jury, the word "*ignoramus*" (we are ignorant), or "not a true bill," or "not found," is written on it by the grand jury, or by their foreman, and it is then, in common parlance, said to be ignored, and the accusation is dismissed, as unfounded. When the grand jury return an indictment as a true bill (*billa vera*), the indictment is said to be *found*, and the party stands indicted, and may be required to be put upon his trial. When the indictment is not found, or is declared to be not true, the accused, if he is in custody, or has been in any way required to appear at the court, and answer to any accusation against him, is entitled to be discharged, or dismissed from any further inquiry or attendance before the court. Every public offence may be properly the subject of an indictment, and taken cognizance of by the grand jury of the county within which it is committed. But there is another mode of proceeding at the common law, at the suit of the king, called an *information*, which is similar to an indictment, except that it is not found by the grand jury, and is filed, *ex officio*, by the proper officer of the government. An information cannot be filed except in cases of mere misdemeanors, or offences not capital; for, whenever any capital offence is charged against a party, he cannot be put upon his trial unless the accusation be made by the grand jury by indictment.

IV. *The Organization of the Grand Jury*. The functions being such as we have stated, it is obvious that the duties require great care in the selection of the persons who are to serve as grand jurors. A precept, commonly called a *venire facias*, issues to the sheriff of every county, some time before any court of criminal jurisdiction is held therein, requiring him to summon twenty-four good and lawful men of his county, to attend the court, to inquire into, and present all offences committed within the body of the county. At the common law, these grand jurors are required to be freeholders of the county, and in England, where the sheriff makes the selection, they are usually gentlemen of the first respectability in the county. In the U. States, different modes prevail in different states in the selection of grand jurors. In some, the grand jurors are chosen, as in England, by the sheriffs; in others, as in the New England States, the grand jurors are drawn by the town officers, from boxes containing the names of all the persons qualified to serve, from time to time, and in such numbers as are required; and the names so drawn are returned to the sheriff, and by him to the court. But, in whatever way the grand jurors are selected, their names are returned on a piece of parchment or paper, by the sheriff, which is called a *panel*, and as many of them as appear in court are sworn on the grand jury, not exceeding twenty-three, so that twelve may constitute a majority. Their oath is, in substance, that they will diligently inquire and true presentment make of all offences committed within the county; that the government's counsel, that of their fellows, and their own, they will keep secret; that they will present no man for envy or malice; neither will they leave any one unrepresented from fear, favor, affection, or hope of reward; but that they will present things truly as they come to their knowledge, according to their best understanding. Usually, the presiding judge of the court instructs them in the matters which are within their jurisdiction, by delivering to them a charge, containing a summary of the offences and other business which may come before them. They then retire to their room, and sit, as has been said, in secret, hearing evidence in favor of the prosecution only, as the main question before them is, whether the party accused ought to be put upon his trial to answer the accusation. But they are always bound to act upon legal evidence, and are instructed that they ought not to find an indictment unless upon their oaths they are persuaded, so far as the evidence goes, that the accusation is true. It has been already stated, that the grand jury is to inquire only into crimes committed in the county for which they sit. And this is regularly true at the common law, for no man was bound to answer for any crime but before his peers in the county and neighborhood where it was committed. But, by sundry statutes, both in England and America, some offences, not committed within a county, have, to prevent a defect of justice, been made cognizable therein. To enumerate these offences would occupy too large a space; and probably no two states in the Union have enacted precisely the same provisions. There are proper powers vested in the courts to compel the attendance of grand jurors; and if any are returned who are not qualified, they may be excluded from the panel; and if an indictment be found by persons not qualified, the accused may except to it on this account. Thus careful has the law been, in the original selection of grand jurors, who are supposed, and indeed required, to be men of integrity, impartiality and intelligence, and above all just objection. And thus a body of men, brought together for the occasion, and for that only, are placed between the government and the citizen, as a shield against oppression and injury, and to afford a reasonable protection to him, if he be not justly suspected of a crime.

V. *As to Petty or Petit Juries*, or, as they are sometimes called, *Traverse Juries*. These consist, as has been already said, of 12 persons, and no more, for the trial of all criminal offences, and of all issues of fact in civil cases at the common law. There are some peculiar modes of trial by jury in England, where a larger number than 12 is required, which may be called the *extraordinary* trial by jury; as, for instance, a grand assize for the trial of issues in writs of right, which consists of 4 knights and 12 other persons; and the jury of attaint, to convict a former jury of a corrupt verdict, which consists of 24 jurors. But these, modes of trial are, at present, wholly disused in America; and, in England, that of a jury of attaint has fallen into neglect, since the general use of the remedy of moving for a new trial, where the verdict is unsatisfactory. And first, as to the trial by jury in civil cases. This is generally confined to issues of fact in proceedings at common law, as contradistinguished from proceedings in equity and admiralty. When, then, the parties have, in their written pleadings, or allegations, come to a fact which is denied on one side, and affirmed on the other, in a regular mode, the cause is said to be *at issue*, and the fact in controversy is to be ascertained by a jury. For this purpose, in England, a precept issues to the sheriff of the proper county, requiring him to select and summon to the court at which the trial is to be had, a suitable number of jurors, for the trial of the cause; and he accordingly makes return of the names of the jurors, on a piece of parchment or paper (thence, as before stated, called a *panel*), who are compellable to attend at the time and place appointed. If the sheriff have any interest in the case, or is not impartial, or is related to the parties, the jurors are selected by some other proper officer, and usually by the coroner of the county. The qualifications of petty jurors do not differ, generally, from those required as to grand jurors, their duties being equally important, and requiring equal intelligence. When the cause is called for trial, if all the jurors do not appear, or any of them are justly objected to and set aside (of which we shall speak hereafter), the deficiency may be supplied from among the bystanders, having suitable qualifications, which is called taking jurors *det alibis circumstantibus*, from which circumstance the persons thus selected are denominated *talesmen*. The jury, being thus full, and above objection, are sworn (severally or together, according to the local usage in each state) well and truly to try the issue between the parties, and a true verdict to give "according to the evidence" (or "according to the law and the evidence given them," by the local usage of some states). In some cases, special juries are allowed to be selected, in a particular mode, for the purpose of trying particular causes; in other cases, the trials are by a jury chosen in the ordinary manner, and thence called a *common* jury. But these distinctions are unknown in some of the states of America, though they are very important in the practice in England. After the jury is sworn, the cause is then tried in open court, the evidence is offered, and the witnesses publicly sworn and examined in the presence of the judges, the counsel on each side, the jury, and all other persons in attendance. The question, whether any evidence is competent to be given to the jury, is, if any objection is made, first decided by the court. If rejected, it is never heard by the jury; if admitted, it is then read, or, if given by a witness, he is then examined before the jury. The party who calls a witness first examines him, and he is then liable to be cross-examined by the other side; and if any question is asked, which either party deems improper, the opinion of the court is taken on it before the witness is allowed to give his answer. So, also, it is, in respect to any written evidence or document offered at the trial. And if either party requests it, the judge who presides at the trial makes a note, in writing, of the objection, so that the party may avail himself of it afterwards, upon a motion for a new trial, or by a writ of error, in a suitable manner. Before the evidence is offered, the counsel for the party who opens the cause, on each side, makes a short introduction, stating the case, the points in controversy, and the facts which he expects to prove, so that the jury may more clearly understand the bearing of the evidence, as it is produced. After all the evidence is gone through, the counsel on each side argue the case to the jury, at large, commenting upon every part of it, and each insisting upon a verdict in his favor. If any questions of law arise (as in most instances they do), the judge is requested, and is bound, publicly to state his opinion on all the points of law applicable to it. This he ordinarily does in summing up the case, after the arguments of the counsel are over; but he may do it before, if he chooses. When the arguments are finished, the presiding judge, in England, and in most of the states in America, proceeds to address the jury, stating to them the questions, recapitulating the evidence, and commenting on it in such a manner as he deems correct, for the purpose of enabling the jury to understand it well, and to apply the law properly to it. In these addresses, he often freely expresses his opinion as to the weight of evidence, the sufficiency of the proofs, the force of particular objections, and the comments of the counsel. But, it being a principle of law, that the jury is to respond as to matters of fact, and the judges as to matters of law (*ad quæstiones facti respondent juratores, ad quæstiones legis respondent judices*), it is always understood, that these comments on matters of fact are not binding on the jury, and that they are given solely with a view of enabling the jury to exercise their functions more perfectly, and that the jury are at liberty to disregard them if they please. But, generally speaking, they do receive great weight from the jury, who naturally place confidence in the judges, from their talents, experience and impartiality, and therefore, unless the judge obviously exhibits some improprieties, or betrays some unjustifiable feeling, they consider him as a friend, aiding and assisting them in their duty; and, his addresses being always in public, and open to the criticism of the public, as well as of the profession, it rarely occurs that his conduct is deemed exceptionable. Still the jury have a right to form, and do form, an independent judgment upon matters of fact; and their judgment is often conclusive. After the judge has finished his summary, the jury withdraw into a private room, where they are kept together for the purpose of deliberation, until they have all agreed in a verdict (*veredictum*) upon the point in controversy. They are not permitted to have any intercourse with any other persons, and are allowed, during their continuance in secret session, to have only such food and other necessaries as are indispensable. Indeed, by the old law, they were to be kept without meat, drink, fire or candle, until they were agreed, unless by permission of the court, which soon, however, became almost a matter of course. When they are agreed, they come into open court, and, their names being called, they deliver in their verdict, which is recorded by the proper officer, who then reads it aloud to the jury, and asks them if they agree to it as recorded, to which they all publicly assent. If either party doubts it, the jurymen are severally asked if they agree, which is called *polling* the jury. Sometimes, when the facts are very complicated, or involve questions of law of great difficulty, the jury, instead of finding a general verdict, that the issue of fact is for the plaintiff or for the defendant, state all the facts at large, and ask the court to decide upon those facts, whether the issue ought to be found for the plaintiff or for the defendant. This is called a *special* verdict. It rarely occurs in criminal cases, and is not very common in civil cases. But the jury are never obliged to find a special verdict, and may, in all cases, give a general verdict, if they choose. If the jury, after being kept together a considerable time, cannot agree they are usually brought into court by the proper officer, and the court, if their difficulty is about any matter of law, often makes additional explanations. But if, after every reasonable effort, the jury continue to disagree, they are discharged by the court, and the cause must then be tried anew. In criminal cases, and especially in capital cases, the court with great reluctance allow the discharge of a jury, after the cause is once committed to them.

Next, as to the trial by jury in *criminal cases*. Here the qualifications of jurors do not differ from those required in civil cases. But the law, with a view to prevent the undue influence of the government in the selection of jurors, and the undue prejudices arising from public opinion, has thrown additional guards round the party accused. He is not only entitled to be tried by good and lawful men, of the neighborhood where the crime is alleged to have been committed, but to be confronted with the witnesses, and to have, in capital cases, some privileges, which are not allowed either in civil cases or in offences of a subordinate character. And, in the first place, the right of challenge, which, though it exists for many purposes in civil trials, is of far more consequence and extent in criminal trials. A challenge is, properly speaking, an objection or exception to a juror, or to the whole jury, as incompetent to sit in a trial. It is of two sorts: the first is a challenge to the array, or an exception to the whole panel or list of jurors, as they are arrayed or set in order by the sheriff in his return. And it may be taken on account of the partiality of the sheriff, when he selects the jury, or of some default, omission or illegality of himself or of some other officer or functionary concerned in arraying or returning the panel. These exceptions are, or may be, various in their nature and extent, in different states; and the particular exceptions, at the common law alone, would not, independently of those provided for or disallowed by statute, be very instructive. This challenge may be either for a principal cause or to the favor, the former of which is founded upon positive proof or presumption of impropriety; the, latter is founded upon less strong presumption or suspicion, and therefore properly to be inquired into, or to be decided by the sound discretion of the triers. Secondly, the other sort of challenge (which also may be for a principal cause or to the favor) is a challenge to the polls, that is, an exception to particular jurors, answering in some degree to the *recusatio judicis* of the civil and canon law. Challenges to the polls, at common law, have been reduced to four sorts:

1. Challenge *propter honoris respectum*, or in respect to nobility; as, if a lord or peer of the realm in England be empanneled on a jury, he may be challenged by either party, or may challenge himself. This cause, of course, does not exist in the U. States, where we have no nobility.

2. Challenge *propter defectum*, or for want of proper qualifications; as if a person be an alien or a slave; or in cases where he is required to be a freeholder, if he is not such; or is not of a suitable age, as a minor; or is a female, for females are not allowed to be jurors; or is convict of an infamous crime, or is otherwise disqualified.

3. Challenge *propter affectum*, for suspicion of bias or partiality. This may be a principal challenge, or to the favor. It is a principal challenge, as has been already stated, when there is pregnant proof or presumption of partiality or of malice, as that a juror is of kindred to either party (at the common law, in the ninth degree); that he has already

prejudged the cause, as an arbitrator; that he has an interest in the cause; that he has taken money for his verdict; that he has formerly, as a juror, tried the same cause; that he is the servant, master, attorney or counsel of one of the parties. A challenge to the polls for favor (which supposes a doubt of impartiality) is where the party has no principal cause of challenge, but has suspicion of favor, and offers circumstances in support of such suspicion. In such a case, the validity of the objection is, by the common law, left to the determination of *triers*, whose office it is to decide whether the juror who is objected to is favorable or unfavorable, or, rather, whether he stand indifferent between the parties. The triers, in case the first man called as a juror is challenged, are two indifferent persons, named by the court; and if they try one man, and find him indifferent, he is sworn, and then he and the two first triers try the next who is objected to; and when a second is found indifferent, those two who are sworn as jurors become the triers of all the others who are objected to, in lieu of the two triers first chosen. This course of proceeding is still common in England and in several of the U. States. But in other of the states, the usual course is for the court to decide upon the indifferency of the persons objected to as jurors.

4. Challenge *propter delictum*, or on account of some crime, of which the person called as a juror has been guilty, and which imports a disability and discredit as a juror. This applies to cases of a capital nature, and other infamous crimes, such as treason, felony, perjury, conspiracy, and other species of the *crimen falsi*. A person called as a juror may be called to say the truth (whence lie is said to be interrogated *voir dire*, *veritatem dicere*) in respect to such causes of challenge as are not to his discredit or dishonor; but he cannot be called upon to acknowledge himself guilty of any crime, or other thing which renders him infamous. These are all the causes, strictly speaking, of challenge by the parties. But many persons are entitled to be excused

from serving on juries, and, on this account, may plead the excuse for themselves, though the parties may not take the exception. Among these are magistrates, aged persons, and person holding particular offices, and others haying special exemptions. The challenges above mentioned equally apply to civil and criminal cases. But in favor of life, in capital trials, the accused is indulged the privilege of challenging a certain number of persons, called as jurors, without assigning any cause; and this privilege is thence called the right of *peremptory* challenge. This is a provision founded in great humanity and tenderness towards persons capitally accused. The reasons commonly assigned for it are,

1. that every person is liable to strong dislikes and prejudices, in respect to particular persons, merely from their appearance, manners and gestures, although they are strangers to him, and that even a caprice or feeling of this kind may, in the course of the trial, embarrass the party in his defence;

2. that upon a challenge for cause shown, the reason may prove insufficient, and, if the party had no right of peremptory challenge, he might be tried by a juror who, from the very circumstance of being objected to, might conceive a prejudice against the accused. On these accounts, he is at liberty to challenge the juror peremptorily, after he has, for an insufficient reason, challenged him for cause; and, as the object of all trials is to allow a fair and full defence, the accused ought, at least, to have his wishes consulted so far as to exclude those whom he distrusts in the first instance. But as it is obvious that the right of peremptory challenge, if not limited by some known boundary, might forever prevent a trial, the law has fixed a definite number, to which the party is confined. The common law fixed this number at 35, or one short of three full juries; and that still remains the rule in all trials for treason. But in other capital offences, the right is now generally restrained, by statute, to 20, both in England and America.

If a person attempts to challenge beyond this number, his challenge is disregarded. If, by reason of peremptory or other challenges, a sufficient number of jurors are not found, talesmen are appointed, as in civil cases. If several persons are tried at the same time, upon one indictment, each one is entitled to his full number of challenges, and one may challenge a juror not objected to by the others, and he must be excluded altogether; for every juryman must be above any objection by any of the persons tried. We have thus far treated of challenges by the party accused. The government has, strictly, no right to challenge, except for cause shown; but for cause shown the government may either challenge the array, or the polls, in the same manner as a private person. However, it is usual, at least in England, if a juror is objected to by the government, not to call upon the government to show cause until the panel is gone through, and then, if sufficient jurors are not found and sworn, the cause of the challenge may be inquired into; for, if there is a full jury without the persons objected to by the government, there is no strong reason to insist upon their being sworn, although no good cause has been showing. There are some other provisions favorable to prisoners accused of capital offences, and especially of political offences, which deserve notice. In England, in cases of treason, the prisoner is entitled to a copy of the indictment five days before his arraignment for trial, and a copy of the panel of jurors who are summoned, and their professions and places of abode, ten days before his trial, and a list of the names of the witnesses to be produced against him, the like length of time before the trial. He is also entitled, at the expense of the government, to have witnesses summoned in his behalf; to establish his defence, and to have counsel assigned to assist him in his defence. In America, in cases of treason, similar provisions in substance exist, with a difference only in respect to the length of time allowed for the copy of the indictment, and lists of jurors and witnesses.

And in many of the states, an equally humane provision exists in respect to all other capital offences. By the laws of the U. States, the prisoner is entitled to have counsel assigned to him, and to have his witnesses summoned at the expense of the government, in all capital cases. In cases of treason, a copy of the indictment is required to be delivered three days before the arraignment, and also a copy of the list of jurors and witnesses summoned by the government, three days before his trial. In other capital cases, the time is two days, instead of three. The right to employ counsel in defence, is also secured to all persons accused of any crimes in the U. States. But in England, it is confined to cases of treason, and to mere misdemeanors. In capital cases, not of treason, counsel are not permitted to be employed in England, except in arguing questions of law. The quaint and unsatisfactory reason given for this exclusion is, that the judges are counsel for the prisoner,—a reason which, if good in any, is sufficient in all cases. But there is more of speciousness than of truth in the remark; for, though the judges ought to take care that the prisoner has a fair and impartial trial it is impossible that they can act as counsel for the prisoner exclusively; and the importance of counsel, exclusively for the prisoner, is admitted in all cases of treason. Why not equally so in other capital cases? Such is a very general outline of the trial by jury under the common law. It is deemed of immense value in England, and among the dearest rights of the people. In America, it is quite as dear, and is deemed of such high importance, that the right to a trial by jury, in all criminal cases, is secured by the constitution of every state in the Union, and is also provided for, in all civil cases at common law, where the amount in controversy is of any considerable value. The constitution of the U. States has provided, "that the trial of all crimes, except in cases of impeachment, shall be by jury; and such trial shall be had in the state where the said crimes shall have been committed. But when not committed within any state, the trial shall be at such place or places as the congress may by law have directed." And farther, "that no person shall be convicted of treason, unless on the testimony of two witnesses to the sane overt act, or on confession in open court." And again, "that no person shall be held to answer for a capital or otherwise infamous crime, unless on a presentment or indictment of a grand jury, except in cases arising in the land or naval forces, or in the militia when in actual service in time of war or public danger. Nor shall any person be subject, for the same offence, to, be twice put in jeopardy of life or limb; nor shall he be compelled, in any, criminal case, to be a witness against himself, nor be deprived of life, liberty, or property, without due process of law." And again, "that in all criminal prosecutions, the accused shall enjoy the right to a speedy and public trial, by an impartial jury of the state and district wherein the crime shall have been committed, which district shall have been previously ascertained by law; and to be informed of the nature and cause of the accusation; to be confronted with the witnesses against him; to have compulsory process for obtaining witnesses in his favor, and to have the assistance of counsel for his defence." And again, "that in suits at common law, where the value in controversy shall exceed twenty dollars, the right of a trial by jury shall be preserved; and no fact, once tried by a jury, shall be otherwise reexamined in any court of the U. States than according to the rules of the common law." Provisions of a similar nature, in substance, will be found in most, if not in all, the state constitutions of the Union. They demonstrate the extreme jealousy of the people of the right of trial by jury, and their extreme solicitude to place it beyond the reach of the passions, and prejudices, and political objects, of those who, as rulers, may be called at any time to administer the government. This strong attachment to the trial by jury, both in England and America, after the experience of it for centuries, furnishes no small argument in favor of its efficacy as a security of right, and a redress of wrongs. It is perpetually spoken of as the palladium of our public rights and liberties; and in all the various fluctuations of public opinions, it has remained untouched and unsuspected. It is not surprising that those, who know it only in theory, or who at present see the administration of its powers and duties in a very imperfect state in the civil law countries, or who are accustomed to a jurisprudence foreign to its principles, should entertain doubts of its advantages, and should feel a deep sense of its defects. The first part of this article shows how difficult it has been found to transfer to France the trial by jury, and to administer it with the same beneficial effects as in England. The errors in France may have resulted, in part, from the imperfect knowledge of the courts, as well as of the juries, from the novelty of this mode of trial, and their want of experience in the management of it. Perhaps, too, there may be something in the other institutions of France, or in the temperament and character of the people, which may disturb its proper operation. It may be useful for us, before concluding this article, to review some of the grounds on which the trial by jury has been hitherto vindicated, and to glance at some of the defects which it is supposed to involve, as well as at some of the objections to which it is supposed to be liable—*Fas est et ab hoste doceri.* And, in the first place, it is not necessary to contend that, as an instrument of public or private justice, it is an institution absolutely perfect; that it is incapable of abuse; or that it never occasions error. That would be to require of it what belongs to no human institution whatsoever. Every work of man is, by his very nature, imperfect. Every form of government involves some inconveniences, and errors, and abuses. Every effort to administer justice must necessarily fall short of perfect correctness, from defects of evidence, from the infirmity of judges, from the wrong biases of human opinion, from errors in reasoning, from ignorance, and passion, and prejudice, independently of all intentional wrong, or corrupt motives, or malice, or dishonesty, or deliberate baseness. The only question is, what, on the whole, is the best means of administering justice, taking human nature as it is, and human infirmity as it must ever operate. If crimes are to be tried and punished, if rights are to be enforced and wrongs redressed by judicial tribunals, what is the best structure of the institution for the purpose of trial and decision? There seems to be but a narrow circle of means, out of which, the choice is to be made. Shall the tribunal be composed of executive officers of the government, or of judges appointed by the government for each case, or of judges holding their office at the pleasure of the government? Or shall the tribunal be composed of judges holding their offices permanently, and independently of the government? Or shall the tribunal be composed of jurors chosen at large, *pro hac vice*, or chosen permanently for that duty, without any previous qualifications of legal experience, learning or superior ability? And if so, by whom, and in what manner, shall they be chosen? Or shall the tribunal be of a mixed character, composed of judges learned in the law, permanent in rank and station, and of jurors selected for the occasion in an impartial manner, and the trial be had before the judges expounding the law, and the juries deciding the facts? In cases of crimes, the object is to protect the innocent and to punish the guilty. Where does the danger chiefly arise? In political accusations, the government not only is a party, but has a strong motive to produce conviction. In other cases, it may not have so strong a motive, but it may be subject to influences of an equally fatal character. If the king or other executive, or officers selected by him for that purpose *pro hac vice*, are to decide upon the guilt or innocence of the party, according to their own discretion and such proofs as are satisfactory to themselves, there is no security whatsoever against unjust convictions. The decision will be arbitrary, and according to the will of the prince or his favorites, or according to state policy, or perhaps public prejudice, actuated by strong resentment. If the trial be by judges solely appointed by the government, and holding their offices permanently, there may be dangers arising from other and different sources, from their political opinions, from their state interests, from their irresponsibility to public opinion, and from influences of character and profession, which insensibly warp the judgment. If the trial be by permanent jurors, there will be still greater dangers from their want of the proper learning, and general weight of character, added to the other objections. So that any of the proposed substitutes does not furnish more safety or certainty, in the administration of criminal justice, than that of a trial by jury. On the other hand, the trial by jury, as known to the common law, affords some checks upon arbitrary power, and enlists many just feelings and reasonable guards against oppression.

1. The jurors are selected from the mass of intelligent citizens, of suitable qualifications, and of the same rank, and having the same general interests, as the accused. They are not permanently employed, and have no common connexion with each other, and no habits of fixed cooperation. They are, or may be, strangers to each other, and to the accused, until the moment when they are enpanneled. They are subject to no reasonable exception, either in point of character or influence, for that would exclude them, at the will of the accused. They are subject to the same laws, and liable to the same prosecution, as the party on trial, and therefore have a natural tendency to sympathize with him.

2. The trial is had in open court, before judges who hold their offices permanently, and who are bound to administer the law, and to give their opinions publicly to the jury. From the moment that they are empanneled, they are

excluded from all intercourse with every person except what takes place in open court; and their subsequent deliberations are private and secret.

3. They are under oath to decide the case upon the evidence given in open court. No testimony can be heard by them, except what is admitted and delivered in open court; so that the court, the counsel, and the bystanders, have a perfect knowledge of every part of it. Thus the whole public become the ultimate judges of the sincerity and justice of their verdict.

4. If they find a verdict against the party, and there has been any error of law or fact, or any misconduct in the jury, the court will grant a new trial; but if they acquit him, there can be no new trial, for the law will not allow a man to be twice put on trial for the same offence, and thus his life, liberty or limb be put in jeopardy. Here we see the humanity of the common law, which leans in favor of the accused, and disables the government from practising oppression upon any citizen, by successive vindictive prosecutions.

5. Again, if the evidence is doubtful, the party is entitled to an acquittal, and the court will so direct the jury; for the common law will not tolerate that any man should be punished, unless there be satisfactory proofs of guilt to the minds of 12 of his peers or equals.

6. It has been said that the facts are often complicated, and the guilt is compounded partly of facts and partly of law. This is true; but here again the wisdom of the common law has provided that the judges shall state to the jury what the law is, as applicable to the various postures of the facts, as they may find them. They are also generally assisted by the arguments of the counsel on each side, in arranging and comparing the facts; and the judge, in his summing up of

the evidence, brings the whole in review, and points out to them the bearings of every part, and strips off the false glosses, if any, which have been made by counsel. But he still leaves them to decide upon it according to their own conscientious belief of it.

7. It is said that the arguments of counsel may deceive them, and blind them to the truth. But the answer is, that they have an equal opportunity to hear the opposite side. and that, generally, the judges assist them, when there is any attempt to misstate the evidence, by referring to their own notes of it, as given in open court. And from long habits, and experience in human life, jurymen learn to disregard the mere efforts of eloquence, and, under a sense of their religious and social obligations, consult the real truth and justice of the case. Would there be more security if no counsel were allowed? No person will say so.

8. It is also said that the judges may have an undue influence with the jury. This is certainly possible, and has actually occurred in corrupt times. In the case of chief-justice Jeffreys, referred to in the preceding part of the article, it should be remembered that he held his office during the pleasure of the crown, and not, as the judges of England now hold, during good behavior, or life. He was a devoted partisan of the crown, and has become infamous by his corrupt administration of the law. But it should be considered, that the jury could scarcely have been free from improper biases of some sort, otherwise they could not have found a verdict against the accused. In our day, and, indeed, at any time since the arbitrary times of king James II and the revolution of 1688, such conduct in a judge would be sure to meet with universal reprobation, and would generally produce an acquittal of the prisoner, and a public impeachment of the judge. Nay, it is well known, that such is the jealousy of juries in this particular, that any undue

interference or solicitude for conviction, exhibited on the part of a judge, would destroy his influence, and produce an opposite verdict. It is his supposed impartiality that gives weight to his opinion; and the jury knows that they have a right to disregard it, if they please.

9. It is said, that juries may be influenced by improper motives, and sometimes disregard the law, and give a false verdict. This is possible, and, indeed, has probably sometimes happened. But the occasions are rare; and where there is a suspicion of that sort, it always injures the character of the jurymen, and subjects them to public scorn and odium. Generally, juries are scrupulous in respecting the law, because it is the only protection of their own rights. Where the law is very harsh, and the punishment is disproportioned to the offence, they have sometimes exhibited a repugnancy to convict; but they rarely have acquitted the party, unless there were circumstances of great doubt, or of great mitigation; and if their conduct, in such cases, is not strictly justifiable, it is generally not such as produces any reproach, either from the court or the public. These occasions, however, are rare, and constitute exceptions of no great moment in the general administration of justice.

10. It is not true, as is sometimes supposed, that juries are ready to convict on slight proofs, or insufficient evidence. Our law declares, on the contrary, that in such cases they ought to acquit the party; and it is always laid down to the jury by the court. Indeed, the judges, in this respect, always act as counsel for the prisoners, and give their advice to the jury, in respect to every reasonable doubt in the evidence. There are so many checks upon juries, in cases of this sort, that it can scarcely happen, that an unjust conviction, at least by the improper bias of the jury, can take place. If there be any error, it is usually on the side of mercy.

11. It is objected, that the jury sometimes find the party guilty of a part, and not of the whole offence, as of manslaughter when he is accused of murder. Certainly the jury do so; and for the best reason, that the law requires it. A jury ought not to find a man guilty of the whole of a charge, unless it is wholly proved. If what is proved amounts to a crime of the same nature, but of inferior enormity, or more mitigated than what is charged, they find their verdict according to the proofs, and the court inflict only the moderated punishment. And any other course would be flagrant injustice. But a jury cannot, upon a trial for one offence, find a man guilty of another offence, not of the nature of the one charged; for instance, upon a charge of murder, they cannot find him guilty of forgery; but if he is charged with stealing two watches, they may find him guilty of stealing one only.

12. It is also objected, that juries often favor criminals. But this is not generally true, except to the extent that the law favors them. There may be cases of a popular cast, or of an odious nature, where juries have occasionally shown improper biases for the accused; but this objection applies to all tribunals, and is founded on human infirmity generally. Juries do not, even in cases of this sort, often depart from their duty; and the exceptions are so few, that they are seldom felt or urged in free governments.

13. But an objection the most pressed by those who are not practically acquainted with the trial by jury, is, that unanimity is required in pronouncing a verdict of acquittal or condemnation. It is true, that no verdict can be received, which has not the assent of all the 12 jurors; and there are no means of compelling an assent; and yet, practically speaking, few cases of disagreement occur, except where there is a solid foundation for real doubts and difficulties. Unanimity is more common than, at first view, might be

suspected. In the first place, the jury reason with each other upon all doubtful points, and if they at first differ, the differences are often removed by further discussion. Pride of opinion is not enlisted on either side, and sometimes each recedes from the first limits of his own opinion. In the next place, the differences of opinion are more often upon inferences and conclusions from known facts than upon the facts themselves; and more often upon doubts as to the proper application of the law to those facts; and still more often upon mere collateral questions, where there is no common standard of measure, as in assessing damages. In criminal cases, fewer difficulties ordinarily arise than in civil cases, because doubts weigh favorably for the accused, and often produce an acquittal. But, after all, there is not probably one in twenty cases, tried by a jury, in which there is a final disagreement; and it is by no means sure, that a decision could be had more just or fair by requiring a majority, or any other number, than by requiring unanimity. The jurors might then be equally divided, or the struggles of the minority to prevent a verdict might be equally violent. Most trials give rise to differences on several points; and, in such cases, the unanimity of a majority, in a general verdict, must be produced in the same manner as unanimity in the whole jury. But the best answer to the objection is, that experience is in favor of requiring unanimity of the whole jury. No practical evil has, as yet, been felt from the rule. And it is no small recommendation of it, that it gives a satisfaction and confidence to the public mind, in England and the U. States, that the decision of a mere majority could scarcely ever give. If unanimity is less easily obtained in France, that proves nothing as to the value of the principle elsewhere. The failure may be from the novelty of the trial in France, or from the habits and character of the people, or from the imperfect comprehension of the proper duties of the judges and the jury.

Most of the remarks above made refer especially to juries of trial in criminal cases; but they are, in a great degree, applicable to civil cases also. It remains only to add, that the other preliminary guards, interposed by the common law in criminal cases, are of inestimable value to every citizen. He cannot be accused, nor be brought to trial, unless upon an indictment found by a grand jury. He is thus saved from prosecutions founded in malice, hatred, political opposition, personal feeling and popular prejudice. The government cannot touch him; the people cannot make him the victim of their jealousy or suspicion. A grand jury of incorruptible and impartial men, who are his equals, must first accuse him, upon the hearing of legal proofs and sworn witnesses, before he can be called to answer for any offence. 12 men, good and true (*probi et legales homines*), must concur in the indictment; and 12 more must concur, upon his trial, in asserting his guilt, before he can be punished. When his guilt is ascertained, the punishment rests, not in the discretion of the king, or of the government, or any mere executive officer; it is to be declared by the judges, before whom he has been tried, or in the same court, according to laws previously passed, and regulating the nature and extent of the punishment. It is not too much; then, to affirm that the trial by jury is justly the boast of England and America; and we may hope that, by the goodness of Providence it may be perpetual.

LIEN

LIEN, in law, in its most usual acceptation, signifies "the right which one person, in certain cases, possesses of detaining property, placed in his possession, belonging to another, until some demand, which the former has, is satisfied." It is, however, not unfrequently used, whenever property, either real or personal, is charged with the payment of any debt or duty, every such charge being styled *a lien on the property*, although the latter be not in the possession of the person to whom the debt or duty is due. This second signification would open too wide a field of discussion. We shall therefore confine ourselves to the explanation of the right of detaining, which is the more technical meaning of the two. Liens are of two kinds:

1. *particular* liens, that is, where the person in possession of goods may detain them until a claim, which accrues to him from those identical goods, is satisfied; and,

2. *general liens*, that is, where the person in possession may detain the goods, not only for his claim accruing from them, but also for the general balance of his account with the owners. Again, some liens are given by the common law, without any agreement between the parties; some are created by express agreement, and some by usage; which latter, indeed, implies an agreement, because, when a man enters into any business, where a particular usage is generally adopted, he is presumed to consent to be bound by that usage, unless, in his dealings with others, he expressly protests against it.

I. The common law gives a lien to the person in possession of goods in three instances:

1. When the common law compels the members of any particular trade or business, without any option on their

part, to accept employment from every person who is willing to pay a reasonable compensation, in recompense for the burden which it thus throws upon them, it allows them to detain such goods as are delivered to them in the course of their business, until the owner has satisfied any debt which may have arisen out of the transaction in which the goods were so delivered. Innkeepers, common carriers and farriers are entitled to this species of lien; for instance, the proprietor of a coach need not give up a parcel until the carriage of it be paid for.

2. When goods are delivered to a tradesman, or any other, to expend his labor upon, he is entitled to detain those goods until he is remunerated for the labor which he so expends. Thus a tailor is not obliged to take a customer's cloth and make it into a coat, but, if he consents to make the coat, the customer cannot compel him to deliver it until he is paid for the making. The first kind seems to be included in the second, but they are kept distinct, because it is supposed that the first was, at one time, the only species of lien allowed by the common law, and that the second was a subsequent invention, adopted on equitable considerations in limitation of it.

3. When goods have been saved from the perils of the sea, the salvor may detain them until his claim for salvage is satisfied; but the finder of goods has in no other case a lien on the goods found, in respect of the trouble and expense to which the finding and preserving of them may have subjected him. All these are particular liens; and, therefore, the coach proprietor may not detain the parcel, nor may the tailor detain the coat, nor the salvor the property saved, until payment of the carriage of a former parcel, or of the price of another coat, or of salvage which accrued for saving other goods. Another rule with regard to particular liens is, that they exist only so long as the possession of

the goods is retained by the person who has the lien. If he once deliver up the goods to the owner, he waves his lien, which is thereby so effectually annihilated, that it will not be revived, even if the same goods, should afterwards return into his possession. Thus, if the tailor deliver the coat, and it is afterwards sent to him to be mended, he cannot then detain it as a security for the original price, but only for the cost of mending. His remedy to recover the price must be by a suit at law and we may here remark, that a creditor can never prejudice his right of maintaining an action for his demand, by insisting on his right of detaining the goods, for the action and the lien are concurrent rights and do not interfere with each other.

II. General liens are only created by express agreement, or by usage. It ha been determined, that attorneys and solicitors, bankers, factors and brokers, insurance-brokers, and some others, are, by the custom of their respective trades and professions, entitled to a lien on the property of their clients, customers and employers, for the general balance of their accounts. Thus an attorney may detain papers which have been delivered to him to assist in the conducting of one cause, as a security for the costs of another; and, if he return them to his client, and they come again into his possession, his lien revives; for, in the case of a general lien, it matters not whether the same or different papers are delivered to the person employed, his right of detaining being the same in both instances.

LAW, LEGISLATION, CODES

[The interest now felt in law and legal reforms must be our apology for the length of the present article. As we have thought that the views entertained respecting legislation and jurisprudence by the civilians on the continent of Europe might be not uninteresting to our readers, the article which treats of them in the *Conversations-Lexikon* has been translated, and forms the first part of the present article, extending as far as the break on page 207. The remainder, giving the common law view of the subject, and treating particularly of codification, is by an eminent American jurist.]

1. Laws are the very soul of a people; not merely those which are contained in the letter of their ordinances and statute books, but still more those which have grown up of themselves from their manners, and religion, and history. Several modern jurists, as John G. Schlosser and Hugo, have shown how little, in legislation, caprice can prevail over the silent but irresistible influence of public opinion. And even the authors of the Code Napoleon have said, with no less elegance than truth, that no legislator can escape that invisible power, that silent judgment of the people, which tends to correct the mistakes of arbitrary legislation, and to defend the people from the law, and the lawgiver from himself. Frequent experiments have shown that laws, at variance with the manners and religious views of a people, cannot be forced upon them, however well meant, and however beneficial may have been their influence upon other nations; and that, by means of laws, a legislator can no more elevate his countrymen to a higher degree of refinement, without passing through the intervening steps, than he can reduce them again to a condition above which they have risen in the natural course of events. Hence Frederic II of Prussia was more happy in his reforms than

Joseph II. For it was by no means the intention of the Prussian legislator to give his subjects a new system of law, but rather to sanction that which they already possessed; to adapt the letter of the ancient laws to the notions of right which had gained a footing in the spirit of the nation, and, above all, to remove those uncertainties which had necessarily sprung from the use of a foreign code, which had checked improvement in practice. Indeed, it is not the duty of a skilful legislator to create new laws; but only to develop those which existed prior to any express recognition, and to introduce, with prudence, those positive rules which cannot be deduced from general principles; as the determination of the length of minority, the period of superannuation, the amount of punishments, &c.; in which the principles of natural right are reduced to a practical application. To the province of the practical legislator belong also those forms which are required in the application of legal principles; as the formalities of contracts and of judicial processes, and the rules of evidence, in all which it should be kept in mind that these positive institutions do not, of themselves, constitute law, but are the mere mechanism to facilitate the use of it. They should be viewed only as the means of promoting a higher end. The view of the original ground of laws is a point on which not only the schools of European jurists differ, but on which the most important principles of public law come into collision.

2. The schools of modern jurisconsults may be reduced, in reference to their Principal characteristics, to four, although these are variously modified, and, in many respects, run into one another. In the last century, with few exceptions, the practical school predominated, which, on the one hand, esteemed the authority of courts and individual jurists higher than the law, and, on the other, was influenced, in an important degree, by philosophy, particularly that of Leibnitz and Wolf. Arguments were, for the

most part, drawn with great logical precision, from the nature of the case. The members of this school felt themselves justified in departing from the letter of the written law, either whenever it seemed not adapted to the existing case, or reference could be made to the decisions of courts on the same point. By this school were introduced a multitude of new opinions, supposed equities, and milder punishments; and their fundamental views were not altogether erroneous. They proceeded on the true notion, that the laws of a people are the result of its own peculiar character, and must take their cue from this. They tried to help the letter of the old laws by deductions from the nature of things, and, by adhering to precedents, to attain to that harmony in the administration of justice, which alone can secure the public confidence. The influence exerted by this school on the legislation of the eighteenth century was very great, particularly through Nettelbladt and Daries; and the code of Prussia, in particular, may be considered as its work. But it wanted a proper system of judicial tribunals, to prevent that fluctuation in practice, in consequence of which all certainty, in regard to law, was lost, so that the result of the decision of the simplest cause could hardly be conjectured beforehand. The practical school was divided again into two parties, which agreed only in this, that the jurisconsults, or the judges, might look beyond positive law; but were opposed to each other in so far that one party recognised nothing but the authority of some favorite casuist, and the usage of courts; the other regarded natural right, and what they called *reasonableness*, as the basis of all their decisions. The former almost always carried the day; for it often happened that the latter opposed them only till they had become familiar with the routine of practice, and felt themselves at home in it. In the last 10 years of the eighteenth century, new views suggested themselves to the *philosophical* jurists. A more perfect and living philosophy had examined afresh the foundations of science. Many a fabric was shattered, which had preserved the appearance of soundness only in consequence of negligence. At the same time, society took a new turn, and every thing seemed aiming at an ideal perfection. All former obstructions in the way of legal reform appeared to be set aside. France became a republican state, and the doctrines of natural right were introduced into practice. But things have changed again, so that philosophical law has made but little advance, and has gained but little influence in courts of justice. Philosophical treatises, however, have appeared on some departments; as on criminal law, on civil process, and particularly on public and ecclesiastical law. But such works can have no real value without a profound and accurate treatment of positive law, and have, therefore, produced but little effect. The difference of opinion, in the two parties above-mentioned, has been of practical importance only on one occasion, viz. when it was proposed to prepare new bodies of law for Germany, or to take from the French legislation (which deserves so much respect in regard to public law), the rules of civil and penal law, and the forms of procedure. This plan presupposed that a code might be formed on purely philosophical principles, which, being adapted to mankind in general, would suit all nations and all times, and become the basis and essence of every other. Corrections might be made in this groundwork by degrees, as the development of the science of law pointed out deviations from the requisitions of natural justice; and the peculiarities of the legislation of each people might be added. For even those who believed that all positive legislation was based on a foundation so unalterable and eternal, could not help seeing that the additions to be made, for the purposes of practical application, must be drawn from empirical premises, which were neither suited to all people, nor constant to any given people; so that such a code, drawn from natural law, must still leave a wide field for positive legislation. This view was taken, particularly in considering the value of the French codes, the adoption of which, in Germany, had been recommended. It was inquired whether the civil code of Napoleon had solved the great problem of how to establish a code based on natural justice, and capable of so universal application as to be equally adapted to people living on the Vistula and the Seine, on the Elbe, and Po, and Tiber. It was soon perceived that the Code Napoléon did not reach this ideal. On this occasion, the contest between the philosophical and historical jurisprudence came up, which was afterwards particularly revived by Savigny's *Vom Beruf unserer Zeit zur Gesetzgebung*, 1815 (the Call for Codification in our Times). The peculiar characteristic of this third school of modern jurists —the *historical*—is, that they regard no legal principles as capable of universal and unconditional application. They view law as a mere result of the accidental relations of a people, and as changing with them. According to the principles of this school, every thing may be right, even slavery and many other things, which the philosophical school declares to be a violation of the universal rights of man, and absolutely wrong. The historical school allows a very narrow sphere to that legislation in which law is based on the will of the law giver, and a very large one, on the contrary, to the customary law, which commences and perpetuates itself by popular usage, and the decisions of courts. Its ideal is the Roman law, as it is presented in the writings of jurists before Justinian. Every innovation in the law, on the part of government, it regards as dangerous; and especially new codes, which interrupt the silent growth of legal rules in a country. So far, this school agrees with the views of the practical school above-mentioned, from which, in fact, it originated. But it rejects all reasons deduced from a supposed nature of things (or, indeed, from philosophical opinions of right), and derives existing law, not from the decisions of courts and colleges, in which it perceives many glaring errors, but from ancient laws and law-books. It regards as truly right, not what modern times have recognised and followed as right, but what they would have esteemed right, if they had properly understood the ancient sources; and therefore considers that all improvement must be the result of a thorough examination of history. Notwithstanding the manifest inconsistency of this reasoning,—since, if the system of law, in any country, is formed by self-development, the newest shape is always the only one that ought to be recognised, and the present cannot be explained from the past,—this view has met with much acceptance, since it avers that whatever is, is right, from the very fact that it is; and in history, by which almost any principle may be proved or refuted at pleasure, it finds a means of crushing every desire of reform but it is most favored because it declares all efforts for something higher to be both foolish and wrong. This view, however, has, doubtless, already reached its acme. It has the merit of having directed to the only successful way of understanding laws by the aid of history; but the erroneous expectation cannot long be maintained, of discovering what should be, from knowing what is, and how that which is, grew up. For, although we may be set in the right way by history, yet nothing but philosophy can direct us to the proper end. History and philosophy supply each other's defects, and either of them, by itself, leads to partial views. It is only together that they can teach us the true science of law, and impart the wisdom requisite for legislation. A fourth view has been advanced, in modern times, which may be termed the *strict judicial* (*legistic*). Justly offended at the authority over the laws assumed by the practical school, and the uncertainty which had resulted from the fluctuations of their practice, impatient of the toilsome researches of a historical jurisprudence, and convinced that the philosophical school could afford materials to the legislator only, and not to the judge, a respectable number of jurists abandoned the authority of existing practice, and returned to the positive laws, though less to the spirit of them than the letter, and frequently to the letter of those laws of which the existence was scarcely known among the people. Much has been said of the injury which attends a sudden change of the laws, by introducing a new code. But, if the object of such a code is to confirm and sanction the ideas of right already prevalent among a people, it can never bring with it consequences so pernicious as followed the calling up from oblivion, and adopting into use, of antiquated laws, Roman forms and subtleties, and the cruel penal laws of the sixteenth century. In case of the literal application of these old laws, no regard can be paid to the circumstances of the age or to the peculiar character of the particular ordinances; and, in consequence of the incompleteness and want of technical accuracy in the ancient legislation, the laws of the empire, the old and new ordinances of particular countries, papal ordinances, Roman constitutions, and fragments of legal writers, are unavoidably mixed up in the most embarrassing confusion, to form a mosaic, which has the outward appearance of an organized whole, but is wholly destitute of inward, living energy. The historical school is right in maintaining that laws can be properly comprehended only by an historical examination of their development; but it has fallen into the error of the *legistic* school, in asserting that the deficiencies which are found in every positive institution should be supplied, not from the fountain of all right, but either by the aid of historical hypotheses, which attribute the most artificial systems to nations in the early periods of civilization, or by heterogeneous additions from wholly different systems of legislation. In so doing, the historical school have particularly forgotten that the objects of their veneration, the juridical classics of Rome, owed their greatness to a perpetual habit of reverting to the maxims of natural law (their *æquitas*). Even the Roman lawyers recognised a universal right, which exists prior to all positive legislation, and without it, and, at the same time, in and with it the rule of conduct wherever the precepts of positive law have not yet reached. There is an important difference between a maxim of law created by a positive ordinance, and one only acknowledged by it as already existing in natural equity. In the first case, the law cannot extend beyond the immediate object, of its creation: in the second, it is of universal application. Of special importance is this distinction in deciding concerning relations and acts without the bounds of a state,—for example, a crime committed abroad,—cases in which positive law has a very limited application. But, however narrow the last-mentioned legistic view may be, it has effected much good, by bringing to light the imperfection, and, in some senses, the utter worthlessness, of the existing positive law, and thus aided to promote the reform, which, in several German states, is so necessary.

3. If the question should arise, From what public organ the improvement of laws should proceed, it may be answered, The various juridical theories exhibit a great practical difference. But, at least, the two principal parties—the historical and philosophical—are perfectly agreed in the opinion, that mere caprice, which sees in laws only a means of promoting its own favorite ends, should be, as far as possible, excluded and it is also agreed, that legislation is an office with which neither the judiciary nor the executive departments can be concerned, without injury to each of them. Nothing can defend men from the arbitrary exercise of power but a separation of the executive, legislative and judicial authorities; for in no other way can each of these three powers be kept within its natural limits. The great discrepancy, both in the intrinsic nature of these powers, and in the character of their results, makes it important that each of them should be administered by a separate organ. To govern is the business of the state. The executive government is the organ of the people's will. The character-

istic of its acts is command. Such commands, however, are not irrevocable, for, at any moment, they may be repealed. Opinions contrary to them may be advanced; and, if they encroach on previous rights, the aid of courts may be enlisted in opposition to them. Law, on the contrary,—and, on this point, the philosophical and historical jurisprudence agree,—is founded, not upon any will, but on the discovery of a right already existing, which is to be drawn either from the internal legislation of human reason, or the historical development of the nation. The law, too, is not irrevocable, nor can any sanction make it so; but, as long as it exists, it is of irresistible and universal force. Finally, the judicial decision is binding only on those who have occasioned its application by resorting to judicial proceedings; but, for such, it is an unchangeable rule, and no power whatever can subvert it. The different character of these public functions must not only be obvious in their external forms, so as to be understood by every one who would know his duty, but the very nature of the provisions which they require for their operation is so different as to furnish sufficient ground for making the executive, legislative and judicial departments distinct in their organization. But it is a great error of modern (constitutional) politics, that they have conceived of this division of duties, as if all connexion and mutual influence of the three powers must be done away; hence the election of judges by the people, and a legislation which could be neither urged nor restrained by the executive (no veto, or only a limited one). This very naturally produced political dissensions, which could only end in the ruin of the state. But, if the executive power is what it ought to be, nothing can be done in the commonwealth without its orders; and both the legislative and judiciary departments must receive from it the impulse of their activity. The convocation of the legislative body, and the proposal of laws, belong to it; and without its consent, no law can become obligatory upon the people. The execution and promulgation of the laws necessarily rest with the executive, and are necessarily joined with an unlimited veto. On the other hand, the influence of the executive government on the legislative should be merely a negative influence, and on the administration of justice, a formal one; i.e. no law should be passed without its consent, and the judges should receive their offices from the executive, while the executive is to see that they do their duty; but how they shall speak cannot be prescribed to them. (See *Courts*.) This is the only means by which unity and harmony, in the action of the public authorities, can be maintained, while every branch of power is supported by the other, and kept in the right path. The entire separation of these three powers is an error which, wherever it has existed, in ancient or modern times, has brought upon the people as great sufferings as if they had been subject to an arbitrary and unlimited dominion.

4. The historico-philosophical view of the sources of laws leads us to results concerning the organization of the legislative authorities, which, it is to be regretted, have been often too much overlooked. The consequence of the unreasonable notion, that legislation is an act of the will, was an idea that the general will of the people might be ascertained, if all the different interests to be found in the people could be brought together; or, as this is, in fact, impossible, it was considered sufficient to unite, in representative assemblies, the most important interests—those of agriculture, commerce and manufactures. In respect to the administration of government, and the judicious choice of means to promote the high ends of the state, this sort of representation may be found sufficient. But, when the question is respecting the establishment of laws, in the highest sense of the word, the most comprehensive intelligence is required. A popular representation, for this purpose, should not represent the fluctuating, capricious will of the people,

influenced, as it is, by interest, prejudice and passion. On the contrary, it should be a mirror to reflect all the intellectual power of the nation, consequently the representatives should be chosen from the most learned, and enlightened, and experienced men, who have the best opportunity to become acquainted with the wants of the people and the defects of the existing laws. That it cannot be concluded that a man possesses these qualifications, because he owns a piece of ground, is very clear. And it is equally manifest, that it is a great mistake to esteem such a possession a security for good intentions. Disinterestedness is no consequence of wealth, but of the habit of self denial; and he learns it much more perfectly who has been inured to it from his youth, than one who has, perhaps, never known a want. To regard landed proprietors as the proper citizens, and others as mere tolerated tenants of the state, is an absurdity. Landed property is the offspring of the state, and not *vice versa*; and the state cannot so distribute the soil, that it may depend on the will of the owner to deprive others of the means of subsistence. The more a natural, distinct interest separates landed proprietors, and, indeed, in some sense, the cultivators of the soil also, from the rest of the community, the more should it be made a main object of public institutions to prevent one party from gaining a decided and permanent superiority. But political institutions now have frequently the opposite tendency—a circumstance which, in some places, has had a remarkable influence on taxation. The second consequence, resulting from the view of legislation here proposed, is, that the number of representatives needs not be proportionate to the number of the people. In a large state, a larger number of deputies is not needed to represent the intellectual capacity of the people; and a small state, if it regards the ends of legislation, properly needs as many persons in its representative assembly as the larger. For it should comprehend so many different kinds of knowledge and talent, that no subject may arise on which a judicious decision cannot be made by the body, by the aid of persons within itself; and that the laws may all have the stamp of moderation, arising from due attention to all interests, which often leads, though by no means necessarily, to half measures. This is the greatest difficulty for smaller states, and they can only prevent it by accommodating their legislation to that of their neighbors. The management of the public affairs of communities, from the village up to the state, cannot be called legislation, in the sense in which we are now considering the subject: these may be suitably administered by even the smallest state. But if a small state undertakes to establish a peculiar system of civil rights, of legal procedure, of penal laws, &c., it will receive less advantage from such an insulated system than of injury, from the bars to intercourse with its neighbors, which must result from such institutions. Hence it is altogether desirable that, in states which are only minor divisions of one nation, having the same religion, manners and cultivation, the municipal laws, and the institutions for their administration, should, as far as possible, be made common to the whole, although matters of political administration might be kept distinct. Thus they might secure to themselves the advantages enjoyed by larger states, in the preparation of like laws by experienced colleges (as the French council), or by juridical commissions, so as to be accommodated to all the existing institutions. Representative assemblies would be freed from the embarrassment of deliberating and deciding upon topics, of which perhaps few, perhaps not a man among them, has any knowledge. But this is not to be observed in small states only: very large ones sometimes suffer still more from this evil; for though, on one side, the mass of knowledge united in the body is greater, on the other, a greater number of ignorant men embarrass and confuse: and while too many take part in making laws, but few take an interest in the subject. The thoughtlessness with which this important duty has been performed in England till the present time, is shown by Miller, in an *Inquiry into the Present State of the Statute and Criminal Law of England* (London, 1822). The people of England, therefore (the paradise of the customary law), are at length beginning to feel the urgent need there is of reducing the chaos of single enactments into general codes. This is called the *consolidation of laws*. Several learned individuals have undertaken to make such compends. [So far the German article.]

We now propose to offer some observations, explanatory of the views of lawyers accustomed to the jurisprudence of the common law, on this interesting subject. Civilians are (it seems from the preceding part of this article) divided into several schools, professing different opinions, and actuated by different principles. The course of the common law naturally leads those who are engaged in its studies to take practical rather than theoretical views of almost every department of it. Hence they can hardly be said to be divided into different schools, or to indulge much in what may be called *philosophical*, *historical* or *antiquarian* inquiries. The actual system, as it exists, is that which they principally seek to administer; and it is only occasionally that very gifted or bold minds strike out into new paths, or propose fundamental, reforms. In the present age, however, a spirit of inquiry is abroad, and the value and extent of codification have, among other topics, been matter of warm controversy among practical lawyers, as well as practical statesmen. We shall speak of this subject in the sequel. Legislation, in its broadest sense, includes those exercises of sovereign power, which permanently regulate the general concerns of society. Its chief object is to establish laws. And by a law, we understand a rule, prescribed by the sovereign power of a state to its citizens or subjects, declaring some right, enforcing some duty, or prohibiting some act. It is its general applicability, which distinguishes it from a single edict, or temporary and fugitive order of the sovereign will. It is supposed to furnish a permanent and settled direction to all who are embraced within its scope. It is not a sudden executive direction, but an annunciation of what is to govern and direct the rights and duties of the persons to whom it applies, in future. The rule being prescribed, it becomes the guide of all those functionaries who are called to administer it, and of all those citizens and subjects upon whom it is to operate. Neither is supposed to be at liberty to vary its obligations, or evade its provisions. But as, in the ordinary course of affairs in free governments, every person has a right, where the matter admits of judicial discussion, to litigate the question, what are the true object and meaning of a law, and how far it bears upon his rights, privileges, or duties, —it is understood, that in free governments, and especially in republics, the ultimate adjudication of what the law is, and how far it applies to a given case, is to be definitively settled by the judicial department of the government. It would be obviously unfit for the legislative department to settle retrospectively, as to past cases, what was its own meaning, its true office being to prescribe rules for the future. And though the executive department may, in the first instance, settle for itself what the law requires, its decisions cannot, and ought not to be final; for it has no means to call the proper parties before it to litigate the question, and no power to decree any judgment. Its proper function is to administer the law, and not to make it; to act upon its true construction, and not to fix it. Otherwise, the fundamental principle of a republican government would be overturned; and laws would be, not settled rules of action to be judged of by courts upon the litigation of parties, deriving their rights from, or in opposition to them; but would be arbitrary decisions of the sovereign power, without appeal and without inquiry. In the American states, this principle is thought so fundamental, that our constitutions of government expressly separate the legislative, executive and judicial departments from each other, and assign to each appropriate duties. It is thought that in no other way can the private rights and the public liberties of the people be secure. A departure from this doctrine would be deemed a direct advancement towards despotism. When, then, in America and England, it is asked what the law is, we are accustomed to consider what it has been declared to be by the judicial department, as the true and final expositor. No one is at liberty to disregard its exposition. No one is deemed above or beyond its reach, as thus declared. If it is supposed to be misconstrued, or rather not to carry into full effect the legislative will, a new or declaratory law is passed, and furnishes the appropriate remedy. And this leads us to remark, that the difference between civilians and common lawyers, in respect to the value and obligatory force of former decisions (which we call *precedents*), is most important. The opinion of no jurist, however high or distinguished is his reputation or ability, is of the least importance in settling the law, or ascertaining its construction, in England or the United States. So far as he may, by his arguments, or counsels, or learning, instruct the court, or enlighten its judgments, they have their proper weight. But if the court decides against his opinion, it falls to the ground. It has no farther effect. The decision becomes conclusive and binding, and other courts are governed by it, as furnishing for them the just rule of decision. No court would feel itself at liberty to disregard it, unless upon the most urgent occasion, and when it interfered with some other known rule or principle; and even then, with the greatest caution and deference. In countries where the common law prevails, it is deemed of infinite importance, that there should be a fixed and certain rule of decision, and that the rights and property of the whole community should not be delivered over to endless doubts and controversies. Our maxim, in truth, and not in form merely, is, *Misera est servitus, ubi jus est vagum aut incertum*. All this (it seems) is different in the civil law countries. There, the celebrity of a particular jurist may introduce a decisive change in the rule, or at least in the administration, of the law; and even different schools of opinion may prevail in different ages. Precedents have not, as with us, a fixed operation and value; and judicial tribunals consider, that a prior decision governs only the particular case, without absolutely fixing the principles involved in it. The practice under the common law has been found to be very beneficial; and, experience having given it a sanction and value which supersede all theory and reasoning about it, it is not often that the matter is discussed upon abstract or philosophical views. But there are many grounds, which might be urged in support of this practice, which are capable of vindicating it in the most philosophical discussions. The question, in its most general form, must involve this inquiry, What is best for society, with a view to its interests, its security, its permanency? Now, it may not be irrelevant to remark, that in every modern government, practically free, the common law rule has prevailed by general consent; and in those of the American states which were formerly under the civil law jurisdiction, there has been no desire ever expressed to retain their own rule. On the contrary, the common law rule has been eagerly adopted. It is not our purpose to enter into a review of all the grounds on which the common law rule might be vindicated; but there are one or two which deserve attention. In the first place, the rule has the advantage of producing certainty as to rights, privileges and property. In the next place, it controls the arbitrary discretion of judges, and puts the case beyond the reach of temporary feelings and prejudices, as well as beyond the peculiar opinions and complexional reasoning of a particular judge; for he is hemmed round by authority on every side. In the next place, the consciousness, that the decision will form a permanent precedent, affecting all future cases, introduces necessarily great caution and deliberation in giving it. If the case only were to be decided, it might be disposed of upon sudden impressions, and upon circumstances of hardship or compassion, or kindness, or special equity. But as the principles involved in it are to govern all future cases, and those principles must be derived from other analogies of the law, and be consistent with them, there are very strong restraints upon the judgment of any single judge. And there can be no permanent evil attendant upon any adjudications of this sort; for the legislative power may always apply the proper amendatory corrective at its will. And if the judges are actuated by corrupt motives, they may be removed by impeachment. It is no small proof that the system works well, that, in the course of many ages, very few decisions (comparatively speaking) have been overturned by the courts themselves, and that the legislature has not often found it necessary to change the rule prescribed by the courts. In fact, positive laws have been amended a hundred times, by the legislature, where one judicial rule has been interfered with. The changes which have been wrought in the fabric of the laws, have not so much arisen from misapplication of principles by the courts, as from the new state of society having rendered the old institutions and laws inexpedient or inconvenient. The circumstances which have been thus alluded to, have introduced a general and settled course of interpreting the laws, in countries governed by the common law. No such thing is known, in our jurisprudence, as a philosophical, or historical, or practical school of interpretation. And our laws are not subject to any varieties of interpretation grounded upon the present predominance of either of them. Certain maxims were early adopted, and they have never been departed from. Supplementary and auxiliary maxims of interpretation have necessarily been introduced. But, when once incorporated into the system, they have been deemed conclusive and obligatory. The sense of a law once fixed by judicial interpretation, is for ever deemed its true and only sense. Among the rules of interpretation belonging to and fixed in the common law, we shall enumerate a few, some of which, indeed, may be truly said to belong to the universal elements of rational jurisprudence. It is, perhaps, the exactness and uniformity with which they are applied, by our judicial tribunals, which give them their principal value.

Laws may be divided into the following classes: declaratory laws; directory laws; remedial laws; and prohibitory and penal laws. Declaratory laws, except so far as they operate upon future rights, are not within the scope of the legislative power in the United States. Our legislatures can only declare what the law shall be, not what it has been, or is; how it shall govern rights in future, not how it shall act upon the past. Directory laws are those which prescribe rules of conduct, or limit or enlarge rights, or point out modes of remedy. Remedial laws are those whose object it is to redress some private injury, or some public inconvenience. Prohibitory and penal laws are those which forbid certain things to be done or omitted, under a penalty, or vindicatory sanction. In the nature of things, there is not any indispensable reason why the same rule should be uniformly applied in the interpretation of all of these different sorts of laws. We shall see that the common law allows some distinction in this respect. The fundamental maxim of the common law, in the interpretation of statutes, or positive laws, is, that the intention of the legislature is to be followed. This intention is to be gathered from the words, the context, the subject matter, the effects and consequences, and the spirit or reason of the law. But the spirit and reason are to be ascertained, not from vague conjecture, but from the motives and language apparent on the face of the law.

1. In respect to words, they are to be understood in their ordinary and natural sense, in their popular meaning and common use, without a strict regard to grammatical propriety or nice criticism. But the ordinary sense may be de-

parted from, if the context or connexion clearly requires it; and then such a sense belonging to the words is to be adopted as best suits the context.

2. Again: terms of art and technical words are to be understood in the sense which they have received in the art or science to which they belong.

3. If words have different meanings, and are capable of a wider or narrower sense, in the given connexion, that is to be adopted which best suits the apparent intention of the legislature, from the scope or the provisions of the law.

4. And this leads us to remark, that the context must often be consulted, in order to arrive at a just conclusion, as to the intent of the legislature. The true sense in which particular words are used in a particular passage, may be often determined by comparing it with other passages and sentences, when there is any ambiguity, or intricacy, or doubt, as to its meaning.

5. And the professed objects of the legislature in making the law often afford an excellent key to unlock its meaning. Hence resort is often had to the preamble of a statute, which usually contains the motives of passing it, in order to explain the meaning, especially where ambiguous phrases are used.

6. For the same purpose, the subject matter of the law is taken into consideration; for the words must necessarily be understood to have regard thereto, and to have a larger or narrower meaning, according as the subject matter requires. It cannot be presumed, that the words of the legislature were designedly used in a manner repugnant to the subject matter.

7. The effects and consequences must also be taken into consideration. If the effects and consequences of a particular construction would be absurd, and apparently repugnant to any legislative intention deducible from the objects or context of the statute, and another construction can be adopted, which harmonizes with the general design, the latter is to be followed. But in all such cases, where the effects and consequences are regarded, they are not permitted to destroy the legislative enactment, or to repeal it, but simply to expound it. If, therefore, the legislature has clearly expressed its will, that is to be followed, let the effects and consequences be what they may. But general expressions, and loose language, are never interpreted so as to include cases which manifestly could not have been in the contemplation of the legislature.

8. The reason and spirit of the law are also regarded; but this is always in subordination to the words, and not to control the natural and fair interpretation of them. In short, the spirit and the reason are derived principally from examining the whole text, and not a single passage; from a close survey of all the other means of interpretation, and not from mere private reasoning as to what a wise or beneficent legislature might or might not intend. Cases, indeed, may readily be put, which are so extreme, that it would be difficult to believe that any rational legislature could intend what their words are capable of including. But these cases furnish little ground for practical reasoning, and are exactly of that class, where, from the generality of the words, they are capable of contraction or extension, according to the real objects of the legislature. These objects once ascertained, the difficulty vanishes. This natural, and sometimes necessary limitation upon the use of words in a law, we often call construing them by their *equity*. In reality, nothing more is meant, than that they are construed in their

mildest, and not in their harshest sense, it being open to adopt either.

9. For the same purpose, in the common law, regard is often had to antecedent and subsequent statutes upon the same subject; for, being *in pari materia,* it is natural to suppose, that the legislature had them all in their view in the last enactment, and that the sense which best harmonizes with the whole, is the true sense.

10. For the like reason, words and phrases in a statute, the meaning of which has been ascertained (especially in a statute on the same subject), are, when used in a subsequent statute, presumed to be used in the same sense, unless something occurs in it to repel the presumption.

11. As a corollary from the two last rules, it is a maxim of the common law, that all the statutes upon the same subject, or having the same object, are to be construed together as one statute; and then every part is to be taken into consideration.

12. Another rule is, to construe a statute as a whole, so as, if possible, or as nearly as possible, to give effect, and reasonable effect, to every clause, sentence, provision, and even word. Nothing is to be rejected, as void, superfluous or insignificant, if a proper place and use can be assigned to it.

13. If a reservation in a statute be utterly repugnant to the purview of it, the reservation is to be rejected; if the preamble and the enacting clauses are different, the latter are to be followed. But the reservation may qualify the purview, if consistent with it, and time preamble control the generality of expression of the enacting clauses, if it gives a complete and satisfactory exposition of the apparent legislative intention.

14. The common law is also regarded, as it stood antecedently to the statute, not only to explain terms, but to point out the nature of the mischief, and the nature of the remedy, and thus to furnish a guide to assist in the interpretation. In all cases of a doubtful nature, the common law will prevail, and the statute not be construed to repeal it.

15. Hence, where a remedy is given by statute for a particular case, it is not construed to extend so as to alter the common law in other cases.

16. Remedial statutes are construed liberally; that is, the words are construed in their largest sense, so far as the context permits, and the mischief to be provided against justifies. By remedial statutes, we understand those whose object is to redress grievances, and injuries to persons, or personal rights and property, in civil cases. Thus, statutes made to suppress frauds, to prevent nuisances, to secure the enjoyment of private rights, are deemed remedial.

17. So statutes are to be construed liberally which concern the public good; such as statutes for the advancement of learning, for the maintenance of religion, for the support of the poor, for the institution of charities.

18. The general rule is, that the sovereign or government is not included within the purview of the general words of a statute, unless named. Thus, a statute respecting all persons generally, is understood not to include the king. He must be specially named. But, nevertheless, in statutes made for the public good, which are construed liberally, the king, although not named, is often included by implication.

19. On the other hand, penal statutes, and statutes for the punishment of crimes, are always construed strictly. The words are construed most favorably for the citizens and

subjects. If they admit of two senses, each of which may well satisfy the intention of the legislature, that construction is always adopted which is most lenient. No case is ever punishable, which is not completely within the words of the statute, whatever may be its enormity. No language is ever strained to impute guilt. If the words are doubtful, that is a defence to the accused; and he is entitled, in such a case, to the most narrow exposition of the terms. This rule pervades the whole criminal jurisprudence of the common law, and is never departed from under any circumstances. It is the great leading principle of that jurisprudence, that men are not to be entangled in the guilt of crimes upon ambiguous expressions. But it is not to be understood, that the statute is to be construed so as to evade its fair operation. It is to have a reasonable exposition, according to its terms; and, though penal, it is not to be deemed odious.

20. Private statutes, also, generally receive a strict construction; for they are passed at the suggestion of the party interested, and are supposed to use his language.

21. Statutes conferring a new jurisdiction, and, especially, a summary jurisdiction contrary to the general course of the common law, are construed strictly. They are deemed to be in derogation of the common rights and liberties of the people under the common law, and are on that account jealously expounded. There are many other rules, of a more special character, for the construction of statutes, which the extreme solicitude of the common law to introduce certainty, and to limit the discretion of judges, has incorporated into its maxims. But they are too numerous to be dwelt upon in this place. They all, however, point to one great object—certainty and uniformity of interpretation; and no court would now be bold enough, or rash enough, to gainsay or discredit them. On the contrary, it is the pride of our judicial tribunals constantly to resort to them for the

purpose of regulating the necessary exercise of discretion in constructing new enactments. The legislative power of a government is generally coëxtensive with its sovereignty; and therefore embraces every thing which respects the concerns of the society. But it is in fact employed, if not universally, at least generally, in mere acts of amendment and supplement to the existing laws and institutions. Its office is ordinarily not so much to create systems of laws, as to supply defects, and cure mischiefs in the systems already existing. The question is often discussed in our day, how far it is practicable to give a complete system of positive law, or a complete code of direct legislation. And, if practicable, the farther question arises, how far it is desirable, of founded in sound policy. These questions have been the subject of ardent controversy among the civilians and jurists of the continent of Europe, living under the civil law; and, as may well be supposed, different sides have been taken by men of distinguished ability and learning; and the controversy is, and probably for a long period will be, pursued with great animation and powers of reasoning. In the countries governed by the common law, and especially in England and the U. States, the same questions have of late been matter of wide discussion among the legal profession, as well as among statesmen, and a great diversity of opinion has been exhibited on the subject. It will be our object, in the sequel of these remarks, to put the reader in possession of some of the main grounds of the controversy. The legislation of no country, probably, ever gave origin to its whole body of laws. In the very formation of society, the principles of natural justice, and the obligations of good faith, must have been recognised before any common legislature was acknowledged. Debts were contracted, obligations created, property, especially personal property, acquired, and lands cultivated, before any positive rules were fixed, as to the rights of possession and enjoyment growing out of them. The first rudiments of jurisprudence resulted from general consent or acquiescence; and when legislation began to act upon it, it was rather to confirm, alter, or add to, than to supersede, the primitive principles adopted into it. We, in fact, know of no nation, or, at least, of no civilized nation, whose history has reached us, in which a positive system of laws for the exigencies of the whole society was coëval with its origin; and it would be astonishing if such a nation could be found. Nations, in their origin, are usually barbarous or rude in their habits, customs and occupations. They are scanty in population and resources, and have neither the leisure, nor the inclination, nor the knowledge, to provide systems for future use, suited to the growing wants of society, or to their own future advancement in the arts. A few positive rules suffice, for the present, to govern them in their most pressing concerns; and the rest are left to be disposed of according to the habits and manners of the people. Habits soon become customs; customs soon become rules; and rules soon fasten themselves as firmly upon the existing institutions, as if they were positive ordinances. Wherever we trace positive laws, in the early stages of society, they are few, and not of any wide extent; directions for special concerns, rather than comprehensive regulations for the universal adjustment of rights. No man can pretend that, in Asia, any such universal rules were established by positive legislation, at the origin of the great nations by which it is peopled. The instructions of Moses, as promulgated by divine authority, for the government of the Jews, are not (as every one perceives) designed for every possible exigency of contract, or right, or injury, or duty, arising in the course of the business and history of that wonderful people. They are rather positive precepts, adapted to great occasions, and to govern those concerns which respected their wants, their spiritual advancement, and their duties as the chosen people of God. The Greeks are not known to us, in their early or later history, as having had a code of universal extent. The

Romans, in their early history, had few positive laws; and those seem to have been borrowed from other sources. We often, indeed, see it stated, that the common law of England was originally formed from statutes now obsolete and unknown. But this assertion is wholly gratuitous. There is no reason to suppose that, in the early history of its jurisprudence, more was done than is usual in other nations, at the same period of their progress, such as the promulgating of some leading regulations, or the forming of some great institutions for the security of the public. In fact, a great portion of the English common law is of modern growth, and can be traced distinctly to sources independent of legislation. The commercial law of England is not two centuries old, and scarcely owes any thing important to positive legislation. In truth, the formation of codes, or systems of general law, for the government of a people, and adapted to their wants, is a business which takes place only in advanced stages of society, when knowledge is consider ably diffused, and legislators have the means of ascertaining the best principles of policy and the best rules for justice, not by mere speculation and theory, but by the results of experience, and the reasoning of the learned and the wise. Those codes with which we are best acquainted, are manifestly of this sort. The institutes, and pandects, and code of Justinian, were made in the latter ages of Roman grandeur—nay, when it was far on the decline, not by instituting a new system, but by embodying the maxims, and rules, and principles, which the ablest jurists had collected in different ages, and from all the various lights of reason, and juridical decision, and general experience. No man imagines that Rome, in her early history, was capable of promulgating, or of acting upon such a system. And this system, large as it was, has no pretension to be deemed complete, even for Rome itself. It left an infinite number of human concerns undecided by its text, which were, of course, to be submitted to judicial decision, and to receive the judgment of the wise men, who should be called, from time to time, to declare the law *ex æquo et bono*. It may indeed be assumed, as a general truth, that the body of every system of law which has hitherto governed human society, had its origin as customary law; and if it has ever assumed the form of positive legislation, it has been to give it greater sanctity and extent, as well as greater uniformity of operation. This is certainly true in respect to the common law. That system, as administered in England and the U. States, is, as compared with the positive code, or statutes, of an immeasurably wider extent, both in its principles and its practical operation. A man may live a century, and feel (comparatively speaking) but in few instances the operation of statutes, either as to his rights or duties; but the common law surrounds him, on every side, like the atmosphere which he breathes. Returning, then, to the question before stated, it may be inquired, whether it be practicable, in a refined and civilized state of society, to introduce a positive code, which shall regulate all its concerns. That such a code could be formed in a rude or barbarous age, so as to be adapted to all their future wants and growth, in passing from barbarism to refinement, seems absolutely incredible. That it could be formed in a refined age, when learning, and large experience, and enlightened views, and a sagacious forecast, might guide the judgments of the legislature, is the point before us. In the first place, it has never yet been done by any people, in any age. The two most illustrious instances of codification are that of Justinian and that of Napoleon. Neither of these purports to be a complete system of laws and principles, superseding all others, and abolishing all others. As far as they go, they purport to lay down positive rules to guide the judgment of all tribunals, in cases within them. But other cases are left to be decided as they may arise, upon such principles as are applicable from analogy, from reasoning, from justice, from the customary law, or from judicial discretion. A positive prohibition to decide in cases not provided for by these codes, is not contained in either. But is it possible to foresee, or to provide beforehand, for all such cases? Society is ever varying in its occupations and concerns, in its objects and its pursuits, in its institutions, its pleasures, its inventions, its intelligence, and, in short, in innumerable relations and diversities of measures and means. How is it possible to foresee, or to limit, these relations or diversities? How is it possible, especially in free governments, to reduce all human acts to the same positive elements? to prevent contracts, and obligations, and rights, and equities, and injuries, and duties, from becoming mixed up in an infinite series of permutations and combinations? Until it has been ascertained what are the utmost limits of human relations, and those limits, with all their intermediate details, can be clearly defined, in every shade of difference, how can any system of laws be adequate to provide for, or to guard them, or to fix the rights growing out of them? To suppose that man is capable of all this, is to suppose that he is omniscient, all-wise, and all-powerful; that he is perfect, or that he can attain perfection; that he can see all the future in the past, and that the past is present to him in all its relations. The statement of such a proposition carries with it its own refutation. While man remains as he is, his powers, and capacities, and acts, must forever be imperfect. But it may be said, that a positive code may be framed, and a declaration made that it shall be deemed the sole guide and rule, and that all other rules shall be prohibited. Certainly this may be done. But the effect of this would be, not to form a perfect code for all the future exigencies of society; but to declare that whatever was left unprovided for in the code, should be neither matter of right nor wrong. It would be to declare, that, as to all other transactions, now and hereafter, society should be utterly lawless; and, of course, it would be to declare, that a system confessedly imperfect, and not meeting the wants or exigencies, the rights or the wishes of society, should still govern it. What would this be, but to provide a bad code for human concerns, which it could not measure or manage? From these considerations, we may assume it as a concession granted on all sides, that a perfect code, to regulate all present, and, *a fortiori*, all future concerns of any civilized society, by positive rules, applicable to them, is morally impossible. The only real question is, whether a positive code can be provided, adequate, in a general sense, to the present known wants of society. That codes may be formed, more or less comprehensive, to regulate many or few concerns, to supply defects, or to give symmetry and order to the law on particular subjects, cannot be doubted. It has been often done. Perhaps no civilized nation has ever existed, in which there was not, at the same time, a written and an unwritten law, or, in other words, a rule of positive institution and a rule of customary law. All special decrees and ordinances of the sovereign power are of the former kind. Many subjects are of such a nature as to require some positive rule, seeing that natural law cannot fix them upon any invariable basis. For example, there is nothing in the nature of things by which we can say, that land shall, in all possible states of society, descend to the possessor's heirs, or who those heirs shall be; that he shall have a right to dispose of them by testament or deed, and how that testament or deed shall be evidenced; whether bills of exchange and promissory notes shall be negotiable or not, and to what extent binding upon the parties. These subjects, in the origin of a society, must either be positively provided for, or no rights can exist (strictly speaking) until they have become, by usage, fixed in a particular form. But most nations, with whose history we are acquainted, have had many positive laws. And to suit their institutions to the exigencies of society, in all its changes, there must be ordinances to change the old and to frame new rides. In ancient Rome, in the modern governments of continental

Europe, and especially in France and in England, great alterations have, from time to time, been made in the existing system of laws. Fundamental laws have been abrogated; amendatory provisions have been established; existing rules have been methodized, confirmed, explained, and limited; and new rules prescribed for new cases. The ordinances of Louis XIV, of 1673 and 1681, on the subject of maritime and commercial affairs, are striking instances of this sort. The abolition of feudal tenures; the regulation of uses and charities; the allowance of last wills and testaments, made in a prescribed mode; the provisions to suppress frauds, in the statute of frauds; the registration of conveyances of lands; the negotiability of promissory notes; and, above all, the positive enactments, various and almost innumerable, in the criminal code, are illustrations of the same fact, in the history of English legislation. All these statutes furnished, to a limited extent, a code on the particular subject. And we have recently seen, in the consolidation of the criminal laws of England into a few statutes, under the auspices of Sir Robert Peel, a striking instance of substantive codification of the criminal law of England, in many of its most important provisions. But the objections often urged against codes, are not meant to be applied to legislation of this sort, but to systems, which are promulgated for the government of the great concerns of nations, in all their various departments and interests. How far this can be done, has been a matter of considerable theoretical discussion. But the question has been practically answered by the celebrity of several positive codes. And among those whose success and wisdom have been most generally acknowledged, are the code of Justinian and the code of Napoleon. That either of them furnishes complete rules for all the concerns of society, or excludes the necessity of judicial interpretation, or positive legislation, cannot be affirmed. That each of them covers a vast mass of the ordinary concerns of society, and fixes, positively and clearly, a great many wrongs and rights, and points out the proper redress, in cases where rights are to be vindicated and wrongs repressed, cannot well be denied. The question, then, is fairly presented, how far codes of this sort (the only ones which, in the actual state, of society, are morally possible) are desirable, and founded in sound policy. It is here, that the advocates and time opponents of codes, under the jurisprudence of the common law, meet on debatable ground. The lovers of ancient institutions, of existing laws, of customary principles, oppose codes as inconvenient and unnecessary. They hold them to be inconvenient, because they fix a stubborn rule, which shall govern future cases, instead of leaving them open to the free operations of the common law, which adapts itself to all the circumstances of the age. They maintain, also, that codes are unnecessary; for, so far as there is any rule, it is already known in the common law; and positive legislation cannot make it more so. It is added (and it is true), that law is gradually formed, and must differ in different ages, according to the different circumstances of society; that it must be varied according to the progress or regress of a nation; that it can rarely settle comprehensive principles, and must, by degrees, thread its way through the intricacies of human actions; and that an inflexible rule might work quite as much mischief as none at all; that no legislature can make a system halfso just, or perfect, or harmonious, both from want of time, and experience, and opportunity of knowledge, as judges, who are successively called to administer justice, and gather light from the wisdom of their predecessors. Most, if not all, of these suggestions, may be admitted to be correct, and yet they do not settle the controversy. In the first place, the objectors must admit, that, under the common law, there are positive statutes, which regulate many great concerns and rights of the countries governed by it. The descent and distribution of real estates, the making of last wills and testaments, the forms and ceremonies attendant upon conveyances of real estate, to say nothing of other important subjects, are, in every one of the U. States, provided for by positive statutes. Here we have a rule, which is absolute and inflexible. To say that, if found inconvenient, it may be altered, so as to suit the future interests of the particular state, is, in effect, no argument at all; for the same may be said as to any provision of a systematic code. No code is supposed to be unalterable. Again, if it be said, that the legislature may, and often does, in an early stage of society, fix great principles and institutions, and then leaves the rest to judicial decisions, and thereby shows its wisdom, the true answer is, that the same reasoning applies to all codes, however extensive, if they leave the judicial tribunals at liberty to decide upon new cases, not governed by, or necessarily included in, the terms of the code. So far as the legislature has laid down principles (whether more or less extensive is of no consequence), these govern; beyond them, all is left as before. Again, the common law is itself, as far as it goes, a system of rules. These rules are fixed, certain, and invariable, as to all cases falling within them. They are quite as unyielding as any code can be. When the common law has declared that the eldest son shall be the sole heir, and that the half-blood shall not inherit, a court has no more liberty, to depart from these rules, or to refuse to apply them to any case falling within them, upon any notion of hardship, or inconvenience, or ill adaptation to the exigencies of society, than it has a right to say, that a last will and testament shall be good, though not executed according to the requirements of a statute. In each case, it is bound, and bound to the same extent. If the question were, whether a positive code should contain a clause prohibiting courts of justice from deciding upon cases not within the purview of the code, there might be much to urge against the policy and reasonableness of such a clause; but it would furnish no objection to other parts of the code. The only point, with reference to a code, which, under this aspect, would deserve consideration, is, how far it would be desirable to provide for cases which may be foreseen, but have not, as yet, actually been subjected to legislative decision. On one side, it may be said, that it would be best to leave all such cases to be decided, as they arise, upon the result of human experience and human judgment, then acting upon all the circumstances. On the other hand, it may be said, that it is better to have a fixed, present rule, to avoid litigation, and to alter it in future, if unexpected inconveniences should arise. The reasoning on each side is sound, when applied to particular cases. On each side, it admits of question, when applied to all cases. It may be best, in many cases, to leave the rule to be made, when the case arises in judicial controversy. In others, it may be far better to establish a present rule, to clear a present doubt, or fix a limit to what is now uncertain. Take the case of a bill of exchange, or promissory note; and suppose the question were, at what time demand of payment should be made, w hen it was payable on time, and no rule existed, and yet there was an immense amount of property dependent upon having a fixed, uniform rule; and, until so fixed, there must be endless litigation. Can anyone doubt of the benefit of a rule, such as is now fixed in the commercial law of our country, for the purpose of securing certainty, viz. that payment must be demanded on the day on which it becomes due. On the other hand, suppose it were now proposed to make a law, fixing what should be the rate of wages in all fixture, times, in all private employments; would it not, at once, occur to be impolitic to act upon a rule, the effects of which might immediately, or in future, press unequally and injuriously upon different interests in society Again, it is said to be unnecessary to reduce the rules of the common law to a code, for they are as certain now as they would be in a positive code. They are even more so, because the legislature cannot be presumed able to lay down a positive rule, with all the limitations and qualifications of the common law. Now, both of these suggestions admit of a satisfactory answer. If the rule exists, and has certainty in the common law, it can be stated. If there are any known exceptions, limitations and qualifications, upon a rule, those also can be stated. If nothing beyond a particular limit is known, then legislation can, at least, go to that limit. And as to all other cases, the same uncertainty exists, both at common law and in legislation. The difficulty of the argument consists in assuming, that, because the legislature has prescribed the same rule as the common law, the courts are thereby prohibited from doing what they possessed the power to do before, in the absence of any rule, viz. to find out what is the rule that ought to govern. Now, the legislature may as well leave this power in the courts, after a code, as the common law; and it will be best, unless there is a positive prohibition to the contrary. The other part of the suggestion applies only to the point, whether the code is well or ill formed by the legislature. If badly formed, it will, of course, be proportionally bad; but that furnishes no objection to a code, but to the mode in which it is executed. Then, again, as to the suggestion that it is unnecessary, because the rule already exists in the common law, and has certainty: to this several answers may be given. In the first place, if it be conceded, that there is entire certainty in the rule, at common law, there can be no harm in making the rule positive. It may do good; for it will instruct many, in and out of the profession, in respect to their rights and duty, who are now sadly ignorant of both, or are liable to be misled by their imperfect inquiries, or their limited sources of information. Every man may be able to peruse a concise text; but every man may not have leisure or ability to study a voluminous commentary. Besides, even in relation to the doctrines of the common l aw, many of them lie scattered in different cases, and many of them are not so clear as not to admit of different interpretations, by minds of different learning and ability. Even lawyers of great research and accuracy, especially where the doctrine, though on the whole clear, is a matter of deduction and inference, may not, at once, come to the correct conclusion; and others of less learning and ability may plunge into serious errors. Now, it would be no small gain to have a positive text, which should give, in such cases, the true rule, instead of leaving it open to conjecture and inference by feeble minds. Again, there are many subjects of great intricacy and complexity, which can be fully mastered only by very able minds, resting, as they do, upon nice, and, sometimes, upon technical reasonings, not seen by the common reader. In such cases, t he text may admit of very exact statement, but the commentaries necessary to deduce it, may be exceedingly elaborate. The demonstration, or last result, may be clear, but the steps in arriving at it, exceedingly perplexed and embarrassing. It may require an analysis by the greatest minds to demonstrate; but, when once announced, it may be understood by the most common minds. For instance, the subject of contingent remainders and executory devises is of uncommon complexity in the common law, and many a lawyer may read Mr. Fearne's admirable treatise on the subject, without feeling competent to expound all its doctrines. And yet, put every principle into a positive text, with all its limitations and restrictions (not to be made out by argument and inference, but given in a direct form), and his labors and his reasoning would be materially abridged, and certainty exist where darkness before overshadowed his mind. Again, the common law has now become an exceedingly voluminous system; and as its expositions rest, not on a positive text, but upon arguments, analogies and commentaries, every person, who desires to know much, must engage in a very extensive system of reading. He may employ half his life in mastering treatises, the substance of which, in a positive code, might occupy but a few hundred pages. The codes of Justinian, for instance, superseded the camel-loads of commentaries, which were antecedently in use, and are all now buried in oblivion. The Napoleon codes have rendered thousands of volumes only works of occasional consultation, which were before required to be studied very diligently, and sometimes in repeated perusals. Again, what is to be done in the common law, where there are conflicting decisions on the same point, or converging series of opposite doctrines, approaching towards a conflict? The rule is here confessedly uncertain. Why should not the legislature interfere, in such a case, and fix a rule, such as, on the whole, stands upon the better reasoning, and the general analogies of the law? In point of fact, this is often done. Declaratory laws, in form, are unusual among us; but laws to clear doubts and difficulties are very common. Such interferences ought, doubtless, to be made with caution and prudence, and great deliberation. But this furnishes no just objection to a reasonable exercise of the power. But in the practice under the common law, there is a still stronger ground for interference. In the first place, what the common law is, is always open to question; and if authorities are suggested on either side, it is common enough to find the rule deduced from them, doubted, denied, or explained a way, by parties in an opposite interest. Courts are bound to hear as well as to decide; and although a court may think t he rule of the common law clear, from their own prior researches and reasoning, it will rarely feel at liberty to stop eminent counsel, when they deny the rule, or seek to overthrow the authorities and reasonings by which it is supported. The spirit of our tribunals, and the anxious desire, not only to do, but to appear to do justice, lead to a vast consumption of time in these discussions. If the legislature had once recognised the rule in a positive code, there would be an end of all such reasoning. The only question which could remain, would be, whether the rule were applicable to the case. In the next place, there are, upon some doctrines of the common law, a vast multitude of authorities to examine, compare and understand, which requires not only great diligence, but great skill. In some cases, there are shades of difference fit for comment; in others, *obiter dicta*, which are to be qualified; in others, doubts thrown out upon collateral heads; in others, reasoning not altogether satisfactory. Under such circumstances, what is to be done? The advocate on the one side comments on every case, and the language of every judge, which furnishes any color of support for his client. His arguments must be met and answered on the other side, not only because no advocate can know what the judges will decide, but what will be the influence upon their minds of a dictum, or doubt, or incidental remark or reason. It is indispensable, therefore, to examine the whole, although, perhaps, if either party doubts what the amount of authority, on the whole, supports. On one point (we believe) a learned English judge said, many years ago, that there were then more than 170 authorities. It is most probable that the number is now doubled; and yet, upon this very point, a legislative enactment of three lines might put controversy at rest forever. Perhaps no man in or out of the legal profession would now doubt what the rule ought to be. The difficulty is, that a rule has either been adopted which works inconveniently in particular cases, or a rule has grown out of a hasty adjudication, which subsequent judicial subtlety has been desirous of escaping from; but it is not easy to do so, without breaking in upon the acknowledged force of the rule. Hence distinctions, nice, and, perhaps, not very satisfactory, are found, as blemishes in some parts of the law, which need the legislative hand to extirpate or correct them. But it has been urged, as has been already incidentally noticed, that it is a great advantage to have law a flexible system, which will yield to the changing circumstances of society; and that a written code gives a permanence to doctrines, which would otherwise be subject to modification, so as to adapt them to the particular character of the times. This objection has been already in part answered. In respect to the common law doctrines, they cannot now be changed, whatever may be the changes of society, without some legislative enactment. They furnish a guide to all cases governed by them, until the legislature shall promulgate a new rule. Courts cannot disturb or vary them; and the question of their application to new cases is equally open, whether there be, or be not a code. The legislature can, with the same ease, vary its code as its common law. It can repeal, amend or modify either. But another principal objection is often suggested, and that is, that all the parts of the common law are not in a state susceptible of codification; and that, as we cannot form a complete system of it, one great object of a code must fail. It may be admitted, that some parts of the common law are too imperfectly settled in principles, and too little understood in practice, to allow of any exact codification. But these parts are principally obsolete, or of rare occurrence and application in the common business of life; so that, if they admitted of being reduced to a text, it may be well doubted if they were important enough to deserve it. There are other parts, again, which have grown up in modern times, which may be admitted to be yet in an immature and forming state, in respect to which, perhaps, it were better to wait the results of experience, than to anticipate them by positive law. Conceding all this, it falls far short of establishing the inutility of a code in other departments of the common law, not open to the like objections. Because we cannot form a perfect system, does it follow that we are to do nothing? Because we cannot, without rashness, give certainty to all possible or probable details of jurisprudence, shall we leave every thing uncertain and open to controversy? There is not a single state of the Union that has not repeatedly revised, changed, and fixed, in a positive code, many of its laws. The criminal code has almost every where received, in some of its principal branches, a methodical form. Virginia, long ago, reduced some important portions of her law to a positive text. New York has recently gone much farther, and, in the form of a revised code, made very extensive alterations in her common law, as well as in her statutable law. England, in our own time, has consolidated the most important heads of her criminal jurisprudence, in a new and methodized text. No man can doubt, that revisions of this sort may be useful, and, indeed, indispensable for the wants and improvements of society, in its progress from one stage to another. The question of more or less is a mere matter of expediency and policy. It is not a little remarkable, that, in England, almost every change in the general structure of her laws, by positive legislation, has, in all ages, met with a similar objection and resistance, and, when once adopted, has been generally, if not universally satisfactory. But there are many branches of the common law which can, without difficulty, be reduced to a positive text. Their main principles are embodied in treatises, accurate and full, and there can be no want of learned men ready to form an outline of them for the consideration of the legislature. Our commercial law is generally in this state. The law of bills of exchange and promissory notes, of insurance, of shipping and navigation, of partnership, of agency and factorage, of sales, of bailments, and many kindred titles, admits of codification to a very high degree of certainty; and yet, in these branches, there is still room enough to controvert particular decisions and authorities, to make it desirable to give a positive sanction to the better doctrine, and thus to save the profession from laborious researches, and the public from expensive litigation. The ordinance of Louis XIV, on commercial law, dried up a thousand sources of disputation; and the present code of commerce of France has settled, in a positive manner, most of the questionable points, which had been found unprovided for by that ordinance, and were resigned to judicial decision in the intermediate period. Besides, a code furnishes the only safe means of incorporating qualifications upon a general principle, which experience has demonstrated to be proper and politic. Courts often lament that a principle is established in too broad terms for the public good, and yet do not feel themselves at liberty to interpose exceptions which the principle does not sanction.

This article has already spread out into a great length, and must now be closed. The result of the whole view, as to codes, is, that neither the friends nor the opponents of them are wholly right in their doctrines or their projects; that, in every civilized country, much may be done to simplify the principles and practice of the law by judicious codification, and to give it uniformity and certainty; that How much ought to be done? is a question not admitting of any universal response, but is, or may be, different as to different countries, or, in different ages, as to the same country; that every code, to be useful, must act upon the existing institutions and jurisprudence, and not, generally, supersede them; that what, with reference to the customs, habits, manners, pursuits, interests, and institutions of one country, may be fit and expedient, may be wholly unfit and inexpedient for another; and that the part of true wisdom is, not so much to search out any abstract theory of universal jurisprudence, as to examine what, for each country in particular, may best promote its substantial interests, preserve its rights, protect its morals, and give permanence to its liberties.

ENCYCLOPÆDIA AMERICANA.

A

POPULAR DICTIONARY

OF

ARTS, SCIENCES, LITERATURE, HISTORY, POLITICS AND BIOGRAPHY,

A NEW EDITION;

INCLUDING

A COPIOUS COLLECTION OF ORIGINAL ARTICLES

IN

AMERICAN BIOGRAPHY;

ON

THE BASIS OF THE SEVENTH EDITION OF THE GERMAN

CONVERSATIONS-LEXICON.

EDITED BY

FRANCIS LIEBER,

ASSISTED BY

E. WIGGLESWORTH.

VOL. IX.

PHILADELPHIA:
LEA & BLANCHARD.
1843.

NATIONS, LAW OF

By *national law*, or, as it is more commonly called, the *law of nations*, we understand that portion of public law which concerns the rights, duties and obligations of nations. This is a very comprehensive subject, and can only be glanced at in this place, since a full and accurate examination would occupy volumes. Nations are considered as moral persons, having duties to perform, as well as rights to enforce, and are bound to the observance of the great principles of justice, which are applicable to the relations which subsist between each nation and its own subjects, and between each nation and every other nation. Vattel has defined the law of nations to be the science which teaches the rights subsisting between nations or states, and the obligations correspondent to those rights. But it is obvious that he here speaks of one branch only of that law, and that he altogether passes by another most important branch, namely, the rights and obligations which subsist between the nation and its own subjects. It would be more correct, therefore, to divide it into two great leading heads, namely, the *internal law of nations*, or that which arises from the relations between the sovereign and the people, and the *external law of nations*, or that which arises from the relations between different nations. The former may be properly called the *public law of the state*, whether it arise from the principles of natural justice, or from positive institution. The latter is appropriately called *international law*, and is again divisible into two heads, the one which regulates the rights, intercourse and obligations of nations, as such, with each other; the other, which regulates the rights and obligations more immediately belonging to their respective subjects. Thus the rights and duties of ambassadors belong to that head which respects the nation in its sovereign capacity; and the rights of the subjects of one nation to property situated within the territory of another nation, belong to the latter head. The former is frequently denominated the *public law of nations*, and the latter the *private law of nations*. The general foundation on which the law of nations rests, is the law of nature, or that system of principles which is deduced by human reason from the nature of man, and his social obligations, for the direction and government of human societies. Not that every principle of natural law is applicable to nations, in the same way and manner as it is to individuals; but that nations, being moral persons, are bound by the same principles, so far as they admit of a just application to them. And among Christian nations, these principles are illustrated and enforced by the superior sanctions and doctrines of divine revelation. It is obvious, that the principles of natural law are not, of themselves, sufficient to regulate, in a fixed and definitive manner, all the complicated relations of society; for, in many cases, no rule is, or can be, furnished by human reason, which is, necessarily, the sole and true rule to govern them. There are many cases in which the rule is a matter of indifference, or of convenience, or of arbitrary regulation; and every nation is free to adopt or reject the rule which is framed by another. There are, again, other cases, in which a nation may justly yield up its own strict rights, or modify them, without any departure from the principles of justice, or moral obligation. The law of nations may, therefore, be divided into two great classes of principles, namely, those which arise from natural or universal law, and those which are of mere positive institution. The former is denominated the universal *law of nations*; the latter, the *positive law of nations*. And the latter is again divisible into the *customary law*, or that which arises from the silent consent of nations, as evidenced by general usages and customs, and habits of intercourse; and the *conventional law*, which arises from express compacts, or treaties between nations, or in a particular state, from the fundamental constitution of such state. We do not propose, in this place, to enter upon any theoretical investigation of the principles of the law of nations, but merely to present a practical summary of the most important of them. Our object is to furnish a guide to the actual state of this branch of public jurisprudence, rather than an exposition of the reasons on which it is founded. In considering this subject, it is our design to treat, first, of the internal law of nations, or that which concerns a nation considered by itself; and, secondly, the external law of nations, or that which concerns its intercourse and relations with other states.

1. *Nations considered in themselves.—*
When any society of men, or body politic, is united for the purposes of government, and for mutual protection, we are accustomed to call such society, or body politic, a *state*, or *nation*. To every state, or nation, we ascribe the attributes of sovereignty, independence, and equality with every other. Every nation which governs itself; without dependence upon any foreign power, is deemed a sovereign state. By *sovereignty*, is meant the absolute right to exercise supreme power, without any responsibility to any superior, except God. This is sovereignty, in its largest sense; and in this view it is despotic and uncontrollable. But it must not be understood that the possession of such an absolute, despotic sovereignty, is indispensable to the existence of a nation, or that it is ordinarily conferred, or proper to be conferred, upon its own functionaries. All that is meant is, that it is competent for the people composing any state, or nation, to exercise such power, or to confide it to their public functionaries; and the exercise of it by either cannot, properly, be questioned by any foreign state or government. Theoretically speaking, this absolute sovereignty may be said to be inherent in every nation, as a potential attribute; but, practically speaking, it rarely has any existence, as an actual

attribute, in the organization of any government. The forms of government are divisible into three sorts: democracies, or governments by the people; aristocracies, or governments of a select few; and monarchies, or governments of a single head; and each of these may be variously mixed up with the others, so as to form a complex government, such as a representative democracy, or republic, or a limited monarchy, or a limited aristocracy. In a pure despotism, indeed, all sovereign power is concentrated in the head; but such a government rarely exists; for, in governments usually styled despotic, the customs and institutions of the society, and the habits, and manners, and opinions of the people generally, interpose some indirect checks, and compel the sovereign to yield a practical obedience to some limits prescribed to his prerogatives. If he does not, there is often an ultimate resort of popular or aristocratical power, which, by cutting him off, administers an effectual, though sanguinary remedy. In free governments, this despotic sovereignty is a mere residuary power in the people, if it can be said to have any positive existence at all. It never is confided to any public functionaries, except for transitory purposes; and it is contrary to the theoretical principles of such governments that it should be intrusted, as a permanent attribute, to the legislative, executive, or judicial departments. Nations, therefore, in a just sense, are deemed sovereign, not so much because they possess the absolute right to exercise, in their actual organization, such transcendent and despotic authority, but because whatever they do exercise is independent of and uncontrollable by any foreign nation. The sovereignty of many nations is, in its actual organization, limited by their own constitutions of government; but, in relation to all foreign states, the sovereignty is, nevertheless, complete and perfect. And a nation may even have a limited connexion with or dependence upon other nations, and yet retain a general sovereignty, in all other respects, and thus entitle itself to be deemed a sovereign nation, if it still possesses the power to govern itself by its own authority and laws. In respect to each other, then, nations possessed of sovereignty, in the limited sense above stated, are deemed equals, and are entitled to the same general rights and privileges. Relative strength is of no consequence; it neither confers nor abstracts any sovereign power. Relative weakness creates no dependence, and, in a just sense, compels to no sacrifice of national attributes. In respect to its own internal concerns, every nation possesses general and supreme authority. How that authority shall be exercised, and by whom, depends upon the particular constitution of each state, and is subject to the modification and control of the national will, expressed in such manner as the people prescribe. The authority of the nation over all its members is, by the very act of association, deemed, in all that concerns the general welfare of the nation, complete and supreme. All the members are bound to obedience and allegiance; and, in return, the nation is bound to protect and preserve its members. It may be proper, however, to express the rights and duties of a nation in a more exact form than can be communicated in such general propositions.

1. Every nation possesses full jurisdiction to create, alter, abolish, and regulate its own form of government, in such a manner as to provide, from time to time, for its own safety and happiness.

2. Every nation possesses an exclusive jurisdiction, within its territory, over all persons and things therein.

3. Every nation possesses a right to demand the allegiance of all its own subjects, and to bind them by its own laws, whether they are at home or abroad.

4. Every nation has a right to the temporary allegiance and obedience of all persons who are strangers and foreigners, so long as they reside within its territorial limits.

5. Every nation has a right to exercise jurisdiction, in common with every other nation, upon the high seas, and in all other places not exclusively belonging to some other nation.

6. Every nation has a right to enforce its own regulations upon its own subjects, and upon all other persons sailing under its flag and protection upon the high seas, and to govern its trade thereon, not interfering with the common rights of other nations.

7. Every nation has a right to hold all persons, born within its limits, and not specially exempted by the law of nations, to be its subjects, and bound thereto by natural allegiance.

8. Every nation has a right to naturalize foreigners residing within its territory, at its own pleasure; but such naturalization cannot impair or destroy the rights of other nations, to whom they may previously owe allegiance.

9. Every nation possesses a supreme legislative, executive and judicial authority, and may confer such portion of these powers upon its public functionaries, for the purposes of its own safety, interest, and happiness, as it may deem proper.

10. Every nation has a right to acquire and hold property, as its own public domain, for public purposes.

11. The rights of persons, and the rights of property, within its territory, are subject to the control and regulation of every nation, according to its own constitution and laws.

12. The territory within the limits of every nation, not owned by any private persons, belongs to the nation, in its sovereign capacity.

13. Every nation, in virtue of its eminent domain, has, in cases of necessity, and for the public safety and happiness, a right to dispose of any portion of the wealth or property of its subjects.

14. Every nation possesses the power, in virtue of its sovereignty, to punish all crimes committed against it, and to enforce all civil obligations due to it from persons subjected to its authority. Such are some of the more important rights of sovereignty, belonging to nations.

We may now enumerate some of their duties.

1. Every nation is bound to protect the rights and possessions of its subjects against all aggressions.

2. Every nation is bound to prevent its subjects from doing any wrong or injustice to the subjects of other countries.

3. Every nation, in virtue of its obligation to preserve the peace, safety, liberty and happiness of its own subjects, is bound to provide for the enactment of all good and wholesome laws for these purposes; and, especially, to provide for the necessities of the nation itself; to promote agriculture, commerce, manufactures, and all lawful pursuits, which are calculated to relieve the wants, promote the prosperity, or encourage the just enterprise of its subjects.

4. Every nation is bound to provide for the due and regular administration of justice; for the redress of wrongs; for the preservation of civil, political and religious liberty;

for the cultivation of piety and sound morals; for the suppression of vice; for public education and instruction; and for all other objects which are essential to the true interests and happiness of the people. Such, in a general view, are some of the more important duties of nations, in respect to their internal concerns.

It has been already stated that every nation possesses a right to all territory within its own limits, not belonging to private persons; and it may be added, that, as all such territory is held for the national benefit, it may be alienated, and disposed of, according to the will of the nation. All property, however acquired by the nation, is subject to the like disposition. Thus all the national revenues arising from taxation, or rents, or other income, or resources, may be applied as the nation deems proper for its own welfare. But there are many things which a nation holds for the public use and benefit, in respect to which all the subjects possess, or may possess, a common right of enjoyment. Thus rivers, lakes, and arms of the sea, within the limits of the territory of a nation, are possessed and owned by the nation, in virtue of its occupation of the adjacent country; and, until alienated, they are held for the common benefit of all the people, and may be used by all the people for the purpose of fishing and navigation. Of the like nature are roads, and highways, and canals, established and supported at the expense of the nation. All these territorial rights and possessions, however, are subject to the municipal regulations of every nation, according to its own choice, and constitution of government.

2. *Of nations, considered in relation to each other.—*
The basis, on which all the rights and duties of nations, in their intercourse with each other, rests, is the fundamental maxims, that they are all moral persons, and that each has a perfect equality, in sovereignty and social rights, with every

other. They are treated as moral persons possessing a sense of right and wrong, and responsible to the common Creator for a just discharge of all the duties common to the human race. They are bound to do justice, to perform the offices of humanity, and to render mutual assistance to each other, in the same manner, and upon the same principles, that bind individuals to like duties. If there is any difference, nations are under a superior obligation to perform all social duties, because their means are more extensive, and their authority more complete, than those of individuals. Hence it is the duty of every nation to succor and assist another, that is suffering by famine, pestilence, or other calamity; to cultivate friendship and good will towards all others; to abstain from all injury and wrong to all others; and to cherish, as far as may be, an honest and frank intercourse with all others, upon principles of reciprocal benevolence. However imperfectly these duties may, in a practical sense, be performed by nations, they are the clear result of undeniable principles of the law of nature, sanctioned and supported by the positive declarations of Christianity. The other maxim, to which we have alluded, is the perfect equality of nations, whether great or small, maritime or inland, strong or weak. In this respect, they are treated like individuals, who, however differing in capacity and strength, are deemed entitled to equal rights and privileges, in the general scale of the human race. In a just sense, then, all nations are of equal rank and dignity, although, by custom and usage, a precedence in mere matters of ceremony and courtesy is often conceded to nations which have a high antiquity, or superior renown, or uncommon power. The rights and duties of nations, in regard to each other, may be divided into two general heads, those which belong to a state of peace, and those which belong to a state of war. We shall first treat of those which belong to a state of peace.

1. Every nation is bound to abstain from all interference with the domain of other nations. That domain extends to everything which a nation is in possession of by a just title, whether it be by purchase, or cession, or conquest, or by a title founded solely on a long possession. In respect to foreign nations, not only the public domain, but all the private property of the subjects of a nation, situated within its limits, is deemed the property of the nation. This right of domain is exclusive; and, consequently, no nation can rightfully exercise any jurisdiction or sovereignty within the territories of another, either over persons or things. If a nation chooses to leave some part of its territory desert and uncultivated, this does not justify any other nation in seizing upon or occupying it. But, where a desert territory has no owner, there the nation that first discovers or occupies it, is generally allowed to possess a just title to it. But if the territory, when discovered, is occupied by inhabitants, no just right exists to expel or to subdue them, upon any recognised principles of national law. Such inhabitants have just as good a title, founded upon possession, as can be claimed by any other people.

2. Where two nations border on a river, or lake, or arm of the sea, it often becomes a matter of dispute how far the limits of each extend, and how far either may exercise exclusive jurisdiction over such places. No principles can be laid down, which will embrace all cases of this sort. But as a nation may acquire exclusive dominion in a river, lake, or arm of the sea, some rules have been laid down as guides on this subject. When a nation takes possession of a country bounded by a river, it is considered as appropriating to itself the river also, if there is no adverse possession or appropriation. In such cases, a priority of possession or occupation is generally allowed to give the superior right. If a nation has long enjoyed the exclusive use of such river, lake, or arm of the sea, for navigation, fishing, &c., that is understood to

strengthen its title of possession. If no priority of occupation is, or can be established, by either of two nations inhabiting the opposite banks of a river, each is considered as having an equal title; and, in such a case, the right of dominion of each will extend to the middle of the stream of the river (*usque adfilurn aquæ*). Where a nation possesses the territory on both sides of a river, so far as such territory extends, it is deemed to be the owner of the river itself; but other nations, owning, in like manner, above or below, on the same river, may have a right of passage, or other servitude. In respect to the main sea, in former times, several nations laid claims to an exclusive dominion, or, at least, to a pre eminence in and over certain parts of it. But the general doctrine now maintained is, that all nations have equal and common rights on the high sea, and they are not bound to admit any superiority there. The sea which washes the coast of a nation, to the extent of a cannon shot, or a marine league, is now deemed to be a part of the territory of the nation, over which it may, for its own protection, exercise an exclusive jurisdiction. And, in respect to persons subjected to its laws, every nation now claims a right to exercise jurisdiction on the high seas, for the purpose of enforcing, not only the law of nations, but its own municipal regulations.

3. From the exclusive jurisdiction and sovereignty of a nation, within its domain, it follows, that no other nation has a right to punish for crimes committed by its own subjects therein. No foreign nation has a right to pursue any criminal, or fugitive from justice, therein; but its claim, if any, is a mere right to demand him from the nation itself. From this peculiar and exclusive jurisdiction, which a nation exercises within its own territory, over persons and things, other nations are accustomed, upon principles of comity and general convenience, to respect the decisions of the local tribunals, and to recognise the rights generally

derived from them. It might otherwise happen that, with every change of domicil, the entire rights of property might be subjected to new litigation; and a judgment, valid where it was rendered, might be set aside by a tribunal having no competency to exercise an appellate jurisdiction.

4. Every nation has a right to regulate its own intercourse and commerce with other nations, not denying them just rights, in such a manner as is most conducive to its own prosperity and interests. It ought not, however, to restrict commerce, which is generally beneficial to all mankind, beyond what a just care of its own interests dictates. And it will not, if it be wise, impose any restrictions upon trade, which tend to a destruction of free commerce, or to create an unjust monopoly. In respect to its conduct towards foreigners, every nation seems under a moral obligation to treat them with respect, kindness, and humanity, during their sojourn within its territories. And though, strictly speaking, no foreigner has any right to claim a permanent domicil, or to exercise his trade or business within its territories, any interference with the ordinary pursuits of such persons is generally deemed a harsh exercise of power. And if a nation allows foreigners to enter into its territory, it is bound to respect their rights, so long as they conduct themselves peaceably; and if, in breach of good faith, it proceeds to punish them vindictively, when they have committed no offence, it is justly responsible for its conduct to the nation to which they belong. Foreigners, however, are bound to obey the laws of a country, as long as they reside within it, and under its protection. And as they are amenable to its laws, so they ought, in reason, to have the assistance of its courts of justice to vindicate their own rights. The property held by foreigners within a country, according to the laws, ought to be protected in the same manner as that of natives. It is a general rule among nations to regulate the descent, distribution and alienation of immovable

property exclusively by the laws of the country wherein it lies. As to movable property, it is now a common custom, and seems most reasonable and just, to allow foreigners the liberty of disposing of it by will, or otherwise, according to the laws of their own country, or of their own permanent domicil. Some governments, in the ease of the death of foreigners within their territory, have exercised a very harsh right of appropriating the property left by such persons to themselves. But this exercise of right, or rather of power, has been generally discountenanced, in latter times, among civilized nations. The rights of foreigners are, however, so much a matter of municipal regulation and policy, that it is difficult to lay down more than a few very general principles on the subject.

5. How far a nation is bound to concede to others the exercise of any rights, within its own territory, has been a matter of much speculation among writers on the law of nations. It has been often asked, whether a nation has a right to demand, in case of necessity, that another shall supply it with provisions, or allow it to procure necessaries therein; whether a nation may insist upon a right of passage through the territory of another nation, either for persons or merchandise; whether it may claim for its subjects a right to reside in the territories of another nation; whether it may, of right, demand from a nation the free use of a thing, within its territory, which is inexhaustible, and is of innocent use, such as of water. To all such questions there can be little more than a general reply, viz. that it is the duty of every nation to concede to the necessities of others whatever may not incommode itself, or affect its interests, or endanger its peace or prosperity.

6. The intercourse between nations can scarcely be beneficially carried on without the instrumentality of some public agents. They may have disputes to adjust, injuries to

redress, rights to ascertain, mutual objects and interests to promote, all of which may require great deliberation and many conferences. It is obviously impossible for the government of a nation to carry on its negotiations at a distance, without the aid of some public functionaries, who shall represent its sovereignty, and have authority to act in regard to its rights. Hence arises the right of every nation to send and to receive ambassadors, and other public ministers. And this right of embassy, inasmuch as its tendency is to promote justice, harmony, peace, and social virtue, among nations, has always been deemed peculiarly sacred. The law of ambassadors forms, therefore, a large head in the law of nations; and it is observed with a jealous and scrupulous care by all civilized nations. As representatives of the nation itself, ambassadors, and other public ministers, are exempted from all responsibility to the civil and criminal jurisdiction of the countries to which they are sent. Their persons are held sacred and inviolable. Their property, and servants, and retinue, enjoy a like privilege. Their houses are deemed, in some sort, asylums; and they have many privileges conceded to them, which do not belong to any other persons in the country where they reside. These rights, and privileges, and immunities, are not, however, to be considered as favors granted to the individual, but as a sovereign claim and public security insisted on by all nations, and refused by none. The peace and safety of all nations are essentially connected with the strict observance of them; and they are rarely infringed, except under circumstances of peculiar aggravation and injury.

7. It is through the medium of ambassadors, and other public ministers, that treaties, conventions, and other compacts between nations, are usually negotiated, thus forming a positive code for the regulation of their mutual rights, duties and interests. In the modern practice of nations, such treaties and compacts are not generally

deemed final and conclusive until they have been ratified by the respective governments to which the negotiators belong. When made, such treaties possess the highest sanctity and obligatory force. They are, indeed, sometimes violated; but they never can be justly violated, except in cases of great and positive wrongs on the side of the other contracting party, or from extreme necessity, or from a change of circumstances, which renders them wholly inapplicable or unjust. Many rules have been laid down for the interpretation of treaties. But they all resolve themselves, ultimately, into one great maxim, which is, that they are to be understood and construed according to their obvious meaning, and the intention of the contracting parties. Treaties may be dissolved in several ways;—first, by the voluntary assent of the parties; secondly, by a formal dissolution, pronounced by one of the parties, acting upon its own responsibility, in the exercise of sovereign authority; thirdly, by operation of law, as in cases where the contracting parties lose their distinct sovereignty, and become incorporated into a single nation; fourthly, by implication, as when new treaties are formed between the parties upon the same subject, or new alliances are contracted, which are incompatible with existing treaties.

8. As to the modes of terminating disputes between nations. These are various,—by compromise; by mediation, by arbitration; by conferences and congresses; by tacit acquiescences in the claims of the other side; and, lastly, on a failure of all these, by an ultimate resort to arms. This resort may be by a limited or by an unlimited warfare; by a limited warfare, as by retaliation, by reprisals, or other modified redress; by an unlimited warfare, as in cases of general hostilities in a public war. It is obvious, that a resort to arms can be properly had only when all peaceable means of redress have been exhausted, and for causes of an important nature.

2. (sic) And this leads us to the consideration of the rights and duties of nations in regard to each other, which belong to a state of war, —First, between the nations at war. The right of declaring war results from the right of a nation to preserve its own existence, its own liberties, and its own essential interests. In a state of nature, men have a right to employ force in self-defence; and, when they enter into society, this right is transferred to the government, and is an incident to sovereignty.

1. What are just causes for entering into war, is a question which has been much discussed by publicists. It is difficult to lay down any general rules on the subject, and nations must be ultimately left to decide for themselves, when the exigency arises. In general, it may be said, that war ought not to be entered into, except for very cogent reasons, as it necessarily involves much personal suffering, and many private as well as public sacrifices. No man can look upon the conflicts of armies and navies, the pillage of cities, the devastation of provinces, and the destruction of property and of life, which it unavoidably involves, without feeling that a deep moral responsibility attaches upon the nation which undertakes it. Defensive wars are necessarily justifiable from the fact, that they involve the existence or safety of the nation and its interests. But offensive wars are of a very different character, and can be justified only in cases of aggravated wrongs, or vital injuries.

2. In respect to the mode of declaring war. It may be formal, as by a public declaration, or informal, as by actual hostilities. In modern times, nations are accustomed, generally, to make a public declaration, and to justify themselves before the world, by a manifesto of their reasons.

3. The effects of a declaration of war. The first effect is to put all the subjects of each of the nations in a state of hostility to each other. All public and all private social intercourse are suspended between them. They are not at liberty to engage in trade, or commerce, or contract, with each other; and they retain the character of enemies, in whatever country they may be found. In the next place, all the property belonging to each is deemed hostile. If it be personal property, it may be captured as prize; if lands, it may be seized, and confiscated, at the pleasure of the sovereign; if it be merely in debts or stock, it may, in the extreme exercise of the laws of war, be equally liable to confiscation. In general, each nation restrains the right to make captures, and to carry on hostilities, to such persons as are in public employment, or to such as receive a public commission for this purpose. Mere private warfare is not allowed, except under many restrictions. Thus the usual modes of carrying on war are by armies, navies, and privateers, acting under the immediate authority of the government.

4. But, although the extreme rights of war are thus rigorous and oppressive, there seems no reason to exclude, even between enemies, the common duties of humanity. While the battle rages, indeed, everything but slaughter and victory are forgotten. But, as soon as it is over, the conquerors are bound to treat the wounded with kindness, and the prisoners with a decent humanity. And they who knowingly offend, in these cases, are guilty of a gross violation of duty in the eyes of God and man. And there are some things which seem positively prohibited from their cruelty and brutal barbarity: such are the violation of female captives, the torturing of prisoners, the poisoning of wells, the use of inhuman instruments of war.

5. In time of war, there is occasionally an intercourse between the belligerents, which should always be held

sacred. Thus the granting of passports, and ransom of prisoners and property; the interchange of prisoners by cartels; the temporary suspension of hostilities by truces; the passage of flags of truce; the engaging in treaties of capitulation, in cases of besieged armies or cities,—all these are matters which are held in great reverence, and demand the exercise of the utmost good faith. *A fortiori*, there should be a total absence of all fraud and stratagem, in cases where preliminary negotiations are entered into for the purpose of restoring peace.

6. In respect to captures made in war, they generally enure to the benefit of the sovereign, unless he has made some other positive distribution of them. When any conquest of territory is made, the inhabitants immediately pass under the dominion of the conqueror, and are subject to such laws as he chooses to impose upon them. Generally, it is for the interest, as it certainly is the common policy, of the conqueror to respect the rights of private persons and private property. But in strictness, his power over each is unlimited, unless, so far as it may be restrained by articles of capitulation, or by moral or religious obligations. In cases of recon- quest, the property, unless previously disposed of, returns to the original owner by the *jus postliminii*, in like manner as the restoration of a prisoner of war to his own country reinstates him in his prior rights.

7. There are also certain rights which war confers on the belligerents in respect to neutrals. Thus they have a right to blockade the ports, or besiege the cities, of their enemies, and to interdict all trade by neutrals with them. They have a right, also, to insist that neutrals shall conduct themselves with good faith, and abstain from all interference in the contest by supplying their enemy with things contraband of war. And if neutrals do so interfere, they have a right to punish them, either personally or by a confiscation of the

property taken *in delicto*. And hence arises the incidental right of search of ships on the high seas, for the detection of contraband goods. Secondly, we next come to the consideration of the rights and duties of neutrals. A neutral nation is bound to observe entire impartiality between the belligerents. It is bound to consider the war just on each side, at least to assume it to be so, so far as regards its own conduct. It should do nothing, therefore, which favors one party at the expense of the other; although, if it has previously entered into treaties with one of them, by which it is bound to lend a limited aid, by supplying stores or troops, it is obliged to conform to its treaty obligations. This becomes often a duty full of peril and difficulty, and, in many instances, will involve the neutral in all the embarrassments of becoming a party to the war; for the other side has a right to treat such interferences as acts of hostility, although, if they are of a very limited extent, they are often silently tolerated. Neutral nations are, strictly speaking, bound to compel their subjects to abstain from every interference in the war, as by carrying contraband goods, serving in the hostile army, furnishing supplies, &c. In practice, however, in cases of contraband goods, the belligerents content themselves with exercising the right of confiscation; and the neutral nation submits to this as a just and fit remedy, without any complaint. Subject to the exceptions above referred to, a neutral has a right to insist upon carrying on its ordinary commerce, with each of the belligerents, in the same manner as it had been accustomed to do in times of peace. Whether it may carry on a trade with either belligerent in war, which is interdicted in peace, is a point which has given rise to very sharp controversy in modern times, and especially between England and America, the former contending for the restriction to the accustomed trade, the latter insisting upon also carrying on the unaccustomed trade. Whether a neutral nation is bound to allow a passage to the troops of either belligerent through its own territory, is a point often discussed. Strictly speaking, neither party has a right to insist on such a passage; and if it is granted to either, and materially affects the fortune of the war, it is almost always construed as an act of hostility to the other party, and is resented accordingly. A neutral nation has also a right to insist, that no hostilities shall be committed by the belligerents within its territorial limits. The persons and the property of enemies, which are within such limits, are deemed inviolable, and entitled to neutral protection. But the property of an enemy, found on board a neutral ship on the high seas, is deemed good prize, and *e converso* the property of a neutral, found on board of an enemy's ship, is deemed neutral. The reason for the difference is, that upon land the neutral sovereign has exclusive jurisdiction, within his own territory, over all persons and property within it. But all nations have a common jurisdiction on the high seas to enforce their rights, and the right of search carries with it an incidental jurisdiction over all enemy's property found therein, in the ships of a neutral. This right of search, however, is strictly confined to merchant ships, and is never extended to ships of war, belonging to the nation itself; for in such ships the national sovereignty is exclusive. In general, too, the character of neutral, or enemy, is decided by the fact of domicil. A native born subject of one belligerent, who resides in a neutral country, is treated, at least for the purposes of trade, as a neutral; and, on the other hand, a neutral subject, domiciled in an enemy's country, is treated, for the like purposes, as an enemy. In cases of civil war, the rights and duties of neutrals are not essentially different. Every neutral is bound to abstain from all active interference in the contest, on one side or the other. If the contest gives rise to the establishment of independent governments, formed out of the severance of the old empire, it is not deemed an act of hostility to recognise each as having a sovereign existence as a nation. But while the contest is dubious, and the affair wears the appearance of a mere private rebellion, such a recognition would be deemed an active interference to promote the civil war, and therefore would, or at least might, be resented as a departure from the neutral character.

Such is a very general outline of some of the more important principles which are recognised in the law of nations. To go into the details would require an entire treatise upon the law of prize, and another upon many complicated questions, growing out of international rights and duties in times of peace.

Natural Law

NATURAL LAW, or, as it is commonly called, the law of nature, is that system of principles, which human reason has discovered to regulate the conduct of man in all his various relations. Doctor Paley defines it to be the science, which teaches men their duty and the reasons of it. In its largest sense, it comprehends natural theology, moral philosophy, and political philosophy; in other words, it comprehends man's duties to God, to himself, to other men, and as a member of political society. The obligatory force of the law of nature upon man is derived from its presumed coincidence with the will of his Creator. God has fashioned man according to his own good pleasure, and has fixed the laws of his being, and determined his powers and faculties. He has the supreme right to prescribe the rules, by which man shall regulate his conduct, and the means, by which he shall obtain happiness and avoid misery. He has given to man the power of discerning between good and evil, and a liberty of choice in the use of those means, which lead to happiness or misery. The whole duty of man therefore consists in two things: first, in making constant efforts to ascertain what is the will of God; and, secondly, in obedience to that will when ascertained. For the purposes of the present article, we shall assume, without undertaking to prove, that there is a God of infinite power, knowledge, wisdom, benevolence, justice and mercy; that he has created man with suitable powers and faculties to pursue and obtain happiness; that man is a moral, dependent and accountable being; that his soul is immortal; that his ultimate happiness or misery is dependent upon his own conduct; that there is a future state of retribution, in which the inequalities of the present life will be adjusted according to supreme wisdom and goodness; that, by a right application of his powers and faculties, man may always discern and pursue his duty; that virtue, or doing good to mankind in obedience to the will of God, has attached to it the reward of everlasting happiness and that vice, or doing wrong in disobedience to that will, is, by the very constitution of man's nature, necessarily connected with suffering and misery, directly or ultimately. In short, that man cannot be permanently happy by the practice of vice, and must be permanently happy by the practice of virtue. We shall assume these propositions, not because they are not susceptible of complete proof, but because, not being intended to be discussed in this place, they nevertheless form the basis of the subsequent remarks.

From the moral government of God, and the moral capacity and accountability of man, we deduce his general rights and duties.

1. His duties towards God. In the just performance of these duties consists piety or devotion. In a large sense, indeed, every performance of our duty is but a performance of some duty towards God; since it is his will which makes it a duty. But in the restrained sense, in which we are accustomed to use the phrase, we refer it to those duties of which God is peculiarly the object. As he is our Creator, we owe him supreme worship and reverence; as he is our Benefactor, we owe him constant gratitude and thankfulness; as he is our Lawgiver and Judge, we owe an unreserved obedience to his commands. We are frail and dependent beings, and we have constant reason to implore his assistance, his mercy and his forgiveness. Hence arises the duty of prayer, as a solemn recognition of our dependence on God; as a means of religious improvement and of cultivating devout affections; as an effectual instrument of communing with our own hearts; as a source of consolation under the afflictions of life; and as an exercise of piety fitted, to give a spiritual elevation to our thoughts, and a livelier and more enduring sense of our duty. From the same

causes also flow the duty of public and social worship; of maintaining religious institutions; of aiding in the diffusion of religious knowledge; and of keeping in view, in all our words and actions, an habitual and reverential fear of God.

2. The duties of man towards himself, or those which terminate in himself. Among these we may enumerate the duty of personal holiness; of self-preservation; of temperance; of humility; of personal improvement in knowledge, wisdom and virtue; and of preserving a conscience void of offence towards God and towards man.

3. The duties of man towards other men, or what are called his *relative* duties, arising from the various relations, which he sustains or may sustain towards others.

Now these duties flow from the correspondent rights of others. And this leads us to the consideration of the different sorts of rights. Rights are usually divided into such as are natural or adventitious, alienable or inalienable, perfect or imperfect. We call those rights *natural*, which belong to all mankind, and result from our very nature and condition; such are a man's right to his life, limbs and liberty, to the produce of his personal labor, at least to the extent of his present wants, and to the use, in common with the rest of mankind, of air, light, water, and the common means of subsistence. *Adventitious* rights are those, which are accidental, or arise from peculiar situations and relations, and presuppose some act of man, from which they spring; such as the rights of a magistrate, of a judge, of electors, of representatives, of legislators, &c. We call those rights *alienable*, which may be transferred, by law, to others, such as the right to property, to debts, houses, lands and money. We call those rights *unalienable*, which are incapable, by law, of such transfer, such as the right to life, liberty and the enjoyment of happiness. We call those rights *perfect*, which are determinate, and which may be asserted by force, or in civil society by the operation of law; and imperfect, those which are indeterminate and vague, and which may not be asserted by force or by law, but are obligatory only upon the consciences of parties. Thus a man has a perfect right to his life, to his personal liberty, and to his property; and he may by force assert and vindicate those rights against every aggressor. But he has but an imperfect right to gratitude for favors bestowed on others, or to charity, if he is in want, or to the affection of others, even if he is truly deserving of it. It is difficult to make any exact enumeration of what may be deemed the general rights of mankind, which may not admit of some exceptions, or which may not be deemed capable of modification under peculiar circumstances. Thus the most general rights, which belong to all mankind, may be said to be the right to life, to liberty, to property, and to the use of air, light, water, and to the fruits of the earth. And yet, under certain circumstances, life, and liberty, and property, may justly be taken away; as, for instance, in order to prevent crimes, to enforce the rights of other persons, or to secure the safety and happiness of society. And in like manner the free use of air, light and water, may be interdicted.

In regard to imperfect rights, although the sanction is wholly upon the conscience of the party under a sense of religious responsibility, the obligation to perform the duties corresponding to them is, nevertheless, to be deemed as imperative, as if they also possessed the strongest earthly sanctions; since they arise from the commands of God, and are to be done in obedience to his will. Every man is therefore bound to exercise charity in its largest sense; to be just, grateful, kind and benevolent; to promote the general happiness; to speak the truth and to abstain from falsehood; to abstain from oppression, anger, revenge, hatred, malice, slander, uncharitableness, persecution, and every other injurious actor passion. These are duties, which are incumbent on him in respect to all the human race. There are others, again, which arise from peculiar relations to others; such are those, which belong to him in the character of master or servant, magistrate or subject, parent or child, husband or wife. Among the duties of masters and servants, we may enumerate, on the part of the master, the duty to enjoin on servants no unnecessary labor or confinement, from caprice, or wantonness, or passion; to insult no servants by harsh, opprobrious or scornful language; to refuse them no harmless pleasures; to promote their welfare by all reasonable means on the part of servants, the duty to be industrious, and punctual in the discharge of their duty, faithful and honest; and to yield a ready obedience to all just commands. On the part of magistrates, the duty of exercising power with moderation and mercy as well as justice. On the part of subjects, the duty of obeying the laws and supporting the institutions of society. On the part of parents, the duty of maintaining, educating, and otherwise providing for the intellectual, moral and physical improvement of their children. On the part of children, the duty to render their parents a just homage, love and reverence, to obey their commands, to lighten their labors, assuage their sorrows, and, as far as may be in their power, to administer to their infirmities, and to support and succor them when in poverty. On the part of husband and wife, the duty to promote domestic peace and harmony; to cultivate mutual love and forbearance; and in prosperity and in adversity, in sickness and in health, in life and in death, to be true, and watchful, and tender, as those whom God has united in bonds of permanent obligation and sanctity. And this leads us to the consideration of the subject of marriage, and some of the rights and duties flowing from it. Marriage is an institution, which may properly be deemed to arise from the law of nature. It promotes the private comfort of both parties, and especially of the female sex. It tends to the procreation of the greatest number of healthy citizens, and to their proper maintenance and education. It secures the peace of society, by cutting off a great source of contention, by assigning to one man the exclusive right to one woman. It promotes the cause of sound morals, by cultivating domestic affections and virtues. It distributes the whole of society into families, and creates a permanent union of interests, and a mutual guardianship of the same. It binds children together by indissoluble ties, and adds new securities to the good order of society, by connecting the happiness of the whole family with the good behavior of all. It furnishes additional motives for honest industry and economy in private life, and for a deeper love of the country of our birth. It has, in short, a deep foundation in all our best interests, feelings, sentiments, and even sensual propensities; and in whatever country it has been introduced, it has always been adhered to with an unfailing and increasing attachment. Polygamy, on the other hand, seems utterly repugnant to the law of nature. It necessarily weakens, and, in most cases, destroys the principle benefits amid good influences resulting from marriage. It generates contests and jealousies among wives; divides the affections of parents, introduces and perpetuates a voluptuous caprice. It has a tendency to dissolve the vigor of the intellectual faculties, and to produce languor and indolence. It stimulates the sensual appetites to an undue extent, and thus impairs the strength and healthiness of the physical functions. It debases the female sex. It retards, rather than advances, a healthy and numerous population. It weakens the motives to female chastity and to exclusive devotion to one husband. Besides, the very equality in point of numbers of the sexes seems to point out the law of God to be, that one woman shall be assigned to one man. And in point of fact, the countries, where polygamy has been allowed, have been uniformly debased, indolent and enervate, having neither great physical, nor great intellectual ability. If marriage be an institution derived from the law of nature, then, whatever has a natural tendency to discourage it, or to destroy its value, is by the same law prohibited. Hence we may deduce the criminality of fornication, incest, adultery, seduction, and other lewdness; although there are many independent grounds, on which such criminality maybe rested. It follows that the right of divorce must be a very limited right; and that divorces are forbidden by the law of nature except for causes of a very extraordinary character. It is manifest, that a power on either side to dissolve the marriage at will, would rob the state of matrimony of many of its principal blessings and advantages. It would deprive one of the parents of the comfort and gratitude of the children of the marriage. It would defeat the main purposes of their union, and weaken all domestic ties between parents and children. On the other hand, a very restricted allowance of divorces has a natural tendency to preserve peace and concord in families, by perpetuating a common interest, and encouraging mutual forbearance and affection. By denying, except for extraordinary reasons, the right of divorce, we discourage, in a proportionate degree, the desire, as well as the means of accomplishing it. Christianity has confined the right of divorce to the single case of adultery; though the law of nature may perhaps be thought to justify some few other exceptions.

4. We next come to the duties of man as a member of political society. And, here, we shall briefly treat of certain rights and duties, which may arise from the law of nature independent of any organization into political societies, but which more naturally find a place here, because they constitute the principal grounds for such organization. Thus the right of property, the obligation of contracts, the duty of speaking the truth, the sanctity of oaths, with other corresponding duties, strictly speaking, may be perfect in a mere state of nature, without the recognition of any fixed society; for they may exist and have a necessary application independent of such society. But their value and importance are

far more felt, and far better provided for, in political society, and, therefore, properly belong to the present head.

1. The origin of political society.— The origin of political society may be traced back to the primitive establishment of families. From the union of a number of related families grew up tribes; and from tribes gradually grew up colonies and nations. Accidental associations for offence or defence may, in some instances, have introduced the first elements of fixed society between strangers; and a sense of mutual interest and mutual dependence may have rendered them permanent. Coeval with the establishment of civil societies was the origin of civil government. Parents, from necessity as well as from prudence, exercised, and were admitted rightfully to exercise, immediate authority and government over their children and families. The patriarch or chief of a tribe, in like manner, exercised authority over those, who were of his blood and lineage. And, silently, the powers of rule or government were either divided as convenience or accident dictated, or were retained by the head, as the common bond of the union of the whole. Sometimes, indeed, government did or might arise from military associations for plunder or protection. And in such cases the strongest, the most intelligent, and the most enterprising and valiant, were the most likely, in the first instance, to be intrusted with the highest powers. The necessity, in all such cases, of prompt submission and obedience, in order to accomplish the immediate objects in view, furnished a sufficient excuse, if not just reason, for intrusting the leaders with summary and despotic authority.

2. Governments, then, may be properly deemed to arise from voluntary consent, or from long acquiescence and prescription, or from superior force. The fundamental objects of all civil governments are, or ought to be, to promote the welfare and safety of the whole society. It is

obvious, that no single individual can protect himself to the sane extent, or by the sane means, as an organized society or government can protect him. The latter has the powers, authority, union and resources of numbers. Men enter, then, into civil societies for the protection) of their persons, and personal rights and property. In a state of nature, if either be invaded, the only redress is by the application of positive force by the individual, who is injured. But under the establishment of civil governments, the redress is taken from the individual, and is administered by the government itself through its own functionaries, and according to its regulations, and by the authority and force of numbers. The entering into civil society, therefore, necessarily, or, at least, naturally, induces the surrender of all those private rights, which are indispensable for the good order, peace and safety of the whole society. And, indeed, unless some surrender of powers and rights were made, there could be no such thing as a regular government, since each person would be at liberty to do as he pleased, and there could be no such thing as lawful authority on one side to give a rule, or, on the other side, any duty of obedience. Civil government, then, may be properly said to consist in the exercise of such delegated powers, as are proper or necessary for the safety, protection and happiness of the whole community. And civil liberty may be said to consist in not being restrained by any laws, which are not conducive to the public welfare. We sometimes see governments existing, in which these objects are but imperfectly obtained, and ask ourselves, why they are not changed. There are several reasons, which may help us to a just understanding of the facts, and enable us satisfactorily to solve the inquiry, how it should happen, that governments should fail of attaining the very objects, on which they are founded, and yet be supported by the acquiescence of the people. In the first place, in every government, there are many persons, who obey from mere prejudice, or the habit of obedience, and from an inherent indisposition to contemplate any thing otherwise than as it at present exists. They do not stop to consider, whether it can be made better or not. They are content, from a *vis inertiœ*, to let things remain as they are. In the next place, those whose obedience is governed by reason, are often persuaded to obedience by the consciousness of their own inability to procure suitable changes; by the dread of civil commotions; by doubts as to the method of curing existing evils; and by the persuasion, that in many instances the form of government has become so interwoven with the habits and institutions of the people, that as much mischief as good might be done by a change. In the next place, in every government, many persons have a direct and positive interest in preserving the government as it is, and even in perpetuating its very corruptions. They may be a favored class, enjoying peculiar privileges, ranks, or patronage; they may have their whole property and importance involved in the existence of the present state of things. In the next place, the actual moral and intellectual power, and even physical power, of the state in its present organization, may be so combined in the structure of the government that they may present insuperable barriers to any change. If, for instance, the whole of the privileged classes should happen to be the only educated persons in the nation; if the whole priesthood should depend upon the government for its influence and support, and its exclusive patronage and privileges; if the whole wealth of the community should be lodged in few hands, and those few should be the very heads of the government; if the military power should be so organized, that it could scarcely find the means, or possess the power, to act except under the existing arrangements; in any, and in all of these cases, it is easy to perceive, that there would be immense difficulties in introducing any fundamental and salutary change. It could scarcely take place but upon some general convulsion, which should break asunder all the common ties of society. But it may be asked, as civil government is formed by the whole people, whether it can ever be justly altered, except by the will of the whole. If by the will of the whole be meant the will of each individual singly, it may be answered in the affirmative; for by entering into society, men necessarily engage to be governed by the will of the majority, since unanimity in all matters of civil polity is impracticable. The will of the majority or the will of the minority must govern. If the latter, by a veto, can stop all measures, the majority are governed by them. All reasoning and all principle, therefore, unavoidably lead to the result, that the will of the majority must be deemed the will of the whole for all practical purposes; and as the interests of the whole society require this, it is binding on every part of it.

3. The origin of property. One of the great objects of political society is the protection of property; and many learned discussions have taken place as to the origin and nature of property. Some things are of common and universal use by all mankind, and to such use all mankind have an equal right. Such, generally speaking, are (as we have seen) air, water, and light. Other things belong, exclusively, to one or more persons, and no others have a right to intermeddle with, possess, or enjoy them. Such an exclusive right in things is called *property*. How did such a right originate. It is plain, that, in a mere state of nature, no man could insist, that he possessed any such exclusive right to things in general; for, if one possessed it, all would equally possess it, which would be the same as to affirm its nonexistence. The earth, and its various fruits, herbage and trees; the various inferior animals, such as birds, fishes, and beasts, either for food, or covering, or pleasure, or labor, seem alike to belong to all mankind, and are for the use of all. To a limited extent, possession and use of a thing must, indeed, confer a temporary or permanent ownership. If, for instance, a man stands or lies on a particular spot of ground,

during the time of such occupation, he must have the exclusive right of occupation, for it is indispensable for his immediate use, and no other person can show a better right to it. So if he gathers fruit, for the purpose of eating it, no other person can have a better right to eat it than himself; and he must, therefore, have an exclusive right, because it is necessary to the use. But if he does not hold the fruit to eat it at present, but lays it aside for future consumption, his right to the exclusive use of it is not so clear; it is somewhat more remote; it does not turn upon immediate possession, and immediate use. It may be said, that he has, by his labor, gathered it, and therefore he has a superior title to it. But, though his labor is his own, it does not follow, that, because he bestows it upon another thing, he thereby acquires any exclusive ownership in that thing. It may be extremely inconvenient, and, perhaps, even injurious to the common claims of others, that he should so bestow his labor upon it. They are not, therefore, bound to respect any claim founded upon such labor. Some persons found the right of property upon a presumed or tacit consent of all mankind, which is a mere theory, and wholly unsupported by any universal facts. Others found it upon mere occupancy; but that, at most, gives only a present and temporary right, during such occupancy. Others, again, found it upon the very equality of all mankind, and contend that, as God has given all things for the use and necessities of all, each may appropriate to himself whatever is proper to satisfy those necessities. But, even here, he must leave sufficient to satisfy the necessities of others; and they may take, of the stores so appropriated, enough to supply their own necessities. The truth, however, seems to be, that, in a state of nature, each man actually appropriates to himself whatever he desires, and can get; and he then holds it by the title of the strongest; and no other person respects his title any longer than it can be so maintained, though no one can show a better title to it. As soon as families are formed, the necessity of providing for their own mutual comforts and wants, gradually leads them to hoard up and appropriate food, and other things, for future use. The convenience, and, sometimes, the necessity of an interchange of commodities with other families, of which each has a superfluity, leads to an increased accumulation. Possession and power are the guardians of these gathered stores; and a sense of convenience and mutual interest induces every family to regard with respect the commodities in possession of the other. Thus the first rudiments of exclusive property begin in the fact of actual possession and power, and the title gains strength and permanence from a sense of the beneficial results to the interests of all the neighborhood, and, ultimately, to the whole society, with which each family and tribe are connected. The advantages of the admission of such an exclusive right are soon felt by all reflecting minds, and gradually prepare the way for a more solemn recognition of it. It is perceived, that its tendency is to increase the products of the earth, by creating inducements to plant, when the planter is secured in his exclusive right to the harvest. It also improves the comforts and conveniences of life, and introduces a fit distribution of labor; and it cuts off a great source of perpetual contest and warfare among those, who would, otherwise, be struggling for the common prize. In the ordinary course of things, movables, such as fruits, and flocks, and herds, and fishes, first become property. Land rarely becomes permanent property until a much later period in the history of nations.

4. But, whatever may be the origin of the right to property, it is very certain, that, as it is now recognised and enforced, it is a creature of civil government. Whatever right a man may have to property, it does not follow, that he has a right to transfer that right to another, or to transmit it, at his decease, to his children, or heirs. The nature and extent of his ownership; the modes in which he may dispose

of it; the course of descent, and distribution of it upon his death; and the remedies for the redress of any violation of it, are, in a great measure, if not altogether, the result of the positive institutions of society. Accordingly, we find that, in different nations, all these subjects are regulated in very different manners. In some nations, all the children inherit the property, upon the death of the ancestor; in others, the eldest son only. In some, there is power to dispose of the whole, or of a part only, by will and testament; in others, this power has been denied. In some, the duration of the right of property is perpetual; in others, it is limited. In some, it may be alienated at all times, and in perpetuity; in others, the power of alienation is restrained. In some, long possession confers title; in others, it confers none. Above all, the capacity to dispose of property is variously regulated by civil institutions. It is obvious, that idiots, and madmen, and infants, ought not to be allowed to dispose of property, since they have no rational discretion. But at what period of life shall a man be deemed to possess such discretion? At ten, or twenty, or thirty years of age? Shall it equally apply, at all times, to both sexes, under all changes of condition? In all nations, some peculiar regulations have been adopted to settle these questions, which, by the law of nature, it would not be easy to settle by any uniform and fixed rule. The power of disposing of property is sometimes allowed at eighteen, sometimes at twenty-one, sometimes at twenty-five, and sometimes at thirty years of age. It is sometimes permitted to married women, but it is more commonly denied to them. Who can say, which of these periods is the true one, or which of these privileges is the proper one.

5. Another great object of society is the protection, not only of property in *things*, but of property (if we may so say) in *actions*. A great portion of the business of human society is founded upon contracts, express or implied; and

these contracts, especially in modern times, constitute the bulk of the fortunes and acquisitions of many persons, from the humblest mechanic up to the most opulent stockholder. The obligation of contracts, or, in other words, the duty of performing them, may, indeed, be deduced from the plainest elements of natural law,—that is, if such contracts are just and moral, and founded upon mutuality of consideration. It is indispensable to the social intercourse of mankind. It is conformable to the will of God, which requires all men to deal with good faith, and truth, and sincerity, in their intercourse with others. It is indispensable, in order to prevent injuries to others, whose acts, and interests, and property, may depend upon a strict fulfillment of such contracts. But, in a state of nature, the obligation of contracts, however perfect in itself; cannot ordinarily be enforced upon the other contracting party to its just extent. The only remedy is positive force; and this, in many cases, is impracticable, and is generally inconvenient. The institution of political society brings the moral, as well as the physical power of the whole in aid of the natural obligation of contracts. The remedy is generally peaceable, perfect and easy. But it may be naturally asked, what contracts are really obligatory. The true answer, in civil societies, is, all such contracts as the law of the land declares to be obligatory, or of which it permits the obligation to been forced. The true answer, independent of the positive recognitions of civil society, is, all such contracts as are moral, just, practicable, and have not been extinguished in any lawful manner. Contracts which are immoral, or which have resulted from fraud or oppression; contracts which require impossible things, or are repugnant to natural justice; or which are founded in essential mistakes; as to persons, characters, or things; or which involve the breach of other paramount obligations, cannot, upon the principles of eternal justice, be obligatory.

6. Without going more at large into the origin and objects of political society, it will be seen, that these objects require the delegation (as has been already intimated) of certain powers and authorities to those, who are to administer the government. The ends required are the preservation of the general rights and the general welfare of the community; and the means to accomplish these ends must be given by the express or implied assent of the governed. The civil powers, which, in every well constituted society, seem indispensable for this purpose, are the legislative, executive and judicial powers. In order to secure the safety and happiness of the society, it is indispensable, that there should be somewhere lodged a power to make laws for the punishment of wrongs, and for the protection of rights, and for the promotion of the peace, health and good order of the society. And, as there is a perpetual change in human affairs, and laws and institutions, which are adapted to one age are frequently unfit for another, there must exist in the government a power to alter, amend and modify existing laws; and, as human legislation must necessarily be imperfect, the power to improve it may always be presumed to be useful, since experience often points out mistakes and deficiencies. The power of legislation must, therefore, in its nature, include the power of abolishing, as well as of enacting laws. Again, as the exigencies of the society must require expenses to be incurred, and revenues to be raised to defray those expenses, the power of taxation naturally belongs to the power of legislation, as a means to accomplish the appropriate ends of society. But, if laws exist, they soon become a dead letter, unless obedience to them can be enforced; for it is found that moral obligation alone is not sufficient to ensure a perfect performance of duty. The existence of an executive authority, to which is intrusted the due and vigilant execution of the laws, seems indispensable. And, as controversies may arise, in a great variety of cases, as to what is the right of one party, and the duty of another;

whether property belongs to one party, or to another; whether a contract has or has not been performed; whether a wrong has or has not been done; whether a crime has or has not been committed, it seems also indispensable, that a power should exist, whose jurisdiction should extend over all controversies of this sort, and should finally decide upon them. This power is the judicial power; and its free, independent and honest exercise is as important to the safety and happiness of society, as either of the other two. In short, without a due administration of civil and criminal justice, society is, and can be, of little value. The merit of every government must, therefore, be subjected to this, as the truest test of its real excellence.

7. In what manner these various powers, legislative, executive and judicial, are to be exercised, and to what functionaries they are to be intrusted, depends upon the particular organization of each society or nation, or what is usually called its form or constitution of government. Where the society is small and within a very limited extent of territory, it is possible to have them all exercised in an assembly of the whole people by the whole people. This would be a pure democracy. But it is obvious, that though possible, in an exact sense it is scarcely practicable; for all the people of even a small territory can rarely be assembled; some will be absent from accidental circumstances of illness, and age, and more pressing duties. And, probably, in no society whatever were these powers ever, in fact, exercised by the whole people, in any single assembly; for idiots, madmen, infants, have been universally excluded; and married women, and persons guilty of crimes, have been usually excluded. The most simple form, in which the powers of government have ever been actually administered, probably is by a majority of that part of the people, which has actually been assembled for such a purpose. And this is, in fact, though in its humblest form, a delegation of

the sovereign power of the whole, since it entrusts the authority of the whole to the part, which is assembled. It is also, though in its humblest form, a *representative* government; for the whole are represented by those, who are present. We ordinarily call such a government a *democracy*, by government of the whole people. But in societies, which are composed of large masses of population, such a form of government is unwieldy, and burthensome, and inefficient. The people are, therefore, driven to a delegation of their authority to a smaller number of persons, who can act as their representatives in the discharge of the legislative, executive and judicial functions. Sometimes all these powers are concentrated in a single person; and then the government assumes the form of a pure despotism; sometimes they are all exercised by one and the same select body, composed of a few select persons, and then the government is, in form, a pure aristocracy. Sometimes the powers are divided, and distributed among various functionaries, and then the government becomes a mixed form of government. If the executive power, in such a case, is delegated to a single person, it is then called a *monarchy*, or a *limited monarchy* if the executive power is exercised by a select body of men, it is called an *aristocracy* or *limited aristocracy*. If the executive power is exercised by a magistrate elected by the people from time to time, and removable by the people, it is sometimes, though not, perhaps, with perfect accuracy, called a *republic*, or a *limited republic*. If, in a monarchy, the power of legislation is shared by the representatives of the people, it is called a *mixed monarchy*; if in an aristocracy it is so shared, it is called a *mixed aristocracy*; if in a republic, it is called a *representative republic*. But it is obvious that all these forms of government may be variously mixed together by delegations and limitations of the executive, legislative and judicial powers, in different proportions; and the actual structure of every government depending upon the choice, or necessities, or prejudices, or accidental combinations, of each society, they do not admit of any determinate classifications. But, whatever be the form of the government, the aggregate exercise of the legislative, executive and judicial powers constitutes what is commonly called the internal sovereignty of a nation.

8. From the nature and objects of civil government, we deduce not only the rights, but the duties of magistracy. These, of course, depend upon the nature of the functions, which belong to the particular department, legislative, executive, or judicial. All magistrates are responsible to God for the due and honest discharge of their duty; and, in republican forms of government, these magistrates are also made, in some shape, directly or indirectly, responsible to the people. Every civil government is bound to promote the interests of agriculture, commerce and manufactures, as conducive to the strength and happiness of the people. Every government is bound to protect the persons, the personal rights and property of its citizens from violation and injury. Every government is bound to establish courts of justice, to provide for the punishment of crimes, to enforce the obligation of legal contracts, to encourage marriages, to prohibit immorality, to cultivate a sense of religious obligation, to allow a free exercise of religious worship, and a free expression of religious opinion, so far as it is not inconsistent with the public peace and safety. Every government may impose oaths or other solemn affirmations, appealing to the consciences of parties, for the purpose of ascertaining the truth of facts, or to secure the just performance of duties. It may, therefore, reasonably require, that witnesses should be sworn, or otherwise solemnly bound to testify the truth; and it may also reasonably require parties to take promissory oaths and affirmations for the future discharge of official and other duties. And here ends our imperfect sketch of some of the leading principles of natural law, in their practical application to the

relations of man to God, to himself, to other men, and to political society. The consideration of the rights and duties of nations to each other, and of their external sovereignty, and independence, and equality, belongs to another head, that of law of nations. (See *Nations, Law of.*)

ENCYCLOPÆDIA AMERICANA.

A

POPULAR DICTIONARY

OF

ARTS, SCIENCES, LITERATURE, HISTORY, POLITICS, AND BIOGRAPHY,

A NEW EDITION;

INCLUDING

A COPIOUS COLLECTION OF ORIGINAL ARTICLES

IN

AMERICAN BIOGRAPHY;

ON

THE BASIS OF THE SEVENTH EDITION OF THE GERMAN

CONVERSATIONS-LEXICON.

EDITED BY

FRANCIS LIEBER,

ASSISTED BY

E. WIGGLESWORTH AND T. G. BRADFORD

VOL. X.

PHILADELPHIA:
LEA & BLANCHARD.
1844.

PRIZE[1]

By the term *prize* is generally understood any thing captured in virtue of the rights of war (*jure belli*). Property captured on land is usually called *booty*, and is generally disposed of at once by the commanding general, or reserved for the disposal of his sovereign, who is accustomed to bestow and distribute it according to his discretion. Few rules are therefore to be found in treatises of public law on the rights of war, in regard to captures on land. The conqueror, indeed, generally respects private property from motives of policy or clemency. He observes, or ought to observe, the terms of capitulation, if there are any; and, ordinarily, he does not give up any place which is conquered to pillage or sack. But property captured in battle of a general or movable nature is commonly subjected to immediate distribution; and the principal question which arises is how it is to be treated upon recapture. Is it to be restored by the law of postliminy (*jus postliminii*) to the original owner, or does it belong to the recaptor? In general, upon principles of strict law, if the capture has been absolute, and the possession complete by the enemy, it is deemed his property, and the title of the original owner is divested, so that he cannot reclaim it. But most nations have introduced into their own laws some modifications of this principle, and, in regard to their own subjects, have given a right of restitution to the original owner, upon his making some compensation. For the most part, however, these modifications are applied more extensively to captures at sea than to captures on land. In regard to maritime captures, a very different course has been pursued by all nations, in modern times, from that which governs in cases of captures on land. As all nations have an equal right to navigate the

[1] The importance of this subject to a commercial community is our apology for the length of the following article.

ocean, and to carry on commerce with each other, belligerents are bound to respect the rights and property of neutrals, whether navigating the ocean or engaged in trade in foreign ports. The right of belligerents to capture the property of their enemies on the sea is admitted, as well as their right to prevent any frauds, or violations of the law of nations on the part of neutrals. But these rights are limited, and must be so exercised as not to trench upon the independence or rights of other nations. Now it is obvious that it is extremely difficult, if not wholly impracticable, to ascertain, with entire certainty, what ships and cargoes sailing on the ocean, or found in belligerent ports, belong to enemies, and what to neutrals. Yet it is the duty of the belligerent sovereign, who exercises the power of capture, to abstain from seizing the one, while he may lawfully seize the other. Some mode of ascertaining the character and genuineness of each must therefore be devised, in order to prevent the abuse of the power, and to secure to neutrals a just protection. The belligerent acts at his peril, and is responsible for every abuse; and, if the wrongs are at once flagrant and frequent, they inevitably produce that state of national irritation and national injury which are the general causes of war. Hence arises the necessity of instituting some tribunals to take cognizance of maritime captures, to ascertain their validity, and, after suitable proceedings, to pronounce a decree of condemnation or acquittal. Accordingly, in modern times, it is settled, as a part of the law of nations, that every belligerent has a right to establish tribunals of prize, to examine into all maritime captures, and judicially to decide upon their validity. The final sentence, when pronounced, is deemed the act of the sovereign, deliberately adopted, and he thereby becomes responsible to all foreign nations for its correctness. But this right would be of little practical value, if other nations were not bound, so far as the property in controversy is concerned, by such a sentence. Hence, as a corollary flowing from this principle, it is another well-settled principle, that the courts of prize of the captors have exclusive jurisdiction over all matters touching captures made under the authority of their sovereign; and the courts of other nations have no jurisdiction, or authority to inquire into, or to adjudicate upon them. And the sentence of a court of competent jurisdiction once pronounced becomes conclusive, and obligatory upon all the world. It changes the property, and devests the former title of the owner, if it is a sentence of condemnation; and all nations are bound to respect the new title acquired under it.

I. It being, then, a fundamental principle that, in matters of prize, exclusive jurisdiction belongs to the prize courts of the captors, whose sentence is conclusive upon all the world, we are next to inquire, under what circumstances this exclusive jurisdiction attaches. It is not permitted to any nation to assume to itself the final adjudication upon all rights of property in which the subjects of other nations are concerned, whenever a court of prize has undertaken to pass sentence upon it. Such a sentence is not obligatory, unless a rightful jurisdiction has attached to such court; and, therefore, in all cases where property, captured and condemned as prize, comes afterwards in judgment before the courts of other nations, and the title is controverted, the first question is, whether the court of prize pronouncing the sentence had jurisdiction over the property. The foundation of its jurisdiction is, that the property has been captured, and is in the possession of the captors, and capable of being reached directly or indirectly through the process of the court. Every court of prize, therefore, proceeds *in rem*, and, in order to maintain its jurisdiction, it must be capable of asserting its claim over the thing or over its proceeds. The jurisdiction, then, gained by capture is lost by a recapture, escape, or voluntary discharge of the property before the court has adjudicated upon it; and if, notwithstanding, it should attempt to bind the property by any subsequent proceedings, its sentence becomes a mere nullity. Upon this ground, it was formerly held that, in order to entitle a court of prize to proceed to adjudication, it was essential that the property or proceeds should be brought within the ports of the capturing power. But this rule was soon found, in practice to be too narrow and inconvenient; and it is now well established, that it is sufficient that the property is in the possession of the captors in the ports of an ally in the war, or even in the ports of a neutral; for, by the capture, the captors acquire such a right and possession as no neutral nation is at liberty to devest or impugn. This rule is so inflexible that even if a belligerent captures a neutral vessel and cargo, and brings it into the ports of the neutral nation to which the vessel and cargo belong, the courts of the latter are bound to abstain from all exercise of jurisdiction over the property, except so far as to inquire whether the captors are entitled to make the capture, or are mere pirates. And this leads to the remark, that the capture must be made in a place where it can, by the law of nations, be rightfully made by the belligerent. Every neutral nation has a right to an exclusive jurisdiction within its own ports, and over its territorial seas to the extent of a marine league on its sea-coast. A belligerent has no right to make any captures within those limits; for it is undertaking to carry on war within the neutral territory, which is a plain violation of neutral rights: so a belligerent has no right to equip, or arm, or man, his ships for war in any neutral port; and, if he does, it is the duty of the neutral to vindicate his own exclusive sovereignty. If, therefore, in either of these cases of violation of territorial sovereignty, or of illegal equipments, the captured property is brought within the neutral jurisdiction, it is the right and duty of the neutral to restore it to the original owner.

A prize court may not only lose its jurisdiction by circumstances occurring after it has once rightfully attached, but it may be incompetent from the locality of the exercise of its jurisdiction. Thus a prize court must sit in the country of the captors, or, at least, in the territory of a co-belligerent; for, if it sits in a neutral country, its sentence of condemnation will be deemed invalid, aid, of course, will be disregarded as a violation of the proper duty of the neutral sovereign.

II. The next inquiry is, Who are entitled to make captures? In general, every belligerent sovereign reserves to himself the exclusive right to grant commissions to make captures in time of war. The object of this regulation is, in the first place, to secure neutrals against predatory warfare and piratical attacks; and, in the next place, to enable the sovereign to limit the operations of war, and control the persons who are engaged in it so as to secure a perfect responsibility to himself for any misconduct. But unless the sovereign actually prohibits any uncommissioned subjects from engaging in the war, they are not absolutely incompetent to make captures; for all the subjects of the hostile nations are deemed enemies to each other. But such captures are always made at the peril of the parties; and the uncommissioned captors acquire no interest therein, but the same are at the free disposal of the sovereign. Indeed, the general principle of the law of nations is, that all captures are for the sovereign; and no beneficial interest can be acquired therein by the captors, except by the grace and bounty of their sovereign. It is usual for the sovereign, in cases of public ships of war, as well as in cases of private commissioned ships, to give the captors, after adjudication, the whole of the proceeds of prizes, according to some stipulated mode of apportionment and distribution. But this is a mere act of grace, and not of duty. In cases of non-commissioned vessels, captures may certainly be made by them in self-defence, if they are attacked; and they are usually permitted to make hostile attacks and captures, which are not in mere self-defence. Indeed, so far as other nations are concerned, such captures are to be deemed lawful, and not piratical; though, if not authorized by their sovereign, the captors may incur an onerous responsibility to him. And, with a view to the exigencies of war, it is a general policy among sovereigns not to allow any rights to vest in the captors until after a final sentence of condemnation, so that, if any intermediate negotiations take place, the prizes may be restored without any infringement of the vested rights of the captors.

III. In the next place, Who are to be deemed enemies? and what property is liable to capture? In general, it may be laid down that all the subjects of the belligerents are to be deemed enemies to each other, and their property is deemed to belong to enemies; but the rule has some qualifications. In cases of prize, the question of enemy or not, depends, not upon the native or adopted country of the party, but upon his actual residence or domicil. (See *Domicil*, appendix, end of vol. iv.) He is deemed to belong to the country in which he has his actual residence or domicil. Hence a neutral domiciled in an enemy's country is deemed an enemy, and a subject of a belligerent domiciled in a neutral country is deemed a neutral; and the masters and officers and crews of ships are deemed to belong to the country, and to possess the national character of the ships in which they are employed, during the time of their employment. And the hostile character may be impressed upon a person who goes into a belligerent country originally for temporary purposes, if other objects of a more permanent nature become engrafted upon that original purpose. *Ambassadors* and *public ministers* are always deemed to retain the national character of their sovereigns; and so *consuls*, while they confine themselves to their mere official duties. But if they engage in commerce, so far as their commerce is concerned, they partake of the national character of their place of domicil. A national character which is acquired solely by domicil ceases with the change of that domicil; and the native character of the party is resumed, the moment he puts himself upon his journey (*in itinere*) to return home. Thus a belligerent subject, domiciled in a neutral country, ceases to hold the character of a neutral as soon as he is on his return to his native country, and becomes an enemy; and, *e converso*, a neutral domiciled in an enemy's country ceases to be an enemy upon his return to his own country. But mere residence in a neutral country is not always sufficient to protect the property of a party from being deemed hostile; for there may be a hostile character impressed upon the property by the mere nature of the trade in which the party is engaged. Thus if a party reside in a neutral country, but has an agent stationed in the enemy's country, who carries on trade there on his account, upon the same footing as a resident merchant and privileged trader, he will, as to such trade, be deemed an enemy. So if a neutral person is a partner in a house of trade in the enemy's country, the partnership is deemed hostile; and his neutral residence will not save his share in the concern from being liable to confiscation as enemy's property. But here the principle of reciprocity is not applied; for if an enemy be a partner in a house of trade in a neutral country, his share in the concern is not protected by the neutral character of the partnership; but his character as enemy attaches to it. There are many other cases in which traffic alone, independent of domicil, stamps upon the party engaged in it a hostile character. Thus if a party be engaged in the navigation of an enemy, or his ships sail under the flag, and pass, and papers of an enemy, the property so employed partakes of the hostile character. There are certain species of trade which are ordinarily confined to the subjects of a nation; and no foreigners are permitted to take part in such trade. Thus, before the late South American revolution, Spain prohibited all foreign intercourse with her continental colonies. In such cases of colonial monopoly, if, by special privilege, or license, a foreigner should, *pro hac vice* be allowed to carry on the trade; or if under color of the names of subjects, he should secretly embark in it, his property so engaged would be deemed hostile. Great Britain has attempted to maintain a further principle, that neutrals shall not be allowed to carry on any trade with colonies in time of war, which is not allowed them in time of peace, contending that if the ports are generally opened during war so as to ward off its pressure, it ought to be deemed a privileged trade, and subject the property to confiscation. America has resisted this extension of the doctrine, asserting it to be new, and not founded in the law of nations. So the coasting trade of a country is so generally confined to its own subjects that it is deemed a privileged trade; and the property of neutrals engaged in it is treated as hostile. And the produce of an estate situated in a hostile colony has been held to be impressed with the character of the soil, although the owner of the estate is resident in a neutral country; and, as to such produce, he is deemed an enemy. A peculiar rule has been applied to certain European factories established in the Eastern and Asiatic nations. These factories are deemed to possess the national character of the countries to which they belong, and not that of the countries where they are situated. The same rule has been applied to European establishments in Smyrna and other Turkish provinces. But the property of enemies is not always liable to capture, for the government itself may limit the operations of war; and certain property is, by the law of nations, exempted from capture. Thus vessels which are cartels, or are sailing under the license flag and pass of the government, cannot be seized as enemy's property; for they are protected by the express or implied authority of the government itself. And it is not uncommon for the government, by special instructions, to limit hostilities. Thus fishing vessels are often exempted from capture, though belonging to the enemy.

IV. Under what circumstances neutral property becomes subject to capture.

1. Belligerents having a right to capture the property of their enemies on the ocean, wherever it can be found, this right would become utterly ineffectual unless they were permitted to visit and search vessels on the ocean, in order to ascertain whether they and their cargoes were neutral or hostile. The right of search is therefore generally admitted as an incident to the right of capture. It has been, indeed, occasionally resisted; but it seems now firmly established as a part of the law of nations, though it is often used as an instrument of vexation to neutrals. Sweden, in the war between France and England, from 1793 to 1802, attempted to establish an exception, where her own ships, being neutral, were navigating under the convoy of her own public ships. But England made captures of them for resistance of the right of search; and, though much irritation existed at the time, the doctrine maintained by England seems now generally admitted. Neutrals taking the advantage of belligerent convoy will, it is said, not be liable to confiscation, unless they receive convoy orders and cooperate in resistance of the right of search. But this doctrine seems questionable; and the judicial opinions in England and America on this subject are irreconcilable. It may, then, be laid down as a general rule, that neutrals are bound to submit to the right of search; and, if they resist it, the property is liable to confiscation.

2. And the right of search draws after it a right to capture and send in the visited ship for adjudication, whenever (though the ship and cargo are under neutral papers) there are circumstances of just suspicion as to their real character. The neutral, under such circumstances, is bound to submit, and wait the regular result of the adjudication of the proper prize tribunals. If, after the capture, the neutral crew rise,

and regain the neutral ship from the possession of the captors, that alone is a hostile act; and however innocent in other respects the ship and cargo may be, they are justly subjected thereby to confiscation.

3. Another cause of the just confiscation of neutral property is that it is contraband of war. (See *Contraband.*) Goods contraband of war are generally those which are peculiarly and exclusively adapted to war, such as military and naval equipments and stores, such as guns, muskets, ammunition, and other articles usually appropriated to war. So ships built for war, and going to the enemy's country for sale, are contraband. Neutrals, being bound to abstain from taking any part in the war, are justly deemed to identify themselves with the enemy by any interposition in it, or by any act against their duty; and if they commit any such acts they are treated as enemies. Many articles of commerce are of promiscuous use, both in war and peace; and, in general, such articles are treated with indulgence, and furnish no ground for capture. And, especially, articles which constitute the produce and export of a neutral nation are, at all times, though applicable to war, treated with indulgence. But if such articles are directly destined for the military or naval use of the enemy, they will then be subject to confiscation, although they are of promiscuous use. Thus ship timber and naval stores, destined to the ports of military equipment of an enemy, are deemed contraband. So provisions in general are not deemed contraband (although there has been much conflicting discussion on the subject), being of promiscuous use; but provisions destined to the military or naval use of the enemy, or sent to his ports of naval and military equipment, are deemed contraband. In modern times, by the conventional law between nations, provisions have been often excepted from the list of contraband, and are subjected to the right of preemption.

4. Another just cause of the confiscation of neutral property is the breach of blockade. Every belligerent has a right to invest the ports of his enemy, to cut off his supplies, and to endeavor thus to compel him to a surrender. And a neutral can have no right to interpose, and relieve the besieged from the pressure of superior force. It is therefore a general rule that a violation of a blockade, by any neutral, subjects his property engaged in it to capture and condemnation. But very important questions grow out of this subject, which have been the occasion of many heated discussions between neutral nations and belligerents. What constitutes a blockade in the sense of the law of nations, has been a disputed question. The principles now established on this point seem to be, that a mere *paper blockade* (as it is sometimes called)—that is, a blockade by proclamation, without any investing force—is not a legal blockade. There must be an actual naval or military force, competent for its object, on the coast and in the vicinity. The port must be actually, and not nominally, invested. If the blockading squadron be withdrawn, or be dispersed by a storm, or, voluntarily relax the siege, the blockade is, for the time, intermitted; and an entry by a neutral, at such a time, ought not to involve any penalty. France and England, during the late continental war, attempted—the former by the Berlin and Milan decrees, the latter by orders in council—to declare whole countries in a state of blockade, and to interdict all traffic with them by neutral nations. But neutral nations resisted these pretensions, with a most decided expression of public opinion, as gross usurpations; and the persistence of Great Britain in enforcing these orders of council, was one of the main causes of the late war between her and the U. States of America.

V. Another inquiry is, What constitutes a breach of blockade on the part of a neutral? A blockade may commence, and be made known by a proclamation or notification of the belligerent government to neutral nations; or it may commence *de facto*, without any such formal notice. In order to affect a neutral with the consequences of a breach of blockade, it should be duly notified to him. Where a blockade is merely *de facto*, the neutral is not in default by approaching the port, if he has no knowledge of the blockade, or if, knowing it, he comes *bona fide* towards the port for the purpose, not of entering in breach of the blockade, but merely of ascertaining, in the neighborhood, if it still exists. But if he is warned off by the blockading squadron, and afterwards attempts to enter the port, that is a breach of blockade. But a mere persistence in this intention, without any act done after such warning off, is not of itself a breach of blockade. There must be some overt act, such as sailing again towards the port, or hovering near it, with an intent to take advantage of some opportunity to enter, to constitute the offence. But where a blockade is known to the neutral, the sailing from the neutral port, with an intent to break it, is of itself a breach of the blockade. In such a case, nothing will save the neutral from the penalty of confiscation, but the fact, that the blockade, though unknown to him, was, at the time of his sailing, withdrawn; for both intent and breach must concur. A blockade by proclamation or notification may be presumed to be intended to endure; and, therefore, notice of such a proclamation is more binding upon the neutral than a mere blockade *de facto*, whose continuance may well be deemed uncertain, temporary, and liable to sudden changes of intention. In respect to cases of contraband and breach of blockade, in order to justify the capture and condemnation of the neutral vessel or cargo, or either engaged therein, it is indispensable that they should be caught *in delicto*. The penalty, therefore, attaches (generally speaking), only while the vessel is engaged in the same voyage. If that is terminated, the offence is deposited with it, and ended. The rule, however, has been held in a somewhat larger extent by Great Britain, and probably will be adopted by other nations. In cases of contraband, if the vessel has sailed under false papers and disguises, the penalty is inflicted on the return voyage. In cases of breach of blockade, the penalty, if not inflicted before, is applied in the next succeeding voyage, but not beyond that. There are other acts which are deemed violations of the duty of neutrals, and subject their property to condemnation. All these acts may be resolved into one general proposition, that if the act be in aid of the objects or interests of the enemy, or if they amount to an actual interposition in the war, they are deemed hostile. Thus, if the neutral is guilty of any fraudulent conduct to defeat belligerent rights; or if he, directly or indirectly, assists in carrying on the war, prejudicing the rights of the other party, he is treated, so far, as a party. Hence, if he is guilty of a spoliation of the ship's papers, or a fraudulent suppression of enemy interests; if he carries enemy goods under false papers; if he carries despatches, or military passengers for the enemy; if he engages in the transport service of the enemy; if he sails under the special license and pass of the enemy;—these, and other acts of a like nature, will subject his property thus employed to confiscation, and he will be thus far held an enemy. And if the neutral mixes up and covers his own property designedly with that of the enemy, the whole will be condemnable. A court of prize will not assist him to unravel the transaction, but will deem the whole forfeited by his own misconduct.

VI. The question has often been discussed by publicists, how far a neutral has a right to carry enemy's goods, and in such case whether the neutrality of the ship gives a neutral character to the cargo; or, in other words, whether free ships make free goods, and enemy ships make enemy goods. There have been many struggles, in modern times, on the part of neutrals, to incorporate into the law of nations the principle, that free ships shall make free goods. But they have wholly failed of their purpose; and the right, whenever it exists at all, is the result of treaty stipulations, and binds those nations only which are parties to them. The general principle now acknowledged in the practice of nations is, that enemy property found on board of neutral ships is liable to capture and condemnation. The neutral flag does not protect it. And, on the other hand, that neutral property found, on board of enemy ships is not liable to condemnation; but the neutral is entitled to restitution. In all these eases, the belligerent is understood, upon the capture, to succeed to the rights of his enemy, and no more, unless there has been some misconduct on the part of the neutral, to make him forfeit the protection of the law of nations. If enemy property is found on board a neutral ship, and the conduct of the neutral is *bona fide*, he is entitled to receive the stipulated freight of carriage from the captors. If neutral property is found on board an enemy ship, the neutral must, if the captors are willing to complete the voyage, pay to the captors the stipulated freight upon due delivery and restitution.

VII. As to the nature and proofs of proprietary interest in ships and cargoes. In the ordinary course of things, the proprietary rights must be judged of by the documents and evidence found on board, and the general principles of national jurisprudence applicable to such subjects. No nation has a right to decide such questions by its own mere municipal regulations, as to the rights of property, but must decide them upon the general doctrines of the law of nations. Every ship navigating the ocean is expected to have on board some papers, which, under proper verifications, shall establish her national character. The usual papers, therefore, which the laws of her own country require as evidence of that character, ought to be on board; and if they are not, that very circumstance creates a suspicion of a false and assumed character. The like rule applies to cargoes; for these are expected to be accompanied by suitable documents to prove the ownership and national character, and to be verified by some public or customary authentications of public officers. The general criterion, therefore, adopted by the law of nations to distinguish the property of different nations found on the sea, is to require the production of such documents as the laws of the nation itself require, as evidence of proprietary interest. But these papers are not deemed conclusive, but only *prima facie*, evidence, until they are impeached. There are, however, some peculiar rules of evidence adopted in prize courts, which require to be mentioned. In the first place, it is a rule of prize courts, in all cases of capture, that the burden of proof is on the claimant to prove a neutral proprietary interest. If he fails so to do, the property is deemed hostile. One reason for this rule is, the difficulty of the captors establishing the contrary, as they have no privity with the shippers; and another is, the extreme facility and frequency of covering belligerent property under neutral disguises in time of war. Another rule is, that the circumstance of property being found on board of an enemy's ship affords a presumption, that it is enemy's property and that presumption will prevail, until it is clearly displaced by satisfactory evidence to the contrary. Another rule is, that where a party claims under a title by capture, he must show a sentence of condemnation; for though, as between belligerents, the property is, or may be changed by mere capture, neutrals or others purchasing from them, must show a good title under the sale, which can only be by such a sentence. Goods are usually accompanied by bills of lading, invoice, and letters of consignment. But a mere consignment to a party is no absolute proof of property; for he may be the mere agent of the shipper. It is, therefore, a rule, that, in such a case, the goods must appear by the documentary evidence to be really shipped on account and risk of the consignee. The consignment must amount to an absolute transfer of the property to the consignee; for if it is contingent, or dependent upon future occurrences, it is deemed to remain still in the shipper. Thus, if the shipment is made on the joint account of the shipper and consignee, or on the sole account of the consignee, at his option, the property, during the voyage, remains in the shipper, and may be captured as his, for, until the option is made, there is no absolute transfer: so, if a sale is made during war be conditional or contingent, or dependent upon future acts or circumstances, the proprietary interest is deemed to belong to the vendor: so, if the goods are sent by the vendor to the vendee without orders, though on account of the latter, the interest remains in the vendor. It is also a rule of the prize court, that property cannot, in time of war, be transferred *in transitu*; so that, for all the purposes of capture, it is treated as belonging to the same party, during the whole voyage, to whom it belonged at its commencement. Another rule is, that no lien upon enemy's property by way of pledge, or hypothecation, or for advances made by the consignee, or in virtue of a general balance of accounts due to the consignee, as factor, is regarded in the prize court as sufficient to defeat the rights of captors; nor, indeed, any liens except such known liens as accompany the very goods by the universal commercial law, such as a lien for freight. The reason for this rule is, that the liens created by private persons must be essentially dependent upon and connected with the municipal laws of the countries where the parties live, and the courts of prize would be involved in endless perplexity in the examination of them, and they would open a wide door for the introduction of false and fraudulent claims, which such courts could have no adequate means to detect.

VIII. Another inquiry is, how far the property of belligerent subjects engaged in trade with their enemies, is liable to capture and condemnation. The declaration of war puts (as has been seen) all the subjects of the different nations at war with each other, as well as the nations themselves in their sovereign capacity: hence all traffic between such subjects, being enemies, is prohibited by the law of nations, and not only all traffic and commerce, strictly so called, but all commercial dealings. Therefore, entering into contracts with an enemy, making remittances to him, or paying debts to him, during the war, is deemed an illegal intercourse, which may interfere with the national policy, and, in some cases, paralyze the operations of the war. A belligerent has no right to go into the enemy's country at all without the license of his own government, even for the purpose of bringing away goods which were purchased before the war commenced. The same principle applies to the subjects of an ally in the war; for the duties of each are the same. Hence the property of a subject, or of an ally, found engaged in commerce with the enemy, is liable to capture, and treated as enemy's property; for no person can be permitted to set up in a court of prize a claim to property founded on a violation of the law of nations. And it matters not whether the trade be carried on directly or indirectly with the enemy, directly with the enemy's ports, or indirectly through a neutral port; or whether there be an actual trade, or only an attempt to trade, for the voyage is itself illegal. And if a belligerent be engaged in any trade in violation of the municipal laws of his own country, and the property so engaged is captured he cannot maintain any claim for it in the courts of prize of his own country; for he cannot be permitted to set up his own offence against the laws to protect his property from condemnation; and his claim being rejected, the property is of course confiscated, as enemy property, for want of a proper claim. If a vessel is captured during the same voyage in which the offence of illegal traffic is committed, although after it has been committed, she is still deemed *in delicto*, and subject to confiscation. And perhaps the same rule of confiscation would be applied to the return voyage, as is applied in cases of breach of blockade and contraband of war.

IX. It is often an important question, how far the acts of the master of the ship bind the owner of the ship and the owner of the cargo. In respect to the owner of the ship, the general rule is, that the acts of the master bind him as much as if the acts were done personally by himself. This rule is established upon the doctrine that the principal is answerable for the acts of his agent, not only civilly, but penally, to the extent of the property intrusted to him. It would be difficult, in any other way, for a court of prize to reach the proprietor himself, however guilty he might be. And, if the rule savors of hardship, it should be remembered, that it is indispensable for the exercise of the just rights of war, and to enforce the just duties of neutrality. If the master has acted in contravention of the instructions of the ship-owner, he will be responsible to the latter. If, therefore, the master deviates into a blockaded port, the owner is bound by his act, and is not permitted to aver his ignorance, or that the master acted against orders. The same principle applies to the carriage of contraband goods. Grotius, and Bynkershoeck, and Pothier, have contended for a more favorable rule, where the owner is ignorant that contraband goods are taken on board. The rule, however, has been established by modern practice against their opinions. But the acts of the master of the ship do not bind the owner of the cargo, unless he is also owner of the ship, or he has knowledge of the unlawful intention, or the master is his agent. In cases of blockade, the deviation into the blockaded port is deemed to be in the service, and for the benefit of the owner of the cargo, and therefore he will be bound by the act, if he had knowledge of the blockade at the time of the sailing of the ship: so if, at the time of time sailing of the ship, the master puts himself under convoy of the enemy, it will be presumed, that it is done with the consent of the owner of the cargo. But where, from the nature of the act occurring during the voyage, upon an emergency which could not have been foreseen by the shipper, it is clear that it is done without the consent of the latter, the act will not bind him, although the master is his agent. But it will be different when the act might have been in the contemplation of the parties at the beginning of the voyage; for, in such a case, ignorance will not be allowed to excuse the shipper from the legal results of the act of his agent. There are many cases in which the acts of the master will bind the owners, both of the ship and the cargo: such are the resistance of the right of search, the rescue or recapture of the ship by the master and crew after capture, and the fraudulent suppression and spoliation of papers. It has been an agitated question, whether the resistance of a right of search by a belligerent master binds neutral property on board, although it is admitted that the resistance of a neutral master will bind all goods on board, to whomsoever belonging. The English prize courts have adhered to the affirmative, and the American prize courts to the negative. And where a person is the general agent of the whole cargo, and he covers enemy property in the ship with his principal's property, the whole will be liable to condemnation, although his principal had no knowledge of the illegal act; so if he uses simulated papers; for the carriage of such papers is emphatically said to be an efficient cause of condemnation.

X. The rights and duties of captors.

1. From what has been already stated, it is manifest that, in many cases, it will be impossible to ascertain, from the examination of the papers on board of a ship, which is visited at sea, whether she is a neutral or belligerent, and whether she is condemnable or not. The captors therefore make the seizure at their peril; and if it turns out to be unjustifiable, they are responsible for all damages and costs arising from their act. If, on the other hand, the capture is justifiable, the captors are exempted from all liability for damages and costs, whatever may be the event, and even

though the property may be restored by the prize court as neutral. They may even be entitled, in case of restitution, to be paid their own costs and expenses, where their conduct has been entirely correct. The captors, upon a justifiable capture, are considered as having a *bona fide* possession; and they are not responsible for any subsequent losses or injuries to the property from mere accident or casualty, as from stress of weather, recapture by the enemy, shipwreck, &c.; but they are responsible for all losses to neutral property which are properly attributable to their own negligence. Probable cause of capture is a perfect justification to captors, even though ultimately a restitution may be decreed. It hence becomes a very important point to ascertain what facts and circumstances constitute such probable cause. These may be almost infinitely varied, and it would be impossible to enumerate all of them; but some of the more common cases may be stated. If the ship pretend to be neutral, and has not the proper and usual documents on board to verify her own character and that of the cargo; if the cargo be without a proper custom-house clearance; if the destination be falsely stated; if the papers on board be false or colorable, or be suppressed, mutilated or spoliated; if the neutrality of the cargo does not clearly appear; if the voyage be to or from a blockaded port; if the traffic be not legal to the parties engaged in it; if the cargo be of an ambiguous character, as to contraband, or its destination be to a port of an ambiguous character, as a port of military and naval equipment; if the conduct of the officers and crew of the vessel give rise to just suspicions of their good faith, —in all such cases (and many others of a like nature might be mentioned), there is sufficient probable cause of capture to justify the captors. If any part of the property is condemnable as prize, though the bulk of the cargo may be restored, that constitutes not merely probable but justifiable cause of capture. But even probable cause of capture will not excuse captors from liability for any loss or damage accruing afterwards from their own negligence or misconduct; for the title of a *bona fide* possessor may be forfeited by such negligence or misconduct. If, therefore, the prize be lost by the negligence or misconduct of the prize officers and crew, from neglect to take a pilot, or from want of a proper prize crew, or from unskillful navigation, or from any impropriety of a similar nature, the captors are responsible to the full amount of the damage. But mere irregularity alone will not make the captors liable for damages, unless there is an irreparable loss properly attributable thereto.

2. Next as to the duties of captors. As soon as the capture of a neutral is complete, it is the duty of the captors to put a proper prize crew on board, and to send the prize into some convenient port for adjudication. The neutral crew, or a part of them, at least, are to be kept on board, and are not to be treated with severity, or handcuffed, or put in irons, unless from extreme necessity. If the neutral crew voluntarily undertake (which they are not bound to do) to assist in the navigation, that may dispense with the necessity of putting on board a full prize crew. Captors are bound to state to the master of the neutral vessel the cause of the capture, so as to give him an opportunity to make suitable explanations, and to show the insufficiency of the reasons to send her in for adjudication. Some stratagems of war are permitted in order to secure captures, as sailing and chasing under false colors; but the law of nations does not permit firing or capturing under false colors. It is the duty, also, of the captors, after capture, to prevent all spoliation and damage by the prize crew, and to abstain from breaking bulk, or removing any of the property, unless in cases of necessity. If any acts of this nature occur, the court of prize will require at their hands a full justification. Upon arrival in the proper port, it is the duty of captors, without delay, to cause proceedings to be instituted in the proper prize court, so that the legality of the capture may be immediately

ascertained. In case of any undue delay, they will be made liable for demurrage, if restitution is decreed. And the neutral may himself, by a proper application to the prize court, compel the captors to proceed to adjudication, if they unreasonably delay. In cases of illegal capture, the inquiry often arises, Who are responsible for the damages and costs? In respect to public ships, the general rule is that the actual wrongdoer, and he alone, is responsible. By the actual wrongdoer is meant the commander who has directed the capture; for the subordinate officers and crew, who have only acted in obedience to his orders, are not responsible. However, when any unauthorized act has been done by a prize master, or by a part of his crew, such actual wrongdoers, thus acting without authority, may, perhaps, be made directly responsible. The rule in relation to the actual wrongdoer is so inflexible that, if the capture has been made by a captain under the instructions of the commodore or admiral commanding the squadron, or the station, who is not present at the time of the capture, the sole remedy lies against the actual captor alone, although he may have his own remedy against his superior officer, under whose instructions he has acted. In respect to private armed vessels, a different rule prevails. There the commander is not only responsible, but the owners of the ship also, for all the illegal acts of the commander and crew. And, for the purpose of making this responsibility effectual on the grant of commissions to privateers, bonds are usually taken, with sureties, as a guaranty against their misconduct.

XI. Recaptures. A recapture may be of the property of a fellow-subject, or of an ally in the war, or of a neutral. It may be from the hands of a pirate or of an enemy. In respect to captures by pirates, no property can be acquired by them, and consequently the capture creates no change of ownership. It is, therefore, to be restored to the original owner, upon the payment of a suitable compensation, commonly called *salvage*, to the recaptors. But, in respect to captures by enemies, the change of property is complete from the time when the capture is deemed firm and secure, whether this be as soon as the surrender (*deditio*) and possession are perfected, or by pernoctation, as holding the possession after capture for a night, or by possession during any other stipulated period, or by carrying the property within the ports and territory (*infra præsidia*) of the capturing power, or by a sentence of condemnation. Various doctrines have, at different times, prevailed among nations, applicable to each of these predicaments of the captured property, the general rule being admitted, that the property is changed as soon as the capture is firm and secure, and the question still remaining open as to the time at which it is to be deemed firm and secure. The right of postliminy (*jus postliminii*) is deemed to attach to all property captured, of which there is not such a firm and secure possession. And, therefore, different nations will withhold, or will grant restitution of property captured, according to the principles adopted in their own codes of practice on this subject. The ordinances of many nations have made special provisions on the subject of recaptures. By the law of France (Ordinance of 1681), if a French vessel is recaptured from the enemy after twenty-four hours' possession, she is a good prize to the recaptors; and if recaptured before twenty-four hours' possession, she is restored to the owner upon the payment of one third of the value as salvage. But this rule is construed to apply solely to recaptures by private armed ships; for if made by public ships, restitution is decreed without payment of any salvage, whether the recapture be before or after the twenty-four hours' possession. France applies a similar rule to the recaptures of the vessels and property of her allies from the enemy. The law of Spain, in regard to recaptures from the enemy, is similar to that of France. By the law of Denmark, in the code of Christian V, if the recapture be before twenty-four hours' possession, the property is equally divided, between the original owner and the recaptors; if afterwards, the recaptors take the whole. By the law of Sweden of 1667, the recaptors are entitled to a salvage of two thirds of the value, and the remaining third is to be restored to the original owner, whatever length of time the vessel may have been in the hands of the enemy. Some alterations have been admitted into the regulations of these nations, in more modern times, either by positive ordinances, or by the practice of their courts, indicating a considerable fluctuation of opinion; but it is not necessary, and scarcely would be useful, to trace out these alterations in detail. Great Britain and the U. States of America have adopted the rule, that the property of the owner is not devested, except by a sentence of condemnation. In respect to recaptures from the enemy of ships belonging to their own subjects or citizens, they are to be restored, upon payment of salvage, if there has been no such sentence. And, by recent statutes (43 Geo. 3, ch. 160, and 45 Geo. 3, ch. 72), British vessels and goods are, upon recapture from the enemy, restored, upon the payment of one eighth of the value, if recaptured by a public ship, and one sixth if recaptured by a privateer or other vessel, without reference to the consideration, whether the property has been condemned by a court of prize or not. There is an exception of vessels which have been set forth by the enemy as ships of war. So that, in Great Britain, the right of postliminy continues forever, or, at least, until the return of peace. In the U. States of America, the act of congress of 1800 has adopted a rule, similar to that of Great Britain, in all cases where there has not been a sentence of condemnation. With us, therefore, the right of postliminy is extinguished by such a sentence. The salvage is one eighth to public ships, and one sixth to private ships, in cases of restitution. But, if the vessel has been set forth and armed for war by the enemy before the recapture, then the salvage is one moiety of the value. In respect to the recapture of vessels, and other property belonging to allies, the rule adopted by Great Britain is the rule of reciprocity. If the ally would restore British vessels and property in a like predicament, then restitution is decreed: if the ally would not restore, then the recaptors are entitled to the whole property. Aid, in the absence of all evidence of any rule adopted by an ally, the British rule is applied in favor of the ally, until it appears that such ally acts towards British property on a less liberal principle. When the rule of the ally is ascertained, Great Britain then adopts the rule of the ally. America has adopted an equally liberal course. In all cases of recaptures from the enemy of property belonging to nations or their subjects in amity with the U. States, where there has been no sentence of condemnation, restitution is decreed, or not, according to the rule which is adopted by such nation in like circumstances towards the U. States. But no restitution is decreed after the property has been condemned by the sentence of a competent tribunal. In respect to recaptures of neutral property, the general rule is to restore the property without the demand of any salvage, if the taking by the enemy was without any reasonable cause, and was merely wrongful. But, if the capture was rightful, and the neutral property was liable to condemnation, or, from the known course of practice of the enemy, was in danger thereof, then, as a beneficial service is rendered to the neutral, salvage is demandable. The ground of this distinction is obvious. If the original capture be wrongful, the neutral is entitled to a decree of restitution, with damages and costs at the hands of the captors; and it is no benefit to him to make a recapture. But if the conduct of the neutral vessel, or the nature of the cargo, would subject, or might probably subject, them to condemnation, then the recapture is a benefit to the neutral, and entitles the recaptors to remuneration. So, if the enemy is in the habit of disregarding the law of nations, and violating all the just rights of neutrals, and refusing them suitable redress, or harassing them with unjust litigation, as, in such cases, there is danger of loss to the neutral, a like remuneration should be paid to the recaptors. Principles of a similar nature are applicable to a *rescue* of a prize by the original crew, or others in aid of them, or by mere strangers. The rescue may be by citizens or subjects of the belligerents, of property belonging to fellow-subjects or fellow-citizens, or by foreigners, of property belonging to foreigners, or by citizens or subjects, of property belonging to foreigners, or by foreigners, of property belonging to citizens or subjects of the belligerents. In all these cases, salvage is due where it would be due in cases of recapture. In cases of derelict by the enemy after capture, the salvors are also entitled to salvage upon restitution; and in like manner upon donations made by the enemy before condemnation, where the donees have brought the property into port, and it is restored (as it ought to be) to the original owner. Where a hostile ship is captured, and is afterwards recaptured by the enemy, and then is recaptured again from the enemy, the original captors are not entitled to restitution upon payment of salvage; for all their rights were devested by the first recapture. The same rule applies where the original captors have voluntarily abandoned their prize, but not where the abandonment has been involuntary, and occasioned by the terror of a superior force of the enemy. In all cases where the amount of salvage is not expressly provided for by law in cases of recapture, the power of courts of prize to award it is discretionary.

XII. Connected with the subject of recapture, that of ransom may properly find a place. It has been already stated that, during war, all intercourse, and right of making contracts, are suspended between belligerents, as interdicted by the law of nations. But an exception has been uniformly recognised in the practice of nations as to contracts of ransom. This contract arises when the enemy, having made capture of a prize, consents to restore it, upon receiving a suitable compensation; and the contract so entered into between the parties is, upon principles of public faith and policy, held valid. It is usual, in such cases, to retain the master, or some of the officers of the prize, as hostages for the strict fulfillment of the contract. The death or escape of the hostages, they being merely security, does not discharge the contract. And although, upon strict principles of law, it has been thought, by the British courts, that actions upon ransom bills cannot be brought against the owners (who, as well as the hostages and master, are bound by the contract) during the war, yet it seems difficult upon principle to perceive why a court of prize might not properly enforce it as a contract of prize excepted from the general rule of hostilities. The effect of a ransom is, that it amounts to a virtual safe-conduct to the vessel and cargo during the remainder of the voyage, so as to prevent the property from a second capture by another belligerent cruiser of the same nation. If it were otherwise, the ransom contract would scarcely be entered into; and, since the validity of the contract is conceded, there is an implied consent on the part of the sovereign of the captors, that it shall be a protection from subsequent capture during the voyage. If the prize, however, deviates from the voyage, she forfeits this protection, and will be liable again to capture. And if she is lost during the voyage, the ransom contract is still obligatory upon the parties; for it is not on the part of the captors a contract for the risk, unless they expressly so engage, but a simple surrender of their own rights acquired by capture. If the prize be a neutral, still, if the capture is not utterly wrongful, but founded upon justifiable cause of capture, such as breach of blockade, carrying contraband, or other violation of neutral duties, or even if it is upon probable cause of capture, and sending in for adjudication, a ransom bill given by the neutral for a release is good, and will be enforced in the tribunals of the neutral country. But suppose, after the ransom bill is taken, the capturing ship, together with the bill, is captured, what becomes of the ransom bill, and to whom does it belong? The answer is, that the ransom bill, is a part of the capture, and the debtors upon it are thus discharged from all claims by the enemy upon it. But it does not necessarily follow, that the recaptors, succeeding to the rights of the ransom holders, might not be entitled to salvage for the benefit rendered to the debtors upon the ransom bill. Pothier says (*De Propriété*, n. 139, n. 140) that, in cases of deviation after the ransom, if a second capture takes place, the ransom holders are entitled to the amount out of the proceeds of the prize, and the second captors can only take the residue. And, under such circumstances, he deems the debtors on the ransom bill discharged from their obligation. His reasoning does not seem very satisfactory. In England, ransom bills are prohibited, and declared by statute to be void, unless in cases of extreme necessity, to be allowed by the court of admiralty. In America, no statute regulations exist; and, therefore, the doctrine stands on the general law of nations.

XIII. Joint captures. Captures may be made by a single vessel, or by an associated force acting together by preconcert, or accidentally cooperating, or by a detached ship belonging to a squadron, by privateers, or by public ships of war, by naval forces alone, or by the conjoint operation of land and naval forces.

1. In relation to public ships, the general rule is, that all public ships in sight at the time of the capture are deemed to be assisting, and are, therefore, entitled to share in the capture. It is otherwise in relation to privateers, for their being in sight is not sufficient, unless they are purposely and previously associated together; but there must be actual intimidation, an actual or constructive assistance. The reason of this distinction is, that public ships are under a constant obligation to attack the enemy; and, therefore,

from the mere circumstance of their being in sight, a presumption arises that they have an intention to capture. But, in the case of privateers, no such obligation exists; and the law does not, therefore, give them the benefit of a like presumption. Besides, in cases of public ships, the rule ensures harmony in the service; and in favor of public ships, the rule prevails even when the actual capture is made by a privateer. There are exceptions, however, to the rule, even in relation to public ships, where the circumstances of the case repel the presumption of constructive assistance. Thus, if the public ship be pursuing a course inconsistent with any notion of capture, or if she have given up the chase, or otherwise abandoned all intention of cooperation or pursuit, the claim of joint capture will be repelled. But, even in cases of public ships, the rule of being in sight is strictly construed. The ship must, at the time of capture, be actually in sight; it is not sufficient that she has been so the day before: she must also be in sight at the commencement of the engagement, or chase, or during its continuance. A convoying ship, notwithstanding her special employment, may be entitled to share as joint captor, if, by chase or intimidation, she aids in a capture, without interfering with convoy duty. In captures made by boats, it is a general rule that the ships to which they belong are entitled to share. In respect to public ships associated in the same service, or engaged in a joint enterprise, the general rule is, that they are entitled to share in each other's prizes made while in such service or enterprise. Thus, where a fleet is engaged in a blockade, the service is considered as joint, and all the fleet are entitled to share in captures made by any one of the ships. But it will be otherwise as to vessels previously detached upon a separate service, or to captures made in another service, for which they were not associated. In regard to conjunct operations by land and naval forces, how far captures made by the latter are to be shared by the former, depends upon circumstances. A mere general cooperation for the same general objects is not sufficient. But an actual cooperation is clearly sufficient. So an ally cooperating by land or sea in a capture is entitled to share in it. In respect to joint captures by public ships, the rule, as to the proportion in which they are to share, is generally settled by statute. In the U. States of America, it is provided by an act of congress, that capturing ships shall share according to the number of men and guns on board each ship in sight. In respect to joint captures by privateers, no statute regulations exist; and the general rule of the prize law, in such cases, is, that they are to share in proportion to their relative strength. In Great Britain and the U. States of America, this relative strength is measured by the number of men on board assisting in the capture. The rule is the same where an ally cooperates in the capture, and in cases of joint capture by a public ship and a private ship, whether commissioned or not.

XIV. The effects of a suspension of hostilities, and a treaty of peace. An armistice, truce, or other suspension of hostilities, is binding between the parties from its date; and all captures made subsequently thereto must be restored by the sovereign. But the actual captors, if they have no notice, are not to be deemed guilty of a wrongful act to the extent of being liable for vindictive costs and damages, at least, if they have not been guilty of gross misconduct or wilful negligence. There may, indeed, be special cases in which ignorance of a treaty of peace, or of a suspension of hostilities, either generally or in particular places, might not excuse a party from responsibility for a capture, or other wrongs done to the injured party, and in which the sovereign would be bound to indemnify him. But such cases are rare, and are governed by their own circumstances. To avoid inconveniences of this sort, it is customary to fix certain distant periods at which hostilities shall cease in different places, so that all parties may have suitable opportunities of notice. In cases where such stipulated periods are fixed, subsequent captures are deemed utterly invalid. But as to captures antecedently made, especially after notice of the existence of the peace, some diversity of opinion exists among writers on public law. The better opinion, however, seems to be, that if the treaty does not otherwise provide, the rule of *uti possidetis* prevails. A treaty of peace has the effect of quieting all titles of possession acquired during the war, unless a different stipulation is made. It therefore operates as conclusively between the belligerents as the most formal sentence of condemnation. And whatever defect may exist in the title, the infirmity is cured, or at least it can no longer be insisted on. And neutrals, who have acquired property from belligerents, under defective titles, have a right to avail themselves of this confirmatory operation, by a treaty of peace. Whatever rights existed antecedent to hostilities between the subjects of the belligerents, if no confiscation or action upon them has taken place during the war, are revived, and may be pursued and claimed, upon the return of peace.

XV. Such is a brief outline of some of the more important principles of prize law, applicable to maritime captures. A full examination of all of them, in their details, could be made only in a large and voluminous treatise. This sketch will be closed by a summary of some of the principles which regulate the general practice of the English and American courts of prize.

1. As soon as the captured ship arrives in port, the prize-master is bound to give notice thereof to the proper court of prize, and to deliver, upon oath, into the registry of the court, all the papers found on board of the ship. It is the duty of the captors to send in, with the ship, the master or some of the principal officers and crew of the ship, in order that their testimony may be taken, upon standing interroga-

tories, which are prepared under the direction of the prize court. The prize-master accordingly gives notice to the commissioners appointed to take the examinations of the master and crew of the captured ship, so brought in, upon these interrogatories; and these examinations are made immediately after the arrival in port; and in order to prevent frauds and concealments, the witnesses, before examination, are not allowed to have any communication with, or to be instructed by, counsel. Each witness is separately examined and his answers written down, and the whole are then subscribed by him, and verified by the commissioners, and then certified, under seal, to the prize court. These examinations being completed, a libel is filed in the prize court, alleging the facts in the most general form, and asserting the property to belong to enemies; and a monition is thereupon issued and duly published, requiring all persons who have any interest or claim to appear, at a given day, in court, and show cause why the ship and goods should not be condemned as prize. This is the American practice, which differs, in the order of the proceedings, from the English, the latter issuing the monition before the filing of the libel.

2. Upon the return of the monition, the parties who have any interest, and mean to assert any claim, appear and put in their claim, under oath; and as soon as such claim is put in, the cause is ripe for a hearing. If the ship or any part of the cargo is neutral, the master usually puts in a claim in behalf of the owners, or it is put in by the consul of his nation, or by the accredited correspondents or agents of the claimant. If the captors have been guilty of any delay in instituting proceedings, the claimant may procure a monition from the court, requiring them to proceed to adjudication. If no claim is put in on the return day of the process, the default is entered on the records; but it is not now usual to proceed to a final decree of condemnation until a year and a day after

the return of the monition, except in cases where, from the evidence, there is a strong presumption that the property belongs to the enemy. But after a year and a day, condemnation goes of course; unless a claim is interposed.

3. No claim is permitted to be put in, unless by the master, or correspondent, or, agent, of the owner, or by the consul of the nation. A mere stranger, having no interest, is not permitted to claim. It has been already stated, that a claimant in a prize court must be the general owner of the property. If he has but a lien, or is a mere insurer, or a mortgagee not in possession, he cannot maintain any claim, for reasons which are founded in the incompetency of such a court satisfactorily to investigate such claims. There are certain other cases, in which claims will not be allowed to be interposed, but are rejected as incompetent: thus no claim is admitted which stands in direct opposition to the ship's papers and documents on board, and preparatory examinations, at least after the war has commenced; no person is permitted to claim, where the transaction is in violation of the municipal laws of his own country; nor in a case where the trade is prohibited by the law of nations, or the law of nature; or is a gross violation of his duties as a belligerent; in all such cases; the claimant is held not to have a *persona standi in judicio*; and, his claim being rejected, the cause stands as if there were no claim at all interposed. The ship's papers, and examinations upon the standing interrogatories, are never allowed to be seen until after the claim is filed, so that the party may not have an opportunity to frame it to meet the exigency of the evidence.

4. Supposing the claim to be interposed by a competent party, and in a valid manner, the cause is then to be heard. The hearing is, in the first instance, confined altogether to the ship's papers and documents on board, and the preparatory examinations taken upon the standing interrogatories.

No extrinsic evidence is admitted on either side; for it is a general rule of the prize courts, that the evidence to acquit or condemn must, in the first instance, come from the papers and parties found on board.

5. If, upon the hearing, a case for condemnation or acquittal is satisfactorily made out, the court will at once proceed to make the proper decree. But if the case be doubtful, and the evidence unsatisfactory, then it becomes a case for further proof. The captors are rarely allowed, unless under special circumstances, to make further proof; but the claimant is allowed to make further proof unless he has forfeited this privilege by his own misconduct, or that of his agents, or the posture of the case shows that he cannot safely be trusted with further proof. The claim to make further proof is a matter not of strict right, but of sound discretion in the court. It is usually allowed where the party has acted with good faith and propriety; it is always denied where he is guilty of gross misconduct or fraud. If further proof is denied in a case which requires it, the result is, that a decree of condemnation follows; for the burden of showing that the property is not good prize rests on the claimant. And where further proof is allowed, it is usually made by affidavits and testimony taken under commission; and if then it proves still unsatisfactory, it is deemed conclusive evidence that the property is hostile, or that there has been some misconduct, which justifies condemnation. Further proof is never allowed where there are false or colorable papers on board; or where any papers are thrown overboard; or where there has been a spoliation of papers; or where there has been a covering and concealment of enemy interests; or where the master and crew, upon the preparatory examinations, have been guilty of gross prevarication or falsehood; or where there is a false destination; or where there is a want of good faith in the

claimant; or where the case appears to be incapable of any fair explanation.

6. During the pendency of the proceedings, which are sometimes protracted to a great length of time, owing to accidental circumstances, an unloading of the cargo often becomes necessary. This may be procured upon a suitable application to the court, for the court has a virtual custody and possession of the property, from the moment of the proceedings *in rem* being commenced. If the property be perishable, the court has also authority to decree a sale of it, upon the application of either party; and it often proceeds to direct a sale upon the consent of both parties, where the property is not perishable. And where a sale has been made, the proceeds are subject to the order of the court, as a substituted fund for the original property; and if not brought into court, they may, in the discretion of the court, be ordered to be deposited in the registry. In cases of the capture of neutrals, application is often made for a delivery of the property upon bail, or security, by way of stipulation for the value; and when so given, the bail becomes a substitute for the property, and is subject, in the same manner, to the orders of the court; but no such delivery will be made, according to the practice of the prize court, until after a hearing of the cause, unless upon the consent of both parties. If, upon the hearing, the case is one for further proof, and the neutral has not disabled himself from producing it by his own misconduct, the court is then in the habit of allowing a delivery of the property to the claimant, upon an appraisement, and giving bail. And if the claimant will not take it, it is sometimes delivered, upon an appraisement and bail, to the captors.

7. After the cause has been finally heard, a decree is entered, either of acquittal or condemnation, of the whole or of part. A decree of acquittal will be with or without

damages and costs to the claimant, according to circumstances. If there was probable cause of capture (as has been already stated), no damages or costs will be given to the claimant; but costs and expenses are usually, in such cases, decreed the captors. If the capture is without probable cause, costs and damages to the claimant usually follow. If a decree of condemnation is pronounced, the claimant is made responsible for the expenses and costs of the captors by reason of the claim.

8. A decree of condemnation being pronounced, it often remains a question to whom the condemnation is to be, whether to the government or to the captors. In cases of captures by public ships, or by non-commissioned vessels, the decree of condemnation is to the government generally. In cases of captures by privateers duly commissioned, the condemnation is to the captors. In England, the lord high admiral is, in certain cases, entitled to the proceeds of captured property, which are called *droits of admiralty*. But in modern times, this office is usually held by the king, or for his benefit, and therefore the distinction is, for the most part, now nominal. In the U. States, no such distinction exists. It is no objection to proceeding to a decree, that any of the parties have died; for, the proceedings being *in rem*, they are not interrupted by such occurrences. Time, however, is usually allowed for the legal representatives of a deceased claimant to appear, if there is any necessity; and in proceedings *in personam*, a monition always issues to the legal representatives, if any, before a decree.

9. A decree of condemnation is usually pronounced by an interlocutory, in the nature of a final decree. But the case rarely ends here; for the prize court, as an incident to the possession of the principal cause, may, and usually does, in cases of controversy, upon the application of any party in interest, proceed to decree distribution of the proceeds. If

the proceeds are not in court, it also acts against prize agents and others having possession of the proceeds of prize, or bound to respond for them, by way of monition, and, orders them to be brought into the registry for distribution. Such is a summary sketch of some of the most important principles of prize law and prize practice. It is necessarily imperfect, for a full discussion of these subjects would be incompatible with the design of a work of this nature.

ENCYCLOPÆDIA AMERICANA.

POPULAR DICTIONARY

OF

ARTS, SCIENCES, LITERATURE, HISTORY, POLITICS AND BIOGRAPHY,

A NEW EDITION;

INCLUDING

A COPIOUS COLLECTION OF ORIGINAL ARTICLES

IN

AMERICAN BIOGRAPHY;

ON

THE BASIS OF THE SEVENTH EDITION OF THE GERMAN

CONVERSATIONS-LEXICON.

EDITED BY

FRANCIS LIEBER,

ASSISTED BY

E. WIGGLESWORTH AND T. G. BRADFORD.

VOL. XII.

PHILADELPHIA:
LEA & BLANCHARD.
1844.

USURY

USURY, in a very general sense, means a compensation or reward for money lent. In this sense, it is equivalent to *interest*. But in the common business of life, it rarely has this signification, but is chiefly used in an odious sense, to express an exorbitant or illegal compensation for money lent, in contradistinction to the common compensation allowed by law, which is called *interest*. Thus a man is commonly called a *usurer*, who lets money for more than legal interest, and who is therefore deemed a hard, oppressive and avaricious creditor. It is singular to what a great extent the prejudice against the receipt of interest upon money lent has prevailed in all ages. That a man should receive a compensation for a thing which he lends to another for a use which is beneficial to the latter, and inconvenient to himself, seems to stand upon the first principles of justice. If A lets his horse to B for a journey for B's pleasure or profit, no one doubts the propriety of A's asking and receiving a compensation for the hire of the horse. Why, then, should not A be equally entitled to a compensation, if he lends money to B for the pleasure or profit of the latter? If the compensation asked be a reasonable recompense only, for the inconvenience to which A is put, or for the hazard which he runs of not receiving back the thing lent, there is no difference in the principle, whether the loan be of the horse or of the money. If it be exorbitant or illegal, the impropriety and injustice equally apply to each case. And yet it has been rare, either in the policy of nations or the opinions of moralists, that the transactions have been viewed in an equally favorable light. One ground of the common prejudice probably has been, that money, being the common medium of trade and commerce, is more generally in demand, and more universally useful to all persons, than any other commodity; and therefore the whole community are eager to borrow upon as cheap terms as possible, and the lenders are as naturally desirous to lend upon as high terms as possible; thus begetting a mutual jealousy, and a strong tendency to hard bargains. In times when money is scarce, the necessity, as well as the difficulty, of borrowing, is greatly increased, and an inflamed spirit of discontent is generated against those who possess the means of relief; and will not afford it, but upon the terms of an exorbitant compensation. They thus become odious, first as individuals, and next, when they become numerous, as a class. In this way, money-lenders are deemed to have a peculiar interest hostile to that of the public at large; and even if the laws do not prohibit the charge of high interest, they are stigmatized as extortioners and usurers. Besides, the poor, the extravagant and the dissolute generally live beyond their means, and therefore have the strongest desire, as well as the strongest necessity, for borrowing. In proportion as their wants rise, they are more ready to contract for high interest; and as they are unable to pay when the proper time for payment arrives, they are compelled to submit to further exactions; and the creditors, as they perceive an increasing hazard of losing the principal, are disposed to indemnify themselves against the risk by additional premiums. From these combined operations, always going on, in such cases, with accelerated force, there is almost a certainty of ultimate ruin to such borrowers. The creditors are thus compelled to more vigilance, and to more effort to obtain or secure payment, until, at last, the borrowers seem to be the victims of misfortunes which they are unable to resist, and the creditors to be the instruments of harsh and vindictive oppression. Thus public sympathy becomes enlisted on the side of the sufferers, without adverting to the rights or the indulgences of the creditors, simply because the latter can bear the loss without as much suffering. But a more extensive ground of prejudice has been derived from religious sources. Those who are enemies to the allowance of interest in general, often make no distinction between that and usury, and hold each to be equally reprehensible. Christians, in an especial manner, have drawn arguments from the prohibition of usury by the law of Moses, among the Jews; and the school divines, partly on this account, and partly on the authority of Aristotle, who has fancifully said that money is naturally barren, and to make it breed money is preposterous, have not hesitated to pronounce it contrary to the divine law, both natural and revealed. The canon law, too, has proscribed the taking of any, even the least, interest for the loan of money, as a mortal sin. It is not surprising, under such circumstances, that men, in the dark ages, should have looked with horror upon the taking of interest, and that the military and feudal lords of those days, who were always needy, and always borrowing, full of the pride of birth and rank, and full of disdain for the humbler avocations of life, and especially of those connected with the accumulation of money, should have looked with contempt upon the usurer, and have augmented the popular delusion. But that, in enlightened times, the religious scruples to which we have alluded should still have prevailed, is one more illustration of, the difficulty of correcting error when it has once fastened itself on the community. Nothing can be clearer, than that the Mosaic precept was merely a political, and not a moral precept. It did not prohibit the Jews from all taking of usury. It only prohibited them from taking it from their own brethren, the Jews. But the Mosaic law, in express words, permitted them to take it of a stranger. The Jews have, accordingly, been great money lenders upon interest in all ages; and this has, probably, in Christian countries, still more augmented the prejudice against this venerable, but unfortunate people. Indeed, so strongly is this prejudice fixed, that a man of a sordid and avaricious character is, even now, proverbially called a *Jew*. There is, however, not the slightest foundation, either in natural or revealed religion, for any prohibition against the taking of interest upon money, any more than against the taking of a profit for the use of any other thing loaned. But the policy of most nations has not suffered the right or rate of interest to rest upon the mere moral law, or the doctrines of religion. In almost all nations, in modern times the legislature have regulated the subject, and prohibited, under severe penalties, all contracts and bargains, by which any excess of interest, beyond the rate prescribed by the law, is secured. In many countries, they have declared all such contracts utterly void, so that even the principal loan cannot be recovered; thus making the supposed want of conscience, on one side, a full justification of the grossest want of conscience on the other. In some countries, they have allowed the interest, if paid, to be recovered back. In other countries, they have refused this, and adopted an intermediate course allowing a recovery of the principal, sometimes with a small interest, and sometimes with no interest. Among statesmen and political economists, it has been for a long time a vexed question, how far the regulation of interest upon money is founded in sound policy, or public convenience. That it should be regulated by the legislature to the extent of declaring, by a general rule, what interest shall be allowed when the parties have been silent, and what shall be allowed where there has been a wilful delay of payment beyond the stipulated period, would seem to be a proposition susceptible of little question or debate. It is far better to have some certain rule, in such cases, to furnish a universal guide, than leave the amount to be ascertained by a judicial decision in every case of difference between the parties. And where the parties have been silent, if such a rule exists, it may fairly be presumed to be acquiesced in or adopted by them. The question, then, is not, whether the law ought, in cases unprovided for by the parties, to adopt some uniform measure of interest, but whether the parties should be prohibited from stipulating for any rate of interest which they may choose. In former ages, it was quite a common practice for legislatures to regulate the rate of buying and selling many commodities, so as to restrain the ratio of profits within certain limits. Such regulations would now be generally deemed unphilosophical and impolitic, as well as oppressive. All that the law would now attempt to accomplish, would be to prevent imposition, fraud and circumvention in such contracts. Why should not the same principles apply to bargains about money? Why should a man, dealing fairly and openly, be prevented by the laws from making as high a profit upon the sale or loan of money as upon the sale or loan of merchandise? The general grounds upon which legislation upon the subject of the interest of money has been justified, as contradistinguished from other profitable contracts, are, the prevention of excessive interest; the prevention of prodigality; the protection of the poor and needy against extortion; the suppression of rash enterprise, and the security of the weak and credulous against imposition. Now, it will be found, upon a careful examination, that some of these grounds are quite unsatisfactory and delusive; and some of them are equally applicable to all other contracts and bargains as well as to loans of money. So far as the object of laws is to prevent oppression and imposition, and undue advantage of the strong over the weak and credulous, the principle should apply to all contracts, not by regulating the terms of every contract *a priori*, and settling what, under all the circumstances, should be just, and reasonable, but by providing, by general principles of law, that unconscionable and oppressive contracts, where undue advantage is taken of the weakness, or credulity, or necessity, of the other party, shall be either wholly set aside, or reduced to moderation, upon a full trial of each particular cause, and an examination of all the facts, so as to make the decision just in itself, *ex æquo et bono*. There is nothing in the nature of contracts for loans of money which, in this respect, makes it either necessary or proper to distinguish them from others. Nor is it easy to see how prodigality would be encouraged by the facility of borrowing any more than of buying. Interest will always bear a steady proportion to the means of repayment, and the punctuality of the performance of the contract. If persons are prodigal and extravagant, they will not be less inclined to borrow because the laws have protected them against paying an undue interest; and if they do borrow under such circumstances, they must either give an extravagant interest, in order to indemnify the lender against the additional risk from its illegality, or else they will borrow upon the usual terms; and in neither case does the prohibition answer its purpose. The interest of money must ordinarily be regulated in practice by the value of the use to the borrower as well as the lender, by the general demand for it, and by the hazard of repayment. If the demand be small, and the security be good, the interest will be low. If the demand be great, the interest will be high, although the security be good. And if the demand be great, and the security doubtful, it is obvious that the price will be proportionally enhanced, since it includes the risk of loss as well as the value of the use. Now, it is certain that these three ingredients admit of very various combinations, and that there are perpetual changes going on in relation to each. Nothing is more uncertain or variable than the demand for money, and the facility of obtaining it. It depends upon a thousand circumstances, political, commercial, and even local. No man can foresee them; and no legislation can suitably provide for them. The very elements upon which to found a rule admit of no arrangement and no certainty. Is it not, therefore, unwise, as well as unjust, to establish a general rule to govern all cases, when the rule itself cannot work the same way any two days in succession throughout the year? On the other hand, there are positive mischiefs attendant upon all absolute regulations of this subject. In the first place, no laws can practically reduce the rate of interest below the lowest ordinary market rate at the time when the money is wanted. It will be borrowed, at all events, if there is a necessity; and in proportion as the demand grows more urgent, there will be a correspondent disposition to evade and break down the restriction. Thus a tendency is created to a habitual disobedience to the laws—a tendency which, in every view, moral as well as political, is deeply to be deprecated. In the next place, it operates greatly to the discouragement of trade and commerce. Nothing more favors the interests of commerce than a general liberty to buy and sell without restraint or obstruction. If the party can always obtain money, while he possesses good credit, without any restraint as to the interest he shall give for it, from the rise or fall of markets, he will naturally be induced to extend his business, and may extend it with comparative security and advantage. But, if he is obliged to calculate all possible chances of relieving his necessities beforehand, with the knowledge that, if money rises in the market, he must borrow upon disadvantageous terms, he will not embark at all in enterprises which go beyond his own present means; or he will take the risk, and, if the exigency arises, he must pay proportionally higher, because the law gives no validity to the contract. He must pay the lender for trusting to his honor and honesty, and not to the authority of the laws. In short, the moment it is admitted (what can hardly be disputed) that commerce cannot well subsist, to a great degree, in any country, without mutual and extensive credits, it is obvious that every measure that facilitates and gives security to such credits must be beneficial. Another evil attendant upon restrictive laws is, that, in any scarcity or extraordinary emergency, they unavoidably enhance the market price of money. They make the pressure heavier, and compel the parties to heavier sacrifices. Many men will not, in such times, lend their money at all upon common interest; and yet they have great scruples about letting it upon any contract for usury, lest they should lose both principal and interest. Others, if they do lend without regard to the laws, demand a higher and perhaps extravagant compensation for the hazard which they run. And conscientious borrowers, rather than incur the imputation of being violators of the laws, make other sacrifices of their property, which sometimes are ruinous, and generally are deeply injurious to their estates. If, under such circumstances, they were free to make their own bargains, they could borrow at lower rates, and could give legal security. In short, the prohibitory system, in many cases, aggravates the very evils which it is intended to mitigate. It makes the prodigal more extravagant, the rash more undistinguishing, the poor more servile and dependent, the rich more irresolute or avaricious, the weak more easy prey to the crafty, the busy and enterprising more timid or more speculative, and thus introduces into social life many perturbations which cannot be calculated, and many immoral practices which silently impair, or openly sap, the foundations of virtue.

APPENDIX

[Review]. Art. XII. Encyclopedia Americana
(*The North American Review (1821–1940)*; Jan. 1832; Vol. XXXIV, No. LXXIV)

Joseph Story's Sketch of American Law
- Kurt H. Nadelmann
(*The American Journal of Comparative Law* Vol. 3, 1954)

American Law
- Joseph Story
(*The American Journal of Comparative Law* Vol. 3, 1954)

Publisher's advertising prospectus for
Encyclopedia Americana

Title page of *Conversations-Lexicon*

Art. XII.—*Encyclopædia Americana.*

Encyclopædia Americana. A Popular Dictionary of Arts, Sciences, Literature, History, Politics and Biography, brought down to the present time; including a copious Collection of Original Articles in American Biography; on the basis of the seventh Edition of the German Conversations-Lexicon. Edited by Francis Lieber, assisted by E. Wigglesworth and T. G. Bradford. Philadelphia. 1829—1831.

This work, which has now proceeded as far as the seventh volume, deserves to be recommended to the great body of our people, as a library of itself;—cheap, comprehensive, exceedingly well executed, and of the highest authority. The German Conversations-Lexicon, which is properly acknowledged to be the basis of the Encyclopædia Americana, is in fact nothing more: a large part of the superstructure, which is made up of biography, politics, and history, having been added here; while even the basis, which contained much that was originally important, but owing to the progress of time, materially diminished in value, has been greatly improved both here and abroad, by the substitution of new and better materials. The articles on the subject of English and American law are entirely new; and, with the treatises in the original on Roman, German and French law, render the work very complete for the historical, and of great use to the professional lawyer. Some articles, those, for example, on the subjects of Zoology, Mineralogy and Chemistry, have been altogether re-written; while others, including the departments of Political Economy and Geography, have been greatly enlarged. Add to this, that the subject of American Biography is wholly new; and those who are acquainted with the original German work will at once perceive the nature, scope and value of the Encyclopædia Americana.

For the information of those who may not be acquainted with the Conversations-Lexicon of Germany, either directly, or through any of its numerous translations, it may be proper very briefly to state a few facts in regard to its origin, history and success, which we have borrowed from the preface to the work before us. The *Allgemeine deutsche Real-Encyklopedie für die gebildeten Stände* originated with Mr. Brockhaus, an eminent bookseller of Leipsic, who was its publisher and principal editor. He called it the Conversations-Lexicon, as being a work chiefly designed for the use of persons, who would take a part in the conversation and society of well-informed circles. The character of the work, however, has been to a certain degree changed by numerous improvements, in each successive edition; and its original title has therefore ceased to be strictly appropriate. But as the book had become known, and had gained its well deserved popularity under that name, it was thought inexpedient to change the title.

The value attached to this undertaking of Mr. Brockhaus is evident from the fact, that about eighty thousand copies of the work, now consisting of twelve volumes, have been published since 1812; besides which, two pirated editions have appeared in Germany. There have been, moreover, Danish, Swedish and Dutch translations of it; and a French one is in progress at Brussels. More than two hundred contributors are enumerated in the preface, most of whom are distinguished not only at home but abroad, while many of them are recognised throughout the scientific and literary world, as among the most eminent men of the age.

'In presenting this work to the public in the English language,' says Dr. Lieber, 'my intention has been, by making such changes and additions as the circumstances of this country required, to render it as useful and acceptable to the general reader here, as the original is in Germany; and I have cherished the hope, that the circumstance of its being an *American* Encyclopædia, not merely in name, but as constituting an extensive repository of information relating to America, as well as to the various branches of general knowledge, would give it a peculiar value with that great European nation, whose language and literature are the common property of themselves and their descendants in the United States.

'In the title-page, this work is stated to be formed upon the basis of the German *Conversation-Lexicon*: and if the reader will compare it with the original, and consider the numerous additions and corrections which have been made, I hope he will not find cause to charge this title with being too pretending. My idea of a good American Encyclopædia has been, that it should contain, besides the most valuable portions of the English Encyclopædias, and the topics of peculiar value to an American reader, information upon all subjects of general interest on the continent of Europe.'

It will be conceded by all, who have bestowed any serious attention upon the subject, that, however numerous may be the Encyclopædias that have hitherto appeared in our language, there is no one, which fully corresponds with this in its principal characteristics, or is at all likely to interfere with it, if this prove what it is designed to be,—a compilation adapted to the use of our country and people, as well as of those abroad, whoever they may be, that speak the same language, and feel interested in the growth of their own distinguishing usages and institutions, though transplanted into another hemisphere. It may be admitted also, that such a work is needed here, and that, if well executed, and placed within the reach of those, who, without the ability to procure large libraries, and without leisure to use, if they had them, are nevertheless able to expend something every year in the purchase of books, and sufficiently inquisitive in regard to the subjects which occur in the course of their general reading, to desire a more extensive, if not a complete knowledge of them. Our citizens, with their abundant leisure, their multitude of newspapers, and their opportunities for acquiring elementary knowledge, appear in fact, to require some such work, more than almost any other people; not excepting the thinking, studious, indefatigable German; nor the shrewd Scot, whose prevailing character is in nothing more evident, than in his efforts to add strength to his understanding; nor the sprightly Frenchman, who is hardly ever so illiterate, as to be ignorant of the principal writers of his own country. A work, which occupies a sort of middle place between our newspapers and our libraries, being more deliberately prepared than the former, and less expensive and more easily mastered than the latter; avoiding the disadvantages, and uniting the benefits of both, at least with most readers, who require summaries and works of reference, rather than voluminous treatises upon the subjects in which they are interested, would appear to be singularly well fitted to our wants and wishes. This is what the editors of the Encyclopædia Americana have attempted to prepare. That there is nothing of this sort within the reach of our people now, may be proved by referring to the Encyclopædias now in use; all of which are too expensive, too bulky, and too learned, or in other respects ill adapted to the use of the many. If we turn to Chambers's Cyclopædia, or the Universal Dictionary of Arts and Sciences, which has already passed through several editions; to the Encyclopædia of Rees, which was re-published in this country, at a very low price, but was disposed of by lottery at last, in consequence of the magnitude and difficulty of the enterprise; to the *Encyclopædia Brittanica,* of which six editions have already appeared, and the seventh is in the course of preparation, containing at different times from ten to twenty volumes, with a supplement of six volumes by Napier; to the Edinburgh Encyclopædia, re-published in Philadelphia, which must consist, when completed, of hardly less than forty volumes; to the *Encyclopædia Londinensis;* to the *Encyclopædia Edinensis;* to the *Encyclopædia Metropolitana,* to consist of twenty-five volumes quarto; and to many more in all the languages of Europe:—or if we run over the list contained in the work before us, we shall be satisfied, that such works are required for the general reader, as well as for those who have libraries, and leisure to enjoy them; and that there is not, as we have already said, one in existence, adapted to the wants of our people. On reviewing the works mentioned above, no one appears to be so well fitted for our purposes, taking all circumstances into consideration, as the German Conversations-Lexicon would be, if translated for us; any improvement, therefore, upon it, would be entirely decisive in its favor. There can be little doubt, that it fully deserves the reputation it enjoys. A work, which has passed through so many editions at home, and has been translated into so many languages abroad, must be,—it cannot be otherwise,—of great value, not only in the country in which it first appeared, but in every other, where it has been allowed to re-appear. Men do not enter into such expensive undertakings without deliberation. They are unlike all others; and they cannot continue, year after year, unless they have something else to depend upon, than merely popular favor. Perhaps two hundred thousand copies of the original work have been distributed through Europe, in different languages, since its publication in 1812; while probably not more than twenty-five thousand copies of the Library of Useful Knówledge have been disposed of. This fact alone is sufficient to convince us, that this age has produced nothing better fitted to the wants of society at large; to the necessities rather; for its circulation could not have been so extended, unless it had been regarded almost as a necessary of life.

One word in regard to the mechanical execution and price of the Encyclopædia Americana; for whatever might be its scientific or literary value, if it were badly printed, or expensive, it would be hardly suitable for us. The price of the whole work is thirty dollars, or two dollars and a half a volume. There are to be twelve volumes, seven of which are already published, each containing between six and seven hundred pages octavo. Owing to the dimensions of the paper, and the mode of printing, they contain as much as three or four English octavos of a similar quality, of which the price would be twelve shillings sterling; so that the whole work will contain as much matter as from thirty-six to forty-eight English octavos, which would cost in this country nearly one hundred and fifty dollars. Nor should it be forgotten, that there are in each volume about fifteen hundred articles, together with a general index. Here then, are nearly twenty thousand articles,—abridged treatises,—upon every subject of inquiry to which the well informed or the ill informed can possibly have occasion to refer; and to be purchased at such a price, that few indeed, in our country, can have the wish, without the means of obtaining the publication which contains them. Six cents a week, laid aside for ten years,—or two dollars and fifty cents a year,—will furnish every individual with a library of his own. Subscribers are found in every part of our country, for the Library of Useful Knowledge, and other cheap publications; and the case will be the same, when the work is properly understood, with the Encyclopædia Americana.

The alterations, omissions, and additions, made by Dr. Lieber, and the gentlemen associated with him, are, as they were designed to be, great improvements upon the original work, so far at least as relates to this country. What interest, for example, is felt here, on the subject of Heraldry, which occupies so large a portion of English Encyclopædias? Occasionally, perhaps, when reading a novel of Sir Walter Scott, or examining a Liverpool coat-of-arms burnt into opaque china, we might wish for something in the shape of a dictionary, to enable us to look into its mysteries; but there are few, indeed, who would care to purchase or possess a work upon the subject. Of course, the place usually occupied by Heraldry, in our Encyclopædias, may be surrendered to something better, in a work which is designed for all classes; and the editors have done wisely, in excluding it from this. It is another material improvement, that they have gone very largely into the subjects of American law, the natural sciences, political economy, American history, and American biography;—subjects of vast importance to ourselves, and to those who are to tread in our footsteps, and inherit our libraries. On the two last, particularly, nothing sufficiently clear, condensed, and satisfactory, is to be found elsewhere. We have Delaplaine's Repository, and Sandford's Biography of the Signers of the Declaration of Independence, together with a few volumes, and only a few, of unconnected individual biography; and in the department of history, we have, perhaps, a hundred volumes, purporting to be histories of these States, many of which are well executed; but we had before no epitome,—no abridgment,—no map of the whole, to which any one may instantly refer, without resorting to a capacious library.

The article, *Statistics of Crime*, may also be mentioned as a particularly valuable paper. We know nothing of the author, and have no means of authenticating his calculations with certainty; but from our general impressions, and the data within our reach, we are inclined to believe, that he has not been led astray by the enthusiast Colquhon, and that he has brought together the substance of much close, thoughtful, and long-continued observation, made under the most advantageous circumstances. Many abridged reports of the House of Commons appear to be still farther abridged, in this brief and very complete summary. If our limits permitted, we should be pleased to follow the author through an inquiry so interesting, not only to the philanthropist, but to the lawgiver, and the philosopher. A very learned paper, embodying in the form of principles, maxims fortified by authorities from every quarter, and comprehending matter enough to fill a volume, as volumes are now made, within the compass of three pages, may be found in the appendix to Volume IV. under the head of *Domicil*. We are satisfied, indeed, by examination of a number of the legal articles, that no lawyer, certainly no lawyer who desires to be acquainted with the Roman law, and its numberless European modifications, ought to think his library complete, without the Encyclopædia Americana. The article *Dyspepsia* is a very original and satisfactory treatise on that subject. The Zoological and Biographical parts, the first prepared by the late Dr. Godman, and the latter by Mr. Walsh, are also executed with great ability.

We conclude with expressing our best wishes for the success

of this valuable publication. In order to secure it a very wide circulation, nothing more is necessary, than that its character should be fully understood, its price known, and specimens of its execution occasionally given in our newspapers. Great things are doing on every side, in the cause of popular education; but none worthier of the object, none better calculated for the safe and certain promotion of it, than the multiplication of cheap standard works, the value of which will not depend upon the caprice or fashion of the day.

KURT H. NADELMANN

Joseph Story's Sketch of American Law

IN THE HISTORY OF LEGAL SCIENCE, THE YEAR 1834 WAS MEMORABLE. During its course, the first modern treatise on conflict of laws made its appearance[1], the first treatise in English not based on the theory of the statutists, and the first to make use—masterly use—of the comparative method.[2] For the author of the work, which brought him world fame,[3] the year was particularly strenuous. Joseph Story had in the early part of 1834 fulfilled his duties as a member of the Supreme Court of the United States, in Washington and on circuit. In the later part, he attended to his heavy teaching obligations as one of the two law professors at Harvard College. During the summer, he delivered an address on "The Science of Government, as a Branch of Popular Education,"[4] and completed a lengthy sketch of American Law for a German legal periodical.[5] This sketch, previously known only in translation,[6] is here presented for the first time in the original text.

How Story came to write this sketch can be reconstructed from correspondence which has been preserved. The account begins with the appearance in Boston in 1827 of the young Francis Lieber, who had left his native Prussia because of political persecution. Lieber had the ambitious plan to produce an American version of Brockhaus' *Conversations-Lexicon.* He managed to secure a publisher in Philadelphia and was able to enlist the active help of many prominent Americans,[7]

KURT H. NADELMANN is a member of the Board of Editors.

[1] Story, Commentaries on the Conflict of Laws, Foreign and Domestic (1834).

[2] In the preface to his Commentaries on the Law of Bailments with Illustrations from the Civil and Foreign Law (1832), Story stated the reasons for making use of foreign sources.

[3] See Lorenzen, Story's Commentaries on the Conflict of Laws—One Hundred Years After, 48 Harv. L. Rev. (1934) 15, 30 Revue Critique de Droit International (1935) 295. There exists a Spanish translation of the Commentaries, by Clodomiro Quiroga, published in Buenos Aires in 1891.

[4] Printed in Story, Miscellaneous Writings (1835) 147.

[5] William W. Story refers to this work of his father in 2 Wm. W. Story, Life and Letters of Joseph Story (1851) 213.

[6] Parts were retranslated from the German in Nadelmann, "De l'organisation et de la jurisprudence des Cours de Justice aux États-Unis d'Amérique, par M. Joseph Story," 30 Boston U. L. Rev. (1950) 382, 390.

[7] Acknowledgment to Joseph Story, John Pickering, Du Ponceau, and others is in the "Notice" with which volume 13 (1833) of the Encyclopaedia Americana opens. On the Encyclopaedia and Lieber, see Freidel, Francis Lieber—Nineteenth Century Liberal (1947) 63.

among them, Joseph Story. Story promised to write, and actually wrote,[8] numerous unsigned articles on legal topics, for example, Courts of the U. States, Domicil, Law, Legislation, Codes, scattered over the thirteen volumes of the *Encyclopaedia Americana* which came out between 1829 and 1833.[9] From that time until his death in 1845, Story took a friendly interest in Lieber's personal and professional affairs.

Lieber had kept in touch with friends in Germany. A description of American prison systems, which he prepared, attracted the attention of the Heidelberg professor of criminal law, Carl Joseph Anton Mittermaier,[10] who requested Lieber in 1832 to provide him with information on American law.[11] In a letter of February 16, 1833, Mittermaier inquired about a new book, of which he had heard, on American constitutional law.[12] He asked Lieber, then located in Philadelphia, to buy it for him and also to bring him in contact with American jurists who might be willing to write articles for the comparative law journal of which he was co-editor.[13] At the time, Story's *Commentaries on the Constitution of the United States* had just appeared.[14] Lieber informed Story of Mittermaier's requests, and, in a letter dated April 24, 1833,[15] Story replied that he would send Lieber for his German friends the abridged edition of the *Commentaries*,[16] adding that he would with pleasure write for Mr. Mittermaier's Journal any judicial essay which he might deem useful in regard to American law.[17] There appeared in the same year a review of the *Commentaries* in Mittermaier's journal.[18]

Lieber had at about the same time tried to induce Carey, the publisher

[8] See 1 Lieber, On Civil Liberty and Self-Government (1853) 232 n. 14; 2 Wm. W. Story, *op. cit. supra* note 5, at 27.

[9] They have never been republished. "Law, Legislation, Codes" is reproduced in Howe, Readings in American Legal History (1949) 460.

[10] See Goldschmidt, Carl Joseph Mittermaier, in Great Jurists of the World (Continental Legal History Series, 1914) 544.

[11] Mittermaier to Lieber, June 24, 1832, Lieber Papers, Henry E. Huntington Library, San Marino, California [hereafter: Lieber Papers].

[12] Lieber Papers.

[13] Together with Zachariä, he published commencing in 1829 the Kritische Zeitschrift für Rechtswissenschaft und Gesetzgebung des Auslandes.

[14] In three volumes, Boston, 1833.

[15] Lieber Papers.

[16] In one volume, Boston, 1833. Translated into French by Paul Odent (Paris, 1843), and from the French into Spanish by Nicolas A. Calvo (Buenos Aires, 1851, 3rd ed. 1860, 4th 1881; Mexican reprints 1871, 1879).

[17] In 1835, Story similarly obliged J.-J. G. Foelix, who had approached him on behalf of the Revue Étrangère et Française de Législation et d'Économie Politique, with a sketch "The Organization and Jurisdiction of the National Courts in the United States." See Nadelmann, *loc. cit. supra* note 6, at 382.

[18] 7 Kritische Zeitschrift (1834) 1. *Cf.* 14 Am. Jurist & L. Mag. (1835) 344; 15 *id.* (1836) 1.

of the *Encyclopaedia Americana*, to bring out a supplement, and he had suggested to Story that the latter write for that volume an article on "American Law." When the publisher decided against the project, Lieber urged Story to write the article nevertheless, as he would send it to Mittermaier.[19] In a letter dated March 27, 1834, Lieber informed Story that Mittermaier was eager to have the article,[20] and Story asked Lieber in his reply of April 5, to tell Mittermaier that he would complete the law article for him as soon as possible.[21] A letter by Story from Cambridge dated August 16th, which is reproduced below,[22] informed Lieber of the completion of the sketch of *American Law* for Mittermaier and that their common friend Charles Sumner had undertaken to transmit the manuscript to Lieber. Story apologized for the state of the manuscript, saying that he had had no time to transcribe it or have it copied and that he was concerned lest it might be found illegible or susceptible of "various readings." On the contents of the sketch, he remarked: "In

[19] Lieber to Story, Jan. 20, 1834, Story Papers, Library of Congress.

[20] Story Papers, Library of Congress.

[21] Lieber Papers.

[22] Letter by Joseph Story to Dr. Francis Lieber, in the Lieber Papers—HM: LI—3262—at the Henry E Huntington Library, San Marino, California. The letter is reproduced by permission of The Huntington Library.

Cambridge Aug. 16, 1834

My Dear Sir

A few days ago I completed the Sketch of American Law, which I promised you for Professor Mittermaier. In drawing it up I have been necessarily compelled to generalize, in order to give any outline; and in what I have inserted I have been mainly governed by your queries and suggestions. Indeed, being aware, that German Jurists could have but little interest in any outline of our jurisprudence, I have confined myself to brief and summary views. The fact, too, is, (as you will know), that each State has in its own system so many pecularities, that little more could be done than to sketch what was common to all. Such as the MSS is, I commend it to your kind indulgence; and must ask you to send it with suitable explanations to Mr. Mittermaier. If he will send me queries on particular topics, I will hereafter answer them as fully as I am able. But really, I have difficulty in precisely seeing what would be dry and uninteresting detail, and what might be useful to know as to Cisatlantic Law.

There is one thing, which gives me no small distress; and that is, the *state* of the *MSS*. I fear, that it may be found illegible, or susceptible of "various readings". My only apology is my want of time and means to copy it, or to send a fairer transcript. I send you that which is in all respects the *original*. I have been, while writing this, engaged in various other tasks, writing judicial opinions, law treatises, and even Lyceum Lectures. I have just completed a Discourse on the Science of Government, as connected with popular education, as a *task duty* for the American Institute of Instruction which I am to deliver in about ten days in Boston. So that you see, that I am compelled to become a handy craft man of all work without time to perfect any.

Our friend Mr. Sumner has undertaken to transmit the MSS to you. But if it shall not go in a few days I shall adhere to my former determination to send it by the mail.

I can scarcely tell you, how much I wish that you lived at Cambridge. I should not even then (so constant are my occupations) see you often; but then I could catch a lazy hour and sit down and talk straight forward with you, on all you thought and wished. I want a mind, that can stir my own.

Yours most truly
Joseph Story

Doctor Francis Lieber

drawing it up, I have been necessarily compelled to generalize, in order to give any outline; and in what I have inserted I have been mainly governed by your queries and suggestions. Indeed, being aware that German jurists could have but little interest in any outline of our jurisprudence, I have confined myself to brief and summary views. The fact, too, is, (as you will know), that each State has in its own system so many pecularities, that little more could be done than to sketch what was common to all."[23]

Lieber mentioned the receipt of the manuscript in a letter to Mittermaier dated September 13, 1834,[24] but a delay occurred in its transmission to Heidelberg, as Mittermaier was still asking for the manuscript in a letter written the 15th of March 1835.[25] The *Life and Letters of Joseph Story*, published by William W. Story after his father's death, reproduces the text of a letter by Mittermaier to Story of November 21, 1835, containing Mittermaier's expression of thanks for the manuscript.[26] In this, Mittermaier stated that the translation had been made and that the paper would appear in two months. Actually a year elapsed before the paper was published as the opening article of volume 9 of the *Kritische Zeitschrift für Rechtswissenschaft und Gesetzgebung des Auslandes.*[27] Mittermaier sent Story a copy of the issue containing the article in a package announced by a letter dated December 30, 1835:[28] "Vous trouverez, aussi, un exemplaire du cahier du journal, qui contient votre article. Le nom de Story est si célèbre en Allemagne, que tout ce qui vient de vous, excite la plus vive attention." The *American Jurist and Law Magazine*,[29] the Boston Law journal published at the time by Sumner, Cushing, and Hillard, noted the appearance of the article. "It will do much," said the editorial,[30] "to diffuse correct information, throughout Germany, in relation to our government and laws, and to the different functions of the federal and State courts, in the administration of Justice." The dissemination of information on American law by the sketch did not remain limited to Germany. There is to be found in

---

[23] See preceding note.

[24] See Mittermaier to Lieber, Nov. 6, 1834, Lieber Papers.

[25] Lieber Papers.

[26] 2 Wm. W. Story, *op. cit. supra* note 5, at 213.

[27] 9 Kritische Zeitschrift (1836) 1.

[28] 2 Wm. W. Story, *op. cit. supra* note 5, at 214; *cf.* Zweigert, "Die Gestalt Joseph Storys," 105 Zeitschrift für die gesamte Staatswissenschaft (1949) 590.

[29] The journal was close to Story. Started in 1829, when Story became Dane Professor of Law at Harvard, it opened with Story's address delivered before the Members of the Suffolk Bar, at their Anniversary, September 5, 1821, one of Story's major speeches on American Law (reprinted in Miscellaneous Writings of Joseph Story).

[30] 17 Am. Jurist & L. Mag. (1837) 496.

volume 8 of the *Juridiskt Arkif*[31] a Swedish version of the sketch, made after the text in the *Kritische Zeitschrift*. No reference to this reprint in Sweden is found in the *Life and Letters of Joseph Story* or in the *American Jurist*, and it may well be that Story never knew of it.

It has already been stated that Lieber received the original manuscript and that Story kept no copy. In the year after Lieber's death (Lieber died in 1872 in New York where he was then professor of History and Law in Columbia College) the University of California acquired[32] from Lieber's widow for $2000 the important library of the "drafter of General Orders No. 100, of 1863."[33] A wealthy German-American from San Francisco had given the University the funds needed for the acquisition.[34] One of the packages contained a manuscript of 31 pages, with the initials *J. S.* and *1834* at the bottom of the last page. The title, *American Law*, appears on the top of the first page. It was bound in 1882 and catalogued as *J[oseph] S[tory], American Law, Mss copy signed J. S.* and has been in the Manuscript Division of the Main Library of the University of California at Berkeley ever since. It is the original text of what appeared in a rather free and often inexact German translation in the *Kritische Zeitschrift*—a manuscript copy[35] that Lieber had had made before he sent the manuscript to Heidelberg.

It is thus possible, after a hundred odd years, to publish the original text of the sketch of *American Law* which Story wrote in the summer of 1834. It is not for us to say whether the text, today, is a mere historical curiosity, from the "formative era"[36] of American law, to be preserved with the respect due to a work from a man who has had a place "in the making of American law"[37] and who "did much to make the law accessible and intelligible,"[38] or whether it is also of contemporaneous interest in that it can shed additional light on problems of American law which still are with the American lawyer. The uninitiated reader abroad will do well to keep in mind that the sketch is an account of American law as of

[31] 8 Juridiskt Arkif (Carl Schmidt ed.) (1837/38) 277.

[32] See Ferrier, Origin and Development of the University of California (1930) 413.

[33] I.e., the "Instructions for the Government of Armies in the Field." See Root, Francis Lieber, 7 Am. J. Int'l L. (1913) 453.

[34] Michael Reese; see Ferrier, *op. cit. supra* note 32, at 431.

[35] The handwriting indicates that several persons were employed to make the copy. Throughout the manuscript, corrections are made, omissions added, and blanks filled in by the same person, presumably Lieber, according to the handwriting.

[36] *Cf.* Pound, The Formative Era of American Law (1938).

[37] See Pound, "The Place of Judge Story in the Making of American Law," 48 Am. L. Rev. (1914) 676.

[38] Mr. Justice Holmes to Laski, August 8, 1924, 1 Holmes-Laski Letters (Howe ed. 1953) 644.

1834, which since then indubitably has developed[39] and might be looked at in a different way today.[40]

This first publication of the original text in the new *American Journal of Comparative Law*, apart from its historical interest, is even more appropriate, as the new journal is devoted to the task thus described in his letter to Lieber of April 5, 1834 by the "American Ancestor of Comparative Law," as Edouard Lambert designated Story.[41] "I hope that the time is coming, when all lovers of the Law, on the Continents of Europe and in America, will be brought closely together for mutual improvement."[42]

---

[39] The Constitution of the United States, for example, has since been amended several times.

[40] The most spectacular and consequential event involving an opinion written by Judge Story has been the overruling by Erie R. R. v. Tompkins, 304 U. S. 64 (1938), of Swift v. Tyson, 16 Pet. 1 (U. S. 1842), involving the question of the extent to which the national (federal) courts have to follow "local" (state) law and the meaning of "local" law in this regard. The domestic literature on the subject would fill a library. For a discussion in French, see Tunc, "L'application du droit des États par les jurisdictions fédérales des États-Unis (Erie Railroad v. Tompkins)," 3 Revue Internationale de Droit Comparé (1951) 5, Spanish text in 67 Revista Jurídica Argentina La Ley (1952) 834.

[41] See Lambert et Xirau, L'ancêtre américain du droit comparé—La doctrine du juge Story (1947). *Cf.* Charles Sumner, "The Scholar, the Jurist, the Artist, the Philantropist," Address before the Phi Beta Kappa Society of Harvard University, August 27, 1846, in 1 The Works of Charles Sumner (1875) 245, 270:

"Story was bred in the common law; but while admiring its vital principles of freedom, he felt how much it would gain, if illuminated by the torch of science, and the light of other systems of jurisprudence. Much of the later labors of his life was specially devoted to this object; and under his hands, we behold the beginning of a new study, the science of *Comparative Jurisprudence*, kindred to those other departments of knowledge which are at once the token and the harbinger of the peaceful association of nations."

As one of the significant statements by Story we may quote: "No nation can be so vain as to imagine that she possesses all wisdom and all excellence. No civilized nation is so humble that her usages, laws and regulations do not present many things for instruction, and some for imitation." Story, Book Review, 20 N. Am. Rev. (1825) 47, 62, reprinted in The Miscellaneous Writings of Joseph Story (1835) 294, 308.

On early comparative law work in the United States, see Pound, "Comparative Law in the Formation of American Law," in 1 Mémoires de l'Académie Internationale de Droit Comparé (1928) 183; Nadelmann, "Peter S. Du Ponceau," 24 Pa. B.A.Q. (1953) 248, 5 Revue Internationale de Droit Comparé (1953) 284.

[42] Lieber Papers, H.M.: LI—3259; reproduced by permission of The Huntington Library.

JOSEPH STORY

American Law

The phrase, American Law, has different senses, or, rather, admits of different interpretations. It may mean (1) the Law, which is peculiar to the U. States, as contradistinguished from European Law; or it may mean (2) the whole body of Law existing in the U. States without any reference to its coincidence with, or departure from, European Law. It is in this latter sense that the phrase will be used in the course of these remarks.

American Law in its largest extent is divisible into two general heads; viz. (1) Public Law, *jus publicum* or *droit public* (2) private Law, or *jus privatum*. The former embraces all rights of a general and public nature, which [concern][1] the whole society and constitute the basis of its political and civil organization. The latter embraces the mere private rights of persons and property. And public law is again divisible into that which regards the Nation as a whole, and that which regards the states comprising it, severally and respectively. Thus, the Constitution and Government of the U. S., is the fundamental law of the whole Union, and ascertains the rights, powers, and duties of the whole nation relative to the states. And the constitutions of the several states which ascertain the rights, powers and duties of the state governments relative to the people of the states respectively are the fundamental laws of the states. Americans are accustomed to call this branch of public law [by][2] the appellation of Constitutional Law.

But without attempting any exact philosophical distribution of the subject, we shall endeavor in the subsequent pages to give a general view of the leading principles of American law, whether public or private, and whether constitutional or otherwise. In order to do this with clearness and accuracy it will be necessary to go back to the origin and history of the American colonies, which now compose the U. States; for their present jurisprudence, as well as their present political organization may be traced up to this source.

The thirteen colonies, which on the 4th of July 1776 declared themselves independent were all of British origin and were settled under British authority and were dependencies upon the British crown until the period above alluded to. Each colony had a distinct organization of government under the authority of the parent country. The colonial governments were of three sorts.

(1) Charter governments, which were created by letters patent of the crown, granting to certain persons, as a corporation, the soil and jurisdiction of the colony, with the powers of legislature and providing for the due organization of the three great departments of government, the Legislative, the Judicial and the Executive. These charters formed the fundamental constitution or basis of the Colony.

(2) Provincial governments. These were establishments existing under the direct and immediate authority of the crown itself with no fixed organization of government, but dependent upon the mere pleasure of the crown. They were, accordingly, governed according to the commissions issued from time to time by the royal governors and the royal instructions given to the latter. Such was their theory. But in point of fact the commissions were always in the same

[1] Omitted in original ms.; "beziehen" in German translation

[2] "as" in ms.

9

* Reprinted with permission.

form, and the actual organization of the departments was practically the same as in the charter governments, the King, however, always appointing the governor, and giving him a negative upon all laws, which was not always the case in the charter governments.

(3) The Proprietory governments. These were grants and letter patent of the crown to one or more Lords Proprietaries of the soil and jurisdiction of the particular Colony, with the power of legislation and appointment of all officers therein, including the Governor. In fact, the Proprietary or Proprietaries possessed the same general authorities and regalities in their respective colonies, as the King possessed within the Provincial Governments.

But, however various were the organizations of the Colonies, and the structures of their powers, the following rights and privileges were conferred on all of them, and were practically exercised, and claimed by all of them, as fundamental. In the first place in all the colonies there existed a Governor, Council and Representative Assembly, the latter being composed of delegates chosen by the people; and by these bodies the legislative and executive functions were respectively exercised. In all of them judicial establishments also were created, separate from, and for the most part independent of the other branches. In the next place the authority of the colonial legislatures extended over all subjects of local legislation, with this limitation only, that the laws made by them should not be repugnant to, but as near as conveniently might be, should be agreeable to the Laws, Statutes and Customs of England. In the next place, all subjects and their children, inhabitants of the Colonies, were declared to be natural born subjects of the realm of England, and entitled to all the rights, privileges and immunities, of free natural born subjects of that realm. In the next place, the common law (that is, the law of England) as far as it was applicable to the circumstances of the Colonies was made the basis of their jurisprudence; and was at all times claimed by them, as their birth right and inheritance. Hence, the Colonists became at once possessed of the invaluable privileges secured by Magna Charta; and the trial by jury in civil and criminal cases, with all its attendant incidents, became incorporated into the very elements of their jurisprudence. In fact their modes of administering justice differed in nothing substantially from those of England. An appellate jurisdiction was established over the final judgments of the highest Courts of the Colonies, to the King of England sitting in Council, so as to preserve an uniformity of principles among all the Colonial Courts. But in point of fact this appellate jurisdiction was rarely exercised, so fully were the principles of the common law recognized and enforced in the Colonies, and so expensive was the prosecution of appeals to England. Hence, we may distinctly trace the origin and source of American Jurisprudence up to the fountains of the English common law, not as a mere matter of voluntary adoption, but as a matter of Constitutional right and duty in the colonies. It is obvious however, that the whole mass of the common law of England was not applicable to the state and condition of the colonies. Much of it could apply only to institutions customs, privileges and feudalities, existing exclusively in the parent country. Thus for instance there was no Church Establishment in America and consequently the whole doctrine of tythes, and the mass of ecclesiastical and common law connected with the Church, could find no home there, and this was foreseen in the very characters of the Colonial governments; for while they required that the laws should not be repugnant to those of England, they at the same time directed, that they should be agreeable to those of England, *only so far as conveniently might be*—thus leaving a wide latitude of discretion, both legislative and judicial, as to the adoption of those Laws. The same remarks are applicable more forcibly to the statutes or positive laws made in England which being generally designed for that realm alone, would, from that very circumstance deviate far more broadly from the system required in the Colonies.

In the administration of justice, the colonial courts at an early period, adopted this general rule of exposition of their authority, that all the common law applicable to the state and condition of the colonies, and all the acts of parliament made in amendment of the common law before the settlement of the Colonies were to be deemed a part of the Common law of the Colonies. The acts of Parliament subsequently made were not obligatory upon the Colonies, unless the latter were expressly named there in. But still many of them, and especially such as were in amendment of the law, were silently adopted in the Colonies by a sort of judicial legislation. Thus for instance the Statute of Queen Ann declaring promissory notes to be negotiable instruments, was admitted into the jurisprudence of most of the Colonies by mere acquiescence, and a sense of its commercial convenience and utility; and it thus became a part of the common law of such colonies.

But from what has been said it may readily be inferred that though the basis of the Jurisprudence in all the Colonies was the same, yet that there must be some diversities in all of them in regard to the extent of the adoption of the principles of the common law. In the first place every portion of it might not be equally applicable to the state or condition of every Colony, or its institutions; in the next place the judicial legislation, which could not fail to be exercised, must in the progress of things, involve differences of opinion among the judges of the different colonies; and each Colony would retain the interpretation given by its own legal tribunals. In the next place the positive enactments of the local legislatures would unavoidably introduce many differences in the laws of each Colony, resulting from its peculiar institutions wants and policy; and in the last place the silent operation of peculiar institutions, habits and customs would gradually incorporate into [the][3] system of each Colony some customary observances which would at length acquire there in the force of law. Considering, however, the extent of the country and the difference of habits, climates and occupations of the inhabitants of the different colonies, it is marvelous how few peculiarities have sprung up from this source.

When the Revolution of 1776 severed the connection between the American Colonies and the Government of Great Britain, no other changes were introduced into the system, except such as related to their political organizations. The Body of their laws remained the same. Some of the Colonies continued to act under their old Charters as a fundamental form of Government with such variations only as in practice were necessary to adapt them to the new state of things. This was the case in the state of Connecticut and Rhode Island. The other states generally formed new constitutions, which in many respects were modelled upon the old colonial Charters; and in the introduction of some of the principles of Magna Charta in the permanent form of a Bill of Rights.

The Jurisprudence, then, of each state in the American Union is at the present time composed of the following Elements: First, of its own fundamental Constitution or organization of Political Government. Secondly, of the common law as actually adopted and administered in it. Thirdly, of its positive or statutable Colonial legislation. Fourthly, of the state legislations since the Revolution. Fifthly, of the fragments (for such only they are) [of][4] customary law which have silently been embodied in the General System. And Sixthly, to all these may be added the Constitution Laws and Treaties of the national

[3] Omitted in ms.

[4] Omitted in ms.

government of the U. States, and all the doctrines of the law of nations resulting from and belonging to that government in common with other foreign governments, and exercising sovereign powers as an independent and coequal community.

Having disposed of these preliminary matters, we shall now proceed to a more minute examination and detail of the leading principles of American law. The Basis of all the American Institutions, state as well as national is that the people themselves possess the supreme power, to form, alter, amend, change and abolish at their pleasure the whole structure of their government and of course to reconstruct it in such manner, as from time to time may be most agreeable to themselves. This is not a mere theoretical principle. It is sometimes (though not frequently) put into execution; not as a measure of violent energy, to suppress great grievances, but as a measure of peaceful deliberation, in order to introduce such improvements, as experience may demonstrate to be useful. Thus many of the states in the Union have, since the adoption of the National Constitution in 1789 established new Constitutions of Government, or have changed some of the provisions of the old Constitutions. The manner in which this change is usually accomplished is by the state legislature passing a law authorizing the People to choose Delegates, or Representatives, in a given form, time and place to assemble in Convention to revise the old Constitution and to propose such amendments, as they think proper. Some times the acts of the Convention [are][6] conclusive without any further ratification by the People. But, more generally, such a ratification is required by the votes of the People subsequently taken in a prescribed manner in their respective municipalities, and the votes being taken, the major vote becomes in the state decisive of the particular measure, that is, of its ratification or rejection. So that, practically speaking, the whole sovereignty belongs to the People, and all power which is exercised by others, is derived from them; and may be increased, diminished, and withdrawn at their pleasure. But the Constitutions of Government until so altered or changed continue the supreme law of the land; and no department of the existing Government has any right to contravene them, or to superceed them.

We shall now proceed in the first place to the consideration of Constitutional law as it exists at present in the United States and it is divisable into two heads (1) That of the nation (2) that of the respective states.

The present National Constitution was adopted by the People of the states, and went into operation in the year 1789. It was formed under the auspices of the thirteen states, and eleven new states have since been admitted into the Union and possess and enjoy its privileges and advantages upon the footing of a complete equality with the original States. This Constitution so far as its powers and rights of sovereignty extend, are by the very terms of the Constitution declared to be the supreme Law of the land, anything in the state constitutions and laws to the contrary notwithstanding. And to secure this obedience all State as well as national officers, Legislative, Executive and Judicial are required to take an oath or affirmation on their entrance into office, to support the Constitution of the United States.

The Constitution of the U. States distributes the powers of the government among three great departments, the Legislative, Executive and Judicial. The legislative power is vested in a Legislature called the Congress consisting of two branches or houses, viz., a Senate composed of members chosen for six years, and a House of Representatives composed of members chosen for two years. Each house is independent of the other in its organization, and it deliberates and decides for itself. Each is the

[6] "are not" in ms.

sole judge of the Elections, Returns, and qualifications of its own members. Each determines the rules of its own proceedings and has a right to punish its members for disorderly behaviour, and with the concurrence of two thirds to expel a member. Each is required to keep a Journal of its own proceedings which is with the exception of such parts as in its judgment require secrecy, published from time to time. A majority of each house constitutes a quorum for business, but a smaller number may adjourn from day to day and may compel the attendance of other members. The yeas and nays on any question at the desire of one fifth of those present must be entered on the Journal. But neither house during the session of Congress can adjourn without the consent of the other for more than three days nor to any other place, than where the Congress is sitting. The members of both houses are entitled to receive a compensation for their services from the Treasury of the United States. They are privileged from arrest (except in cases of treason, felony, or breach of the peace) during their attendance in the sessions and in going and returning from them; and for any speech or debate in either house, they are not to be questioned in any other place. No Law or Resolve can be passed, except it shall be by the consent and approbation of both Houses. There are some peculiarities belonging to each. The House of Representatives chooses its own speaker, and all its other officers; the presiding officer of the Senate is the Vice President of the United States; but in his absence or disability the Senate may appoint a president pro tempore; and it appoints its other officers. All bills for raising revenue must originate in the House of Representatives. The House of Representatives possesses the sole power of impeachments; and the Senate the sole power to try impeachments. When vacancies happen in the representation of a state the Executive of that state is to issue writs of Election to fill the vacancies. But when a vacancy occurs in the Senate during the recess of the State Legislature the Executive of the State may move an appointment, which will continue good until the next meeting of the legislature. The Senate also (as we shall see) have a voice in executive appointments, and in making treaties. The Senate is chosen by the state legislatures. Each state has a right to choose two Senators, and each senator has one vote, so that in the Senate there is a perfect equality in the votes of the States. One third of the Senate goes out of office every two years, and is then replaced by new Senators. But the Senate is so arranged that ever since the first elections, the succeeding members are chosen for six years. The qualifications of a Senator are, being 30 years of age, being an inhabitant of the State at the time of the election, and being a native citizen or a citizen nine years before the election. The House of Representatives is composed of members, chosen in each State by the People thereof, who are voters in the most numerous branch of the state legislature. The number of Representatives in each state is apportioned according to its population, including free blacks and two fifths of those not free. The number of Representatives is not to exceed one for every 30,000 persons. But each state is entitled[6] to have at least one representative. A census or enumeration of the population is taken under the authority of Congress every ten years; and Congress are then to apportion the representatives according to such ratio as they may choose, not below the constitutional ratio of one for every 30,000 persons. The qualifications of a representative are that he shall be twenty five years of age, that he shall be an inhabitant of the state from which he is chosen, and shall have been a citizen of the United States seven years. The times, places, and manner of holding elections for senators, and representatives are prescribed by the state legislatures respectively. But Congress may by law make or alter such regulations except as

[6] "entitle" in ms.

to the place of choosing Senators. Both Senators and Representatives are disqualified from holding any office under the national government, while they act in their legislative capacity; and they cannot during the time for which they are elected, take any office created, or increased in emolument, during the same period.

The Congress are to meet annually, and on the first Monday of December, unless they shall by law appoint a different day. The powers confided to the Congress are specially enumerated in the Constitution. These powers are as follows: to levy and collect taxes, duties imposts and excises (which must be uniform throughout the United States) for the payment of the publick debts, and for the common defence and general welfare; to borrow money on the credit of the United States; to regulate commerce with foreign nations, and among the states, and with the Indian Tribes; to establish an uniform rule of naturalization, and uniform Laws on the subject of Bankruptcies; to coin money, and regulate its value, and that of foreign coins; to fix the standard of weights and measures; to punish the counterfeiting of the publick securities and coin; to establish post offices and post roads; to secure to authors and inventors, for limited times, the exclusive right to their writings and discoveries; to constitute tribunals inferior to the Supreme Court of the U. States; and regulate the appellate jurisdiction of the latter; to define and punish piracies and felonies on the high seas, and offences against the law of nations; to declare war, grant letters of marke and reprisal, and make rules concerning captures; to raise and support armies; but no appropriation of money for such a purpose is to be for a longer term than two years; to provide and maintain a navy; to make rules for the government for the land and naval forces; to provide for calling forth the militia to execute the laws of the Union; to suppress insurrections, and repel invasions; to provide for organizing armies and disciplining the militia and governing them when in the service of the United States, reserving to the States the appointment of officers; and of training the militia according to the discipline prescribed by Congress; to exercise exclusive jurisdiction over places ceded to the United States for the seat of Government, or for forts, arsenals, and other public objects; to dispose of and make regulations respecting the public territory and other property of the U. States; to admit new States into the Union; to prescribe the manner in which the acts records and proceedings of the state shall be proved and the effect thereof in other states; to declare the punishment of treason; to determine the time of choosing the electors of President and Vice President, and the day when they shall give their votes; and finally to make all laws which shall be necessary and proper for carrying into effect the foregoing powers, and all other powers vested by the Constitution in the Government of the United States, or in any department or office thereof.

There are also certain prohibitions restrictions, and limitations upon the exercise of power by the National Government specially provided for. Among these are the following. The privilege of the writ of *Habeas Corpus* is not to be suspended, unless in cases of rebellion or invasion when the public safety may require it; no bill of attainder or ex post facto law is to be passed; no capitation or other direct tax is to be laid unless in proportion[7] to the last census or enumeration of the inhabitants; no tax or duty is to be laid on any exports from any state; no preference is to be given by any regulation of commerce or revenue, to the ports of one state over those of another; vessels bound to, or from one state are not obliged to enter, or pay duties in another; no money is to be drawn from the Treasury but in consequence of appropriations by law; no title of nobility is to be granted by the United States; no person holding office can without the

[7] "proper time" in ms.

consent of the Congress accept any present, emolument, office or title, from any foreign princes or states; and no private property can be taken for public use without just compensation. The Congress are also prohibited from making any law respecting an establishment of religion, or prohibiting the free exercise thereof, or abridging the freedom of speech or of the Press, or the right of the people peaceably to assemble, and to petition the government for a redress of grievances. The right of the people to keep or bear arms, is not to be infringed; and no soldier in time of peace can be quartered in any house without the consent of the owner, nor in time of war but in a manner to be described by law. No religious test can be required as a qualification to any office or public trust under the United States.

There are also certain prohibitions restrictions, and limitations upon the exercise of power by the respective states. No state can enter into any treaty, alliance or confederation, grant letters of marque and reprisal, coin money, emit bills of credit (that is paper money) make anything, but gold and silver coin a tender in[8] payment of debts, pass any bill of attainder, ex post facto law, or law impairing[9] the obligation of contracts or grant any title of nobility. No state can without the consent of the Congress lay any imposts or duties on imports or exports except to execute its own inspection laws and such laws are subject to the revision[10] and control of the Congress. No state can lay any duty on tonnage, keep troops or ships of war in time of peace, enter into a compact with another state, or with a foreign power or engage in war unless actually invaded, or in imminent danger thereof.

We next come to the Executive Power under the National Constitution. It is vested in a President who (together with a Vice President) is chosen for four years in the following manner. Each state is to appoint in such manner as the Legislature thereof may direct a number of Electors equal to its Senators and Representatives in the Congress. The choice is sometimes by the legislature itself, sometimes by the people of the state at large, and sometimes by them in districts. On a given day which is the same throughout all the United States, the Electors of each state meet therein, and vote by ballot for two persons, one as President the other as Vice President. The votes are all returned to the seat of Government under seal; and on a given day the President of the Senate in the presence of the House of Representatives, opens them, and the votes are counted. If any person has a majority of all the votes, he is chosen the President, if no person has such a majority, then the House of Representatives, (the whole Representation from each state having one vote) are to choose from the persons (not exceeding three) having the highest number of votes, the President. But the person chosen must have a majority of all the votes, and a quorum of the House must consist of a member or members from two thirds of the states. If no choice is made before the 4th day of March following, then the Vice President who is chosen acts as President. If no person is chosen Vice President by a majority of the Electors, then from the two highest on the list the Senate choose the Vice President. But a quorum is required of two thirds of the whole number of the Senators for the purpose, and a majority is necessary to a choice. The qualifications of President and Vice President are the same, they must be 35 years of age, have been fourteen years resident in the United States and be native citizen or citizens at the time of the adoption of the Constitution. The Vice President is ex officio president of the Senate, except when he acts as President. He acts as President when the latter is removed from office, or dies, or resigns, or is unable to perform his duties, and the Congress have power to provide for cases of the removal, death,

[8] "and" in ms.

[9] "imposing" in ms.

[10] "division" in ms.

resignation or incapacity of both the President and Vice President.

The President is to receive a compensation which cannot be increased or diminished during the period for which he is chosen, and he cannot receive within that period any other emolument from the U States, or any of them. On entering upon his office he takes an oath faithfully to perform the duties thereof, and to support the Constitution.

His Constitutional powers and duties are as follows. He is Commander in Chief of the Army and Navy, and of the Militia in the public service. He may require the opinions in writing of the heads of the executive departments; He has power to grant pardons and reprieves for offences against the U States, except in cases of impeachment. He may by and with the advice and consent of the Senate (two thirds of the Senators present concurring) make treaties; he is to nominate and by and with the advice and consent of the Senate appoints, ambassadors, other public ministers and consuls judges of the Supreme Court, and all other officers of the United States, whose appointments are not in the Constitution otherwise provided for. But the Congress may by law vest the appointment of inferior officers in the President alone, in the Courts of Law or in the heads of departments. The President may during the recess of the Senate grant temporary commissions to fill up vacancies in office then happening; and such commissions to expire at the end of the next session. He is to commission all officers of the United States. The President is also from time to time to give to the Congress information of the state of the Union, and to recommend measures; he may on extraordinary occasions convene both Houses, or either of them; and in cases of disagreement between them, with respect to the time of adjournment, he may adjourn them to such time, as he shall think proper. He is to receive Ambassadors and other publick ministers; and he is to take care, that the laws be faithfully executed.

The President has also a qualified veto on all Laws and Resolutions (except on a question of adjournment) passed by the two Houses. If he disapproves any Law or Resolution, it is to be within ten days returned with his objections, to the House, in which it originated. If upon reconsideration it is passed by two thirds of each House, the vote being taken by yeas and nays and entered on the public Journals, it becomes a law, otherwise it is rejected.

The President and Vice President, and all civil officers of the United States (Senators and Representatives are not included) are liable to removal from office upon impeachment for, and conviction of high crimes and misdemeanors. But as the judgment in the cases of impeachment can extend no farther than to a removal from office and disqualification to hold office, the party is still liable to an indictment, trial, judgment, and punishment for his offence in the proper court according to law. When trying impeachments, the Senate are on oath or affirmation. When the President is on trial, the Chief Justice of the United States is to preside, and no conviction can be on impeachment without two thirds of the Senators present concur there in.

We next come to the consideration of the national Judiciary. By the Constitution the judicial power of the United States extends to all cases in law and equity arising under the Constitution, laws, and treaties of the United States; to all cases affecting ambassadors, other public ministers, and consuls; to all cases of Admiralty and maritime jurisdiction; to controversies, to which the United States are a party; to controversies between two or more states; between a state and citizens of another state; between citizens of different states; between citizens of the same state, claiming lands under grants of different states, and between a state or the citizens thereof and foreign states, citizens, or subjects. But the jurisdiction does not extend to any suits brought by citizens of another state, or by citizens or subjects of any foreign state, *against* any state.

The judicial power is vested in one Supreme Court, and in such inferior courts as the Congress shall from time to time ordain and establish. The judges of the Supreme and inferior courts hold their office during good behavior, and receive at stated times for their services a compensation, which cannot be diminished during their continuance in office. The Supreme Court has *original* or primary jurisdiction in all cases affecting ambassadors, other public ministers and Consuls, and cases in which a state is a party. In other cases the Supreme Court has appellate jurisdiction only, and this latter is subject to the regulation of Congress.

The trial of all crimes, except in cases of impeachment, is required to be by jury. The trial must be in the state where the offence is committed; but if not committed in any state, then in such place as Congress may have directed by law. In all criminal prosecutions the accused is entitled to a speedy and public trial; to be informed of the nature and cause of his accusation; to be confronted with the witnesses against him, to have compulsive process for obtaining witnesses in his favour, and to have the assistance of counsel for his defence.

He is not held to answer for any capital or otherwise infamous crime, unless on a presentment or indictment of a grand jury (except in cases arising in the land or naval forces or in the militia while in the public service). He is not to be subject for the same offence to be twice put in jeopardy of life or limb, he is not compellable to be a witness against himself; and he cannot be deprived of life, liberty, or property without due process of law. Besides these great privileges secured, as it were, by a Bill of Rights, there are provisions which secure the rights of the people in their persons houses papers and effects against unreasonable searches and seizures; and no warrants are to issue but upon probable cause supported by oath or affirmation describing particularly the place to be searched, and the persons or things to be seized. Excessive bail is not to be required, nor excessive fines imposed, nor cruel or unusual punishments inflicted.

In civil suits also, at the common law, the right of a trial by jury is preserved in all cases, where the value in controversy exceeds twenty dollars. And no fact tried by a jury can be reexamined otherwise than according to the rules of the common law, that is, by a writ of error, which leaves the facts to be determined by the Jury, and subjects the law of the case only for the Revision of the Courts.

And in order to shield persons against the charge of the highest political offences arising from prejudice, malice and oppression, the offence of treason is declared to consist only in levying war against the U. States, or in adhering to their enemies, giving them aid and comfort; thus cutting off all constructive treasons. No person can be convicted of treason, unless upon the testimony of two witnesses to the same overt act, or on confession of the party himself, in open court. And although the Congress may declare the punishment of treason, no attainder of it can work corruption of blood, or forfeiture of property, except during the life of the person attainted.

Some few provisions of a general nature remain to be mentioned. The public Acts, Records, and judicial proceedings of each state, are to have full faith and credit in every other state. The citizens of each state are entitled to all privileges and immunities of citizen in the several states. Fugitives charged with crimes and flying to another state are to be delivered up to justice, and so fugitive slaves are to be delivered up to their owners. No new state can be formed within the limits of another state nor any state formed by the junction of two or more states without the consent of the state legislatures as well as of the Congress.

The United States are to guarantee to every state a Republican form of government, and are to protect it against invasion and, when required, against domestic violence. The Constitution, Treaties and Laws of the U. States, are declared to be the supreme law of the land. It is further declared that the enumeration of certain rights in the Constitution shall not be construed to deny or disparage others retained by the People; and the powers not delegated to the United States by the Constitution nor prohibited by it to the States, are reserved to the States respectively, or to the people.

And finally to secure such alterations and amendments as experience may show to be useful, the Congress when two thirds of both Houses shall deem it necessary, may propose amendments to the Constitution, or,[11] on the application of the legislatures of two thirds of the several states, shall call a Convention for proposing amendments; and any amendment so proposed, when ratified by the legislatures or conventions of three fourths of the States, as the one or the other mode of ratification may be proposed by the Congress are to be valid, as a part of the Constitution. But there is this permanent exception that no state shall without its own consent, be deprived of its equal suffrage in the Senate.

Such is the national Constitution, in all its important provisions. But it may be asked if Congress, or the Executive, or other authority, shall violate its provisions, in what manner is redress to be sought. The answer is that if the grievance admits of judicial inquiry and decision, it will be redressed by the state and the national courts by declaring the law to be unconstitutional, a function which has been often exercised by the state authorities, the same resort can be had, and many cases have occurred in which the state acts have been declared to be unconstitutional by the Supreme Court of the United States. Indeed, in all judicial questions of infringement of the national Constitution, Treaties and Laws, whether the case originates in a state court or in a national court, the Supreme Court can exercise a final appellate jurisdiction, and its judgment as to the constitutionality of the act or law becomes conclusive. If the grievance be not of a judicial character, or capable of a judicial investigation, it is to be redressed, first by the power of impeachment, if that applies; if that does not apply, then by the people themselves by displacing the offenders, when a new election occurs. And lastly if all these means should fail, then the power of Amendment may be resorted to; and then the grievance may in one way or another be suppressed. In fact, this last mode of redress, has on several occasions been applied in a very quiet and beneficial manner, not so much to the positive evils as to guard against their occurrences, as soon as they have been foreseen.

It is to be observed that the powers conferred on the national Government, are sometimes declared to be exclusive, and sometimes they are manifestly *concurrent*, with those of the state governments. The great difficulty is to ascertain when they are exclusive by implication (though not declared to be so) and when not. The rule of interpretation generally adopted is to construe the powers to be exclusive (though not expressly declared so) when they are in their own nature and exercise incompatible and repugnant to like powers in the states; and in all other cases to consider them concurrent. But in cases of concurrent powers if there should arise an actual conflict in the exercise of them the state must under such circumstances yield to the national Government. An instance of a power not expressly declared to be exclusive, and yet judicially held to be so, is the power "to regulate commerce," on the other hand a power held to be concurrent, but not expressly declared to be so, is the power "to lay taxes." Most of the questions of constitutional law which have from time

[11] Omitted in ms.

to time agitated the whole nation have arisen from the exercise of powers given to the national Government by implication, as necessary and proper to carry into effect the express powers, or from the exercise of powers by the state governments, where there has been a supposed conflict with the powers exercised by the national government or a virtual repugnance to the powers of the latter. The lines of distinction between state and national powers[12] in many cases, are very clear and well defined; in other cases, the powers approach so near to each other, that it [is][13] extremely difficult to say to which government the exercise appropriately belongs, or whether it does not belong to each. These embarrassments necessarily grow out of written constitutions of government and of divided sovereignties. But hitherto, the questions have been disposed of in a peaceable manner; and the decisions made by the Judiciary in the last resort, have been acquiesced in and generally approved.

We may next pass to the consideration of the constitutions of the several states —and here it will not be necessary to go into such minute details since they are generally formed on the same mode, and contain the same fundamental principles[14] with such peculiarities only, as make them more acceptable to the people or more consonant with the existing institutions and habits of the particular state. It is proposed therefore to give only a leading outline of the general principles, and organization, applicable to the constitutions of each of the states, as the minute differences among them are very numerous, but at the same time are comparatively unimportant.

In all the state constitutions, there is a division of the great departments of government into Legislative Executive and Judicial. The state legislatures (with the exception of that of Vermont) consist of two branches, generally called a Senate and House of Representatives. The Senators of each state (with the exception of Maryland) are directly chosen by the people for various terms of service, in some states for one year, in others for two years; in others again for three years, in others for four years and in some for five years, in some states part of the Senators go out every year. The Representatives are uniformly chosen directly by the people and generally for one year. But in Rhode Island they are chosen for six months only and in South Carolina Tennessee Illinois and Louisiana biennially. The legislative powers are not specified in the state constitutions; but they are given in general terms or by the mere delegation of the Legislative power; and when they are intended to be restrained, it is done by express prohibitions and restrictions, so that the state governments are not (like the national Government) governments of special, enumerated powers; but of general powers specially restricted. They are subject, however to the national Constitution, and all are open to amendments by the people. The Executive Power is universally vested in a Governor, sometimes with and sometimes without the aid of a council. The Governor has in some states very effective powers a qualified negative on laws and a substantial patronage in appointments to office. In other States his powers are very limited; and in some he is a mere shadow of sovereignty having little more than a nominal authority as the official head of the government. In most of the States, he is chosen by the People; in a few by the legislature, his term of office varies in different states from one to four years. The Judiciary in every state, is organized as a different Branch. The Judges are appointed in some states by the Governor; in others by the Legislature. They hold their offices in most of the states during good behaviour, in some states for a period of seven years; and in others for a shorter period. The organization of the Judicial Department in different states is effected in a very different

[12] "powers are" in ms.

[13] Omitted in ms.

[14] "principals" in ms.

manner. In some of them there are distinct courts of Law and Equity. In others, the forms of each are united in the same court; and in others, no such distinction as Law or Equity is finally known but the principles of Equity are administered in connection with Law or in specified cases only. In some states the highest courts exercise appellate jurisdiction, only from the judgments and decrees of subordinate courts, in others they exercise original jurisdiction (that is principally, in the institution of suits). The jurisdiction of the state courts, is not like that of the national courts, limited to particular classes of persons or cases but is general, and extends to all persons and cases which are not prohibited by the constitution and laws of the State and which it is competent for any territorial sovereignty to assume.

Every State Constitution contains in form or in substance, a Bill of Rights, and other prohibitory and restrictive provisions upon the exercise of power by the respective departments of the government. Among these the most important and general, are the following: That all men are born free and equal, and have certain unalienable Rights; that the people have a right to make and alter their forms of Government; that they have a right to worship God according to the dictates of their conscience; that they have a right to freedom of speech and of the press; that they have a right to trial by Jury in all criminal cases; and in civil cases when they desire it; that the citizens have a right to bear arms; and peaceably to assemble and petition for redress of grievances; that the writ of *Habeas Corpus* shall not be suspended unless in cases of rebellion or invasion, when the public safety may require it; that ex post facto laws shall not be passed, nor bills of attainder; that private property shall not be taken for public use without compensation; that no taxes shall be raised without the consent of the legislature. And generally the same auxiliary provisions in the virtue of a Bill of Rights, exist in the state constitutions, as in the national Constitution. The qualifications of voters in the choice of public officers, though very various, in the different states, are such as enable the great mass of the male population to be voters. In some states all free persons of full age who are inhabitants, are voters. In others the payment of taxes or other equivalent service is added, in others a small pecuniary qualification exists; in others again a freehold qualification or some title to or possession of land is necessary. A like diversity exists as to the qualifications of persons to hold office; but it may be generally stated, that the qualifications, whatever they may be, as to age, property, inhabitancy, are of such mixture as to give the people at large a full opportunity to vote for officers, and to hold offices. For violations of the state constitutions the like remedies exist, as [for][16] the violations of the national Constitution. If the subject be capable of judicial inquiry and redress, the state courts will entertain the suit and grant suitable redress. If not capable of judicial inquiry and redress, then the remedy must be sought in new elections of rulers, and in the conservative power of amendments of the constitution.

Having given this general outline of the principles of American Constitutional Law, we shall next endeavor to lay before the reader a concise view of American municipal law. The basis of that law in all the states and territories, except Louisiana and Florida, is (as we have seen) the common law of England. Louisiana and Florida are governed by a different jurisprudence, the former by the laws of France, whose Civil code has been expressly adopted into its own, and the latter by the laws of Spain, all whose civil codes may be deemed in full vigour and force there in.

But although the basis of American municipal law (with the exceptions above mentioned) is the common law of England, many important differences exist in the actual state of jurisprudence between England and America, some of

[16] "far as" in ms.

which we shall now proceed to point out. In the first place, no church establishment (as has been already stated) exists in America; and therefore the whole law of tithes and compulsive contributions for public worship, and the various rights and privileges of the Church, under the Ecclesiastical and Canon law, are unknown. In the next place, the great law of inheritances of Estate or immovable property in America differs from that of the common law. In England the Eldest son is the sole heir of all the real Estate, in America all the children male, and female, inherit equally. And in inheritances among collateral heirs the same rule prevails; all persons in the same degree of kindred taking equal shares of the Estate. The father and mother also (contrary to the common law) can inherit directly the Estates of their children; the half blood (for the most part but not universally) inherit equally with the whole blood. And though in some states there is a distinction made of Estates divided "ex parte paterna," and "ex parte materna," so that the estate descends to those who are kin only on the side of the parent from whom the estate came; yet this distinction is not generally adopted. Personal estate, movable property is distributable among the next of kin generally in the same modes, as real estate mutatis mutandis. In the next place, real or immovable property is universally held in America by one tenure (if indeed, there can be said to be any tenure at all) that of free and common socage. In other words, all real property is held in absolute property, free of any contributions, or tax to or superior right by any Lord Paramount. There are no copyhold estates (as they are called in England); and no feudal rights or privileges. The great mass of all the lands is held by persons in fee simple, in pleno dominio, without any payment of rents, to any other proprietor, under long leases. In short, there are few tenants except in our cities, who hold estates upon rent, and then hold for very short periods, rarely exceeding seven years, and often for one year only, or even less. Land is, comparatively speaking, so cheap, that few farmers exist who are not the owners of the soil. So that properly speaking, a dependent peasantry is almost unknown in America. This circumstance combined with the equal distribution of all real property by inheritance prevents any undue accumulation of property in particular families for successive generations, and silently preserves great uniformity and simplicity in the system of transfers of real property. The mode of conveyance is so easy and inexpensive that the humblest magistrate can frame the proper deed, and in every township there are many persons who occasionally perform the duty of conveyancers. Estates tail (so well known in the English law) are still allowed in some states; in others they are abolished by a very simple provision, which declares that Estates Tail, shall be deemed Estates in fee simple. And where they are not thus abolished, they are so easily barred or destroyed by the tenant in tail for the time being that this species of estate is scarcely known as any obstruction to the sale of real property. Estates for life or for any determinate period of years may be created at the pleasure of parties, and are valid in point of law, but they rarely exist unless created by the operation of law, as in the case of a husband [who][16] upon the death of his wife is entitled to an estate for life in the real property of his wife or of a widow who is entitled to an estate for life in one third part of the real estate of her husband.

In respect to *persons* as contradistinguished from *things*, the American law differs far less from the law of England. The general rights and duties of Husband and Wife, Parent and Child, Master and Servant, and Guardian and Ward, are in a great measure the same. But though the law is not changed, the gradual change of [manners][17] has had

[16] Omitted in ms.

[17] "names" in ms.

great influence in relaxing the powers incident to these relations. There is however one leading distinction between the law of England, and that generally (not universally) prevalent in the American States. Marriages are more easily contracted in America with fewer ceremonies, and are treated more as civil than as religious contracts. In England divorces *a vinculo matrimonii* are grantable only by Parliament, and generally for one cause only, adultery. But in most of the American States, divorces are grantable for adultery by Courts of Justice upon a proper hearing and trial by the Court. And in some of the American States divorces a vinculo are allowed for other causes, such as desertion and cruelty of conduct; and indeed, the causes are sometimes so loose and indefinite in some States, that they seem ill adapted to the preservation of this great bond of social life.

The law with regard to personal or movable property, and contracts, (often called in the language of common law, *choses in action*) is in substance that of England. The same principles and distinctions exist as to the formation, obligation, interpretation, and execution of contracts. The Law of Bailments, of Agency, of Partnership, of Insurance, of Bottomry, of Promissory Notes, of Bills of Exchange, of Shipping and Navigation, and of other maritime and commercial contracts, is generally, (not universally) the same as that of England, except that the American law on these subjects is more expansive and comprehensive, and liberal, borrowing freely from the law of Continental Europe, and more disposed to avail itself of the best principles of commerce, which can be gathered from all foreign sources not excluding even the civil law.

The modes of civil remedy and remedial justice are for the most part the same in America as in England. The same forms of action generally exist; the pleadings and practice are generally the same, except that in America all the proceedings are far more simple, direct expeditious, and cheap, than in England. In some of the States, (as in Massachusetts, and Maine) the forms of real actions (as they are called) for the recovery of immovable property are still used, though they are obsolete in England. But in most of the States modern English action of Ejectment substituted for the same purpose, is in use. The complex forms of process in England do not exist; but forms borrowed from them, but in a far more simple character, are adopted.

The modes of trial in civil cases are the same as in England; in *common law suits* by a Jury; in Equity and in Admiralty cases by the Judges alone. The trial by Jury in civil cases is precisely the same, except, that the Jury in England is always selected and returned by the Sheriff; that in America there is a diversity of practice. In some States the Jury are selected by the Sheriff, and in others they are drawn from sealed boxes containing the names of all the principal citizens; and in others again they are drawn in a more peculiar manner. The Rules of Evidence and of competency of witnesses to give testimony are generally the same in America, as in England. Persons who are interested in the event of the cause, or are infamous, or are unbelievers in the existence of God, and of responsibility to God, by way of future rewards or punishments, are not competent witnesses. All other persons of reasonable age and discretion are required to give testimony, unless they stand in the relation of Husband and Wife, or client and attorney to each other. But, generally, no person is admissible to give testimony in his own person in his own cause. In England the written depositions of witnesses, are rarely admissible in civil cases, but in America they are far more liberally admitted, especially in cases of bodily infirmity, and where the witnesses live at considerable distances from the place of trial, or are about to go abroad. Presumptive evidence in all its legal forms, is generally admitted; but what we call Hearsay (that is, the statements of other persons not under oath in

Court) is generally inadmissible, and is admitted only as to matters of general reputation, such as local boundaries, heirship and lineage. The mode of conducting civil trials is the same as in England. It is in open court in the presence of the people at large; with the assistance of counsel for each party. The judge, after all the evidence is heard, and all the counsel have spoken, usually gives his own opinion as to matters of law to the Jury, and sometimes sums up, (that is recapitulates) the facts and evidence to the Jury with such observations as he thinks pertinent to make the matter more clear or impressive. The Jury then retire, from the Courts, consult by themselves, and give their verdict or decision according to their own opinions. But, still, if there has been any mistake in point of law the court may grant a new trial; and sometimes it is granted for a supposed mistake in matters of fact, when the court think injustice has been done. But interference in the latter class of cases (of facts) is quite rare, and is never interposed but upon any strong circumstances, the court preferring to leave matters of fact expressly to the Jury. On this account the verdicts of juries as to matters of fact are generally satisfactory, and of great weight.

In criminal cases the system is generally the same as in England. The same crimes, (known as crimes at the common law), exist. Thus, whatever crime would be a breach of peace of the King in England is treated as a breach of the public peace, and peace of the State, in America, and is punishable by fine or imprisonment, or by both. In general the punishments for crimes in America are far more mild and moderate in America than in England. There are very few capital offences. In the Code of the National Government nine offences only, are punishable with death, viz., Treason, Murder, Rape, Arson or Maliciously burning a dwelling house, Maliciously burning public ships, Robbery of the mail Casting away or destroying ships on the high seas for fraudulent purposes, Piracy and the Rescue of persons capitally convicted, before or during execution. In some of the states a still smaller number of crimes only are capital; and in none of them (it is believed) are a greater number of crimes punishable. Treason, Murder, Highway Robbery, Arson, Burglary, or Breaking open a dwelling house in the night time for the purpose of Theft and Rape are the crimes [now][18] commonly punished capitally in the jurisprudence of the States.

In general no person can be tried, unless upon an indictment found by a Grand Jury, composed of any number, not less than *twelve* persons, and not more than *twenty three.* Twelve of them must agree in an indictment, which is a written statement describing the person, the offence, the time, place, and mode of committing it, with reasonable certainty. The Grand Jury is composed of respectable citizens chosen or drawn in the same manner as common jurors. They are under oath to perform their duty faithfully and impartially. They examine in secret witnesses, who are under oath, and generally only the witnesses in behalf of the Government. If they think the crime has not been committed, or is not proved against the party, they say so, and the party, if he is in custody, is immediately discharged. If they find an indictment against him, he is then at a proper time put upon his trial in open court; and all the witnesses both for and against him give their testimony in open court on oath, and no depositions of any witnesses are admitted. On his trial he is entitled to employ counsel to assist him in his defence (very different from the practice in the English Court) and the counsel are fully heard, as to all matters before the Jury. The Court after all the evidence is heard generally sums up the facts and states the law to the Jury who then return a verdict of Guilty or not guilty. But if they cannot all agree in a verdict, one way or the other, then the Jury may be discharged, and the cause may be tried by another Jury, until

[18] "not" in ms.

there is a verdict of acquittal or conviction. If the party is acquitted, he can never be tried again for the same offence. But if he is convicted, and any error has been committed in point of law, or fact he may have a new trial by order of the court. He is not at the trial admitted to give his own testimony in his own favour; and he cannot be compelled to give his own testimony against himself. In general the same testimony and evidence are admissible in criminal cases as in civil cases. But in criminal cases the person, who is injured, as for instance the owner of goods stolen, the party stabbed, the party who has been robbed or whose house has been burnt, is admissible as a witness. But husband and wife cannot testify for or against each other; and the same immunity is allowed as between client and attorney. In short the trial is conducted in the same way, except as to counsel as in England.

In respect to punishments, the distinction between capital and secondary punishments is not particularly felt, because it is not admitted that capital punishments are rightfully to be deemed primary in their nature and other punishments mere substitutes. The most usual punishments, not capital, are fine, simple imprisonment, solitary confinement, in a penitentiary and confinement to hard labour in a penitentiary. Other punishments, although formerly known, and used are now abolished, or are in a course of abolition; such, for instance, as public whipping, branding with a hot iron, for forgery and other fraudulent crimes, and sitting in the public pillory or stocks. Indeed these punishments are now generally so revolting to the feelings of Americans, that they exist in but few of the States, and even there they are not often inflicted. The penitentiary system is in general favour in America. It has two objects, first, as a punishment, to deter offenders; secondly, as a means of reformation. In the former view it is probably now, or may be made as effective as any system of punishment can be; in the latter view, the experiment has not been as yet sufficiently tried to justify any conclusive judgment upon its efficacy. A discussion of this subject would require a large treatise; and does not properly fall within the limits of the present sketch.

In treating the subject of American Law thus far, it has been necessary to state many propositions with the qualifications, that they are *generally* not *universally* true. The reason is that in the jurisprudence of almost every state there are some positive or customary peculiarities; and the differences would require volumes to develop; and even then, these peculiarities would hardly be found to produce much effect in the general system. They are for the most part the result of accident rather than of design, of old habits and institutions and prejudices rather than of philosophy, or deep meditation. Every where in American jurisprudence one may trace the same family likeness and characters. It is everywhere, *alter et idem*. Upon leading doctrines and principles there is throughout all America great uniformity, especially in the decisions of judicial questions upon given law. On minor topics there is almost an endless diversity. There is no state, which has not much local law, which requires great industry and caution to understand and apply it. And yet in a vast variety of cases, standing upon general principles of the common or commercial law, a lawyer of one state may without inconvenience or embarrassment pass into another state to argue a cause before judicial tribunals without any fear of gross error in regard to the jurisprudence of the latter. Of course, the administration of national law is, or ought to be the same throughout all the states. The national courts, sitting in the states, and deciding upon the rights and property of citizens thereof, administer the local law in the same manner, and upon the same principles, as the state tribunals. In administering constitutional and public law, the law *inter gentes*, or the principles applicable to private rights growing out of international principles, the courts decide upon universal reasoning, and in the same manner, that the same questions ought to be decided by a court, sitting in England, in France, or in Germany. A national court exists in every state in the Union; and then administers the justice belonging to the national government. This court is called a District Court, and has a single Judge. In most of the States another higher national Court exists called the Circuit Court, composed of the District Judge, and a Judge of the Supreme Court of the United States. From the decisions of each of these courts an appeal, in cases of considerable value and importance,[19] (viz. two thousand dollars in value) lies to the Supreme Court, which is composed of seven judges and sits annually for nearly three months at Washington. And it is to the Supreme Court, thus sitting, that appeals from the state courts in questions of constitutional law are brought and decided at the last resort.

These remarks will now be concluded by a slight sketch of the literature of American Law, and the sources, in which it is to be explored and studied. The positive or statute Codes of the Union, as well as of the several states may be found in the printed collections of the Constitutions and Laws of each, which are from time to time published under the authority of the legislatures respectively. Of the public statutes various editions and revisions exist and they are generally collected in a compendious form and being in general use, new editions are constantly published, as fast, as the public demand requires. The latest edition is, of course the best for practical purposes; but, as it generally omits all the laws, which have been repealed or become obsolete, it is for historical purposes generally the least valuable. In such cases resort must be had to the original collections and the supplements published at short intervals, and generally every year. The other branches of law must be obtained from more general sources. Before the American Revolution there did not exist a single book on American law; and it could not be said, until the appearance of Mr. Chancellor Kent's Commentaries on American Law (which was first published in 1826) that there existed any work comprehending any full outline of it, in all its various branches. That admirable work which has done for America what Mr. Justice Blackstone, in his Commentaries has done for England, is now in the hands of all lawyers in America and will afford very ample information to foreign jurists, who may be disposed to examine the subject at large. Upon particular heads of the law, there are now various American treatises, which are in general use, though the more common course is to republish the English treatises on particular subjects, with notes on the American law the coincidences or deviations from the English doctrines. But the most full and complete stock of judicial materials is to be found in the reports, (as they are technically called) that is, in the collections of the cases argued and decided in the various courts within the United States. The earliest Reports (which have been published) were by Mr. Dallas in the year 1790. Since that period there has been a constant accumulation of works of this sort; and at the present time there are periodically published Reports of the Decisions of the Supreme Courts in all the states except four or five in the Union. Besides these the decisions of the Supreme Court of the United States are annually published, as well as many decisions of the Circuit and other national courts. So that at the present time the whole number of American Reports already printed approaches near to three hundred volumes; and there are not less than twenty volumes annually published. Among these, the most important and valuable to foreign jurists are the Reports of the decisions of the Supreme Court of the United States printed by Dallas, Cranch, Wheaton, and Peters, of the State courts of New York by Caines, Johnson, Cowen, and Wendall; the state courts of Pennsylvania

[19] "important" in ms.

by Dallas, Binney, Sergeant and Rawle, and Rawle alone; and of the state courts of Massachusetts by Tyng and Pickering.

Foreign Continental law and the civil law are not extensively studied, except in Louisiana and Florida. But there is a growing taste for both and there are many American jurists, who study with profound interest the leading works of the Continental Jurists and especially of the French Jurists; and they are daily by their example, as well as by their precepts recommending the most enlarged and comprehensive examinations of the writings of the civilians, as well as of the great masters upon municipal law of France Germany Holland Italy and Spain.

J. S.

1834

In July will be Published

BY CAREY, LEA AND CAREY,

THE FIRST VOLUME

(To be continued at intervals of three months)

OF THE

ENCYCLOPÆDIA AMERICANA:

A

POPULAR DICTIONARY

OF

ARTS, SCIENCES, LITERATURE, HISTORY, AND POLITICS,

BROUGHT DOWN TO THE PRESENT TIME,

ON THE BASIS OF THE SEVENTH EDITION OF THE GERMAN

CONVERSATIONS-LEXICON:

AND INCLUDING A COPIOUS COLLECTION OF ORIGINAL ARTICLES IN

AMERICAN BIOGRAPHY.

EDITED BY

DR. FRANCIS LIEBER,

ASSISTED BY

EDWARD WIGGLESWORTH, ESQ.

TO BE COMPLETED IN TWELVE LARGE VOLUMES OCTAVO,

PRICE TWO DOLLARS AND A HALF EACH.

To convey an idea of the nature of this work, the publishers deem it proper to give the following account of the German original, and of what may be expected in the *Encyclopædia Americana*.

The *Conversations-Lexicon*, of which the seventh edition in twelve volumes has lately been published in Germany, had its origin about fifteen years since. It was intended to supply a want occasioned by the character of the age, in which the sciences, arts, trades, and the various forms of knowledge and of active life, had become so much extended and diversified, that no individual, certainly no one engaged in business, could become well acquainted with all subjects of general interest; while, on the other hand, the wide diffusion of in-

2

formation rendered such knowledge essential to the character of an accomplished man. The want thus created, was one which no existing works were adequate to supply. Books treating of particular branches, such as gazetteers, &c. were of too confined a character; while voluminous Encyclopædias were too learned, scientific, and cumbersome, their articles being usually elaborate treatises requiring much study or previous acquaintance with the subject discussed. The object of the conductors of the *Conversations-Lexicon* was to select from every branch of knowledge what was necessary to be known by a well-informed man, and to give popular views of the more abstruse branches of learning and science, so that their readers might not be incommoded, and deprived of pleasure or improvement, by ignorance of facts or expressions occurring in books of conversation. Such a work, it is obvious, must be of great utility to every class of readers. It has been found so much so in Germany, that it is met with every where, among the learned, the lawyers, the military, artists, merchants, mechanics, and in short among men of all stations. The reader may judge how well it is adapted to its object, from the circumstance that though it now consists of twelve volumes, seven editions, comprising about one hundred thousand copies, have been printed in less than fifteen years. A French translation is now preparing in Brussels. Germany afforded peculiar advantages for the execution of this work, since its object requires that it should be cheap in price, and at the same time contain an immense amount and variety of information. One great advantage of this work is, that when any matter is treated, which has been the subject of dispute and animadversion, the article is written by an advocate of the point in question, and afterwards the various conflicting opinions are stated. In this way, a liberal and impartial character has been given to the work.

In regard to the work now about to be published, the public may rest assured that every exertion has been used to make it as interesting and valuable to American and English readers, as the original is to readers in Germany. Such articles, as have little interest out of Germany, have been omitted, and their places supplied by others adapted to the wants of the American and English public. In all cases this information is brought down to the present time, thus giving the work a very decided advantage over even the very extensive Encyclopædias heretofore published in this country. The great improvements that have taken place since the chief part of Rees's and the Edinburgh Encyclopædia was published, will render it desirable even for those who possess those works.

There can be no doubt that a work like the *Encyclopædia Americana* will be found peculiarly useful in this country, where the wide diffusion of the blessings of education, and the constant intercourse of all classes, create a great demand for general information.

The Publishers feel satisfied, that, by the efforts of the Editors, the work will be so prepared for publication, as to justify in this country the reputation it has obtained in Europe. Dr. Lieber is connected with many of the principal men of letters in Germany; he has resided for a considerable period in England, and is possessed of the talents,

3

knowledge, and industry, needful to carry on such a work with success. Mr. Wigglesworth is a gentleman of ability and acquirements, acquainted with the condition and wants of his own country, and with the literature of Europe; and the Publishers feel assured he is fully competent to give all needful assistance in fitting the work to the present condition of the United States. But, while they feel confident that the task of translating and arranging the *Conversations-Lexicon* for publication in America, is in safe and suitable hands, they have not neglected, and will not neglect, any other means, that may come within their power, to make it as complete as possible.

In the preparation of the work thus far, the Editors have been aided by many gentlemen of distinguished ability, and for the continuation, no efforts shall be spared to secure the aid of all who can, in any way, contribute to render it worthy of patronage.

The American Biography, which is very extensive, will be furnished by Mr. Walsh, who has long paid particular attention to that branch of our literature, and from materials in the collection of which he has been engaged for some years. For obvious reasons, the notices of distinguished Americans will be confined to deceased individuals: the European Biography contains notices of all distinguished living characters, as well as those of past times.

In the department of the Fine Arts, the work will be exceedingly rich. Great attention was given to this in the German work, and the Editors have been anxious to render it, by the necessary additions, as perfect as possible.

To Gentlemen of the Bar, the work will be desirable, as in cases where legal subjects are treated, an account is given of the provisions of American, English, French, Prussian, Austrian, and Civil Law.

The Publishers believe it will be admitted, that this work is one of the cheapest ever published in this country. They have been desirous to render it worthy of a place in the best libraries, while at the same time they have fixed the price so low as to put it within the reach of all who read, with the hope that they may, by an extensive sale, be compensated for the great expenditure incurred in its preparation.

Conditions of Publication.

I. It will be completed in twelve volumes, of from six to seven hundred pages each, handsomely printed on fine paper, and upon the same type as the pages annexed to this prospectus.

II. The first volume will appear in July, 1829; and a volume will be published every three months, until completed. The work is now so far advanced as to enable the publishers to assure the subscribers, that no delay shall take place.

III. The price to subscribers will be two dollars and a half per volume, strongly done up in muslin.

⁂ **Orders for the work will be received by the publishers, or by any of the agents in the annexed list.**

(4)

Letter from George Ticknor, Esq. of Boston.

Boston, Nov. 25, 1827.

SIR,—I am not acquainted with any book in a foreign language, which, I think, may be translated into English and published in the United States, with the needful alterations, with so much success as the Conversations-Lexicon, of which so many editions have been published in Germany. It seems to me to be suited, in a particular manner, to the present condition and wants of this country, because it contains more of that information which is useful and interesting to well-educated persons of all classes, than any other work with which I am conversant. It has made the fortunes of its publishers in Germany. It is about to be adapted to the wants of the rest of the continent, in a French translation just undertaken at Brussels; and I do not doubt, a similar adaptation of it to the United States, would be as fortunate and as successful as was the original work; because, the class of persons to whom it would be interesting, is much greater in this country than it is in Germany.

GEORGE TICKNOR.

DR. FRANCIS LIEBER.

Letter from Dr. Charles Follen, Instructer in German, in Harvard University.

Cambridge, Nov. 23, 1827.

SIR,—My opinion with respect to the translation of the Dictionary for Conversation into English, as proposed by Dr. Lieber, coincides entirely with the views which this gentleman and several eminent literary men of this country have already expressed. The Dictionary for Conversation owes its excellence, as well as its signal success, principally to this circumstance, that in Germany every one who aims at distinction in any science or art, commonly devotes himself almost exclusively to his particular pursuit. This devotedness to a single object is apt to be attended with a very imperfect acquaintance with other branches of knowledge, and it is this defect which occasioned the edition of a work which brought within the reach of every one the most interesting results of all the different departments of learning and industry. On the other hand, the profound knowledge contained in the works of those who have made a particular pursuit the object of their life, has enabled the compilers of that Dictionary to present to the public, in a concise manner, a great number of articles which are generally interesting, without being superficial. It is satisfactory not only to the general reader and scholar, to the philosopher and the historian, but to those also who are engaged in any particular business or profession, as farmers, mechanics, merchants, physicians, lawyers or theologians. Those articles of the work which do not fully deserve this praise, will certainly be improved in usefulness and interest for this country, by the translator and those literary men who are expected to assist him in this useful and patriotic undertaking.

CHARLES FOLLEN.

Letter from George Bancroft, Esq. one of the Principals of Round-Hill Seminary, Northampton.

Northampton, Dec. 22, 1827.

SIR,—I am very glad to hear that you seriously propose to publish the Conversations-Lexicon among us. It is the most convenient book for general reference, with which I am acquainted; and as for its popularity, the sale of more than seventy or a hundred thousand copies of it in Germany, establishes that point. It is for the past, what a newspaper is designed to be for the present,—a general summary of the most interesting things known, stated on the best authority, to which access could readily be had. There is one circumstance which I think is much in its favour. We have had Encyclopædias, compiled in France and Great Britain, each containing the current views on matters of science and letters, prevailing respectively in those countries. In the Ger-

(5)

man work we shall have the materials a little differently wrought. There has been nothing of the kind at once so popular and so trustworthy.

I remain, with best wishes and sincere regards,

Respectfully yours,

GEORGE BANCROFT.

From Edward Everett, Esq. Member of the House of Representatives of the United States.

Winter-Hill, Charlestown, Nov. 17, 1827.

I entirely concur in the opinion expressed in the foregoing pages, of the merit of the Lexicon for Conversation. It is somewhat of the nature of an Encyclopædia, intended, however, for convenient and popular use. Although, of the great number of articles contained in it, all are not equally well executed, no work, that I am acquainted with, contains such an amount and variety of information, in a form so accessible and commodious. The alterations proposed by Dr. Lieber, seem to me calculated to render it still more valuable in this country; and with them, it will be, in my opinion, the best work for convenient general reference, in the English language. So deeply impressed have I been with the merit of the work, that, without having heard of Dr. Lieber's proposal to undertake a translation, I had determined to recommend to some of the principal booksellers to endeavour to procure a translator of it.

EDWARD EVERETT.

Extract from a Letter from Joseph Story, Esq. one of the Judges of the Supreme Court of the United States.

Salem, April 26, 1826.

Dear Sir,—I wish every success to your excellent undertaking. It will supply a desideratum in our libraries, which I have almost despaired of seeing supplied in my day. Please to consider me a subscriber to the work.

Dr. Francis Lieber.

New-York, July 18, 1828.

Gentlemen,—It gives me pleasure to hear of your proposed publication of the *Conversations-Lexicon* in English. It has long been a very popular work in Germany; has passed through seven large editions there, and is soon to appear in a French translation, at Brussels. The articles are generally comprehensive, and for the most part very satisfactory; and the work may properly be entitled, a well digested summary and general dictionary of interesting and useful information, in all departments of knowledge. It will meet the wants of a large portion of our community, and be received, I think, with very general approbation and encouragement.

J. F. SCHROEDER.

Extract from a Letter from the Rev. Dr. F. C. Shaeffer, of New-York.

"Since the first appearance of the *Allgemiene deutsche Real-Encyclopædie, oder Conversations-Lexicon* in its present form, I have had occasion to use it as a book of reference, and have frequently expressed the opinion, that an English translation of this valuable work, with necessary emendations, would be a great benefit to American readers who are unacquainted with the language of the original. In passing through several editions, it has been much improved; and, on comparing the sixth and seventh edition, it is readily perceived, that the latter, the ground work of the 'Popular Encyclopædia,' to be edited by the able Dr. Lieber, is to be considered as far better than a mere reprint."

Neues

Conversations-Lexicon

oder

encyclopädisches Handwörterbuch

für

gebildete Stände.

Herausgegeben

von

einer Gesellschaft rheinländischer Gelehrten.

(In zwölf Bänden.)

Erster Band.

A – Az.

Original-Ausgabe.

Mit Genehmigung einer Königl. Preuß. Censur-Behörde.

Köln und Bonn,
im Comptoir für Kunst und Literatur.
1824.

INDEX

www.ingramcontent.com/pod-product-compliance
Lightning Source LLC
LaVergne TN
LVHW101455200926
848483LV00001B/134

* 9 7 8 1 6 1 6 1 9 4 5 4 3 *